TUDOR INTERLUDES

General Editors
Marie Axton   Richard Axton

THREE RASTELL PLAYS

TUDOR INTERLUDES

In preparation

The Plays of Henry Medwall, ed. A. H. Nelson
Thersites, Horestes, Jack Juggler, ed. M. Axton
The Winchester Morality Plays, ed. R. Beadle
The Complete Plays of John Bale, ed. P. Happé

THREE RASTELL PLAYS

Four Elements, Calisto and Mélebea, Gentleness and Nobility

Edited by Richard Axton

D. S. BREWER · ROWMAN & LITTLEFIELD

Introduction and notes © Richard Axton 1979

First published 1979 by D. S. Brewer Ltd, 240 Hills Road,
Cambridge, and P.O. Box 24, Ipswich IP1 1JJ,
and by Rowman and Littlefield Inc., 81 Adams Drive,
Totowa, NJ 07512, U.S.A.

ISBN 0-85991-047-4

British Library Cataloguing in Publication Data

Three Rastell Plays (Tudor Interludes)
   1. English drama – Early modern and Elizabethan, 1500–1600.
   I. Axton, Richard   II. Rastell, John, d. 1536. Four Elements
   III. Calisto and Melebea
   IV. Heywood, John, b. ca 1497. Gentleness and Nobility   V. Series
822'.2'08   PR1262

181333

Phototypesetting by Galleon Photosetting, Ipswich.
Printed by Redwood Burn, Yeoman Way, Trowbridge, Wiltshire,
in Great Britain.

Contents

Acknowledgements

The editor wishes to express his gratitude to the British Library, for permission to print the text of the unique copy of *Four Elements*; to the Bodleian Library, for permission to print the text of the unique copy of *Calisto and Melebea*; to the Master and Fellows of Magdalene College, Cambridge, for permission to print the text of *Gentleness and Nobility* from the copy in the Pepys Library; to Tamesis Books Ltd, for permission to quote from James Mabbe's translation of *Celestine*, edited by Miss Guadalupe Martinez Lacalle in 1972.

The general editors wish to thank the Trustees of the Una Ellis Fermor Research Fund of Bedford College, London, for a grant which has aided the launching of the series.

Abbreviations

EETS	Early English Text Society.
Greg, *Bibliography*	W. W. Greg, *A Bibliography of the English Printed Drama to the Restoration*, vol. 1, Stationers' Records. Plays to 1616, London, 1939.
OED	*The Oxford English Dictionary.*
STC	*A Short-Title Catalogue of Books Printed in England, Scotland, and Ireland, and of English Books Printed Abroad, 1475–1640*, compiled by A. W. Pollard and G. R. Redgrave (London, 1926). Second Edition, revised and enlarged by W. A. Jackson, F. S. Ferguson, and K. F. Pantzer, vol. 2, I–Z (London, 1976).
TFT	Tudor Facsimile Texts, ed. J. S. Farmer (146 vols. London, 1907–14, reprinted N.Y., 1970).
Tilley, *Prov.*	M. P. Tilley, *A Dictionary of the Proverbs in England in the Sixteenth and Seventeenth Centuries* (Ann Arbor, 1950).
Whiting, *Prov.*	B. J. Whiting and H. W. Whiting, *Proverbs, Sentences, and Proverbial Phrases from English Writings Mainly Before 1500* (Cambridge, Mass., and London, 1968).

Introduction

John Rastell published all three plays in this volume. *The Nature of the Four Elements* he composed at the midpoint (c.1518) of an energetic career pursued in the law, in printing, in a variety of commercial ventures, as member of parliament, and in Cromwell's service. It reflects Rastell's own special interest in science ('natural philosophy') and geography ('cosmography'). The comedy of *Calisto and Melebea* is the work of an anonymous English poet who adapted the earliest European novel, *La Celestina*, 'in the manner of an interlude'. *Gentleness and Nobility* treats a favourite humanist topic in a spirited, three-cornered dialogue; it was probably written by Rastell's son-in-law, John Heywood. The diversity and novelty of the three interludes partly hide their formal and thematic links. The epilogues to the later two plays take up the theme of social responsibility first struck in the prologue to *Four Elements* and resounding through the prefaces to the law text books that were the heavyweight daily business of Rastell's printing house. It is likely that these moral conclusions to the plays are Rastell's own writing, plain in style and earnest in its democratic message; for his interest was primarily, though not wholly, in the educational possibilities of the drama, and he was the first English printer to realise them on any significant scale.

No plays in English had been printed in the fifteenth century, when the bulk of drama was sacred and traditional, performed at set times of year by amateurs and churchmen, locally oriented and identified by regional dialect. London-based printing hastened the formation of a standard English language which had a new and growing prestige in the schools. At the same time, acting troupes proliferated, mostly the liveried servants of noble households and by no means ill-educated, offering small-scale 'portable' plays.[1] For the first time conditions existed for an English national drama that could be secular, socially engaged, and experimental. The clerical playwrights and preaching friars of the fourteenth and fifteenth centuries had evolved a viable formula for popular dramatic entertainment in the notion of sermon-and-game, that is, expository instruction interspersed with comic, 'folksy' entertainment (the fifteenth-century *Mankind* is a lively and intelligent example).[2] Their successors of the early sixteenth century, many of them educated London humanists, explored the newly

---

[1] See D. M. Bevington, *From Mankind to Marlowe* (Cambridge, Mass., 1962).

[2] R. Axton, 'Popular modes in the earliest plays' in *Medieval Drama*, ed. Neville Denny (Stratford-upon-Avon Studies 16, 1973), pp. 28–39; *European Drama of the Early Middle Ages* (1974), ch. 10.

1

available book learning for fresh material to cast in dramatic form. They adapted and 'compiled' (a favourite printers' term) from learned sources, experimenting with traditional forms and with the possibilities of the English language. The original audiences for many interludes were probably London coteries, although by dint of publication, repeated playing and reprinting, some plays, like *Youth*, achieved popular status.[3]

Most early Tudor plays are advertised to readers or players as 'interludes' or as being put together 'in manner of an interlude'. Presumably the authors and printers knew roughly what they meant, but a generic description is notoriously difficult from a historical viewpoint. Etymology is little help. The medieval Latin title *Interludium* given to an English comic wooing play of about 1300 may be evidence of an early attempt to dignify native traditions of secular 'playing' with the banquet entertainments of ancient Rome.[4] It is also possible that the English spelling *enterlude* (found as early as 1418) implies a false etymological association with *entering*: the players come in to a hall, they visit the audience, rather than vice-versa. But *interlude* is perhaps most safely taken in a neutral sense as a 'play between two or more speakers'.[5] There are usually about six players. The plays are short (an hour or hour-and-a-half) and sometimes broken into two or three sections that might have accompanied dinner or supper on the same day (as is the case with Henry Medwall's *Fulgens and Lucrece*, c.1495), or have divided courses at a feast. Indoor performance is envisaged in a single 'place' occupied by actors in turn or together, rather than on an elaborate 'simultaneous' set (as is the case with most medieval religious drama). The actors often announce their arrivals and departures and are solicitous of the audience's attention. The plays themselves are extremely varied, but often alternate grave and trivial matter ('toys and gests'), and are typically described as 'merry'.

A sense of the conventions and possibilities of interludes could readily be acquired by anyone with access to the court, the universities, the inns of court, the household of a wealthy magnate, or a civic mayoral banquet. John Rastell's contacts at court, his law practice and various employments would have brought him in touch with most of the intelligentsia in London's population of about 50,000. He married

[3] Greg, *Bibliography*, No. 20. See C. R. Baskervill, 'Mummers' Wooing Plays in England', *Modern Philology*, 21 (1924), 225–72, pp. 232–4.
[4] Glynne Wickham, in his introduction to *English Moral Interludes* (1976), pp. vii–viii.
[5] E. K. Chambers, *The Medieval Stage* (2 vols., Oxford, 1903), II, 181–90.

the sister of Thomas More, whose legendary playing in interludes was celebrated in the Elizabethan play about him that was partly written by Shakespeare.[6] Rastell's daughter Joan married John Heywood, musician at Henry VIII's court and the wittiest of the interlude makers. Fortunate social contacts also brought practical experience; Rastell was the maker of street pageants, the erector of stages and awnings for royal entertainments. At his own house in London's suburbs he had a stage, and a wardrobe of costumes that were hired out to acting companies. It is the scope of Rastell's interest in the drama that is unique at this period. Above all, it was his practical concern to treat plays as more than ephemera and to make play texts available as books to a reading public.

The plays Rastell chose to print all have some intellectual weight – they are full of ideas. The first (printed before 1516) was Henry Medwall's *Fulgens and Lucrece*. Next, *Four Elements*, *Calisto and Melebea*, and *Gentleness and Nobility* were printed in the 1520s, after which Rastell published Skelton's *Magnificence*.[7] William Rastell continued his father's tradition by printing Medwall's ethical morality *Nature*, a play of *The Prodigal Son*, and four plays of Heywood's.[8] John Rastell's publications reinforce the impression gained from his own play *Four Elements* of a strongly secular cast of mind, a man who insists that all knowledge must begin with 'these vysyble thyngys inferyall', and who is constantly concerned with the rationality and justice of human society. Three great themes are stated in the prologue to *Four Elements*: the 'sufficiency' of the English language to unlock the 'subtell sciens' contained in learned Latin books and convey it to all people; the responsibility that learned men have to propagate knowledge; man's ultimate duty to his fellows and to the 'common wele'. For Rastell himself this meant exploring the physical world, seeking to create wealth, to educate the ignorant and vicious, to reform the law and administration, to make men know their rights and duties. His ideals and interests are in many ways typically humanist and protestant, and the moral face of his work, for all its paternalism and optimism, is recognisably modern.

[6] *Sir Thomas More*, ed. W. W. Greg (MSR, Oxford, 1911). The relevant scene is printed by P. Happé, *Tudor Interludes* (Harmondsworth, 1972), p. 368. See also William Roper's *Lyfe of Sir Thomas Moore* (EETS, 1935), p. 5.

[7] *Magnyfycence* (printed by P. Treveris for J. Rastell, ?1530). The dates given here and subsequently are those in *STC*.

[8] *Nature* (1530–4). *Pater, Filius, et Uxor* (?1530) survives only as a fragment (*STC* 20765.5). *The Pardoner and the Frere* (1533), *Johan Johan* (1533), *The Play of the Wether* (1533), *A Play of Love* (1534).

John Rastell's career

A brief account of a life so active and diverse can hardly do it justice. Some areas, for instance, bibliographical study of Rastell's entire printing output to determine an exact chronology, await full and detailed investigation. But an outline was established by A. W. Reed in 1926 and, though it needs correction in points of detail, serves as a guide.[9]

Rastell's father was city coroner in Coventry. He entered his son John in the Guild of Corpus Christi in 1489, when the boy may have been about fourteen. Like many of his contemporaries who aspired to public office, including Thomas More, his future brother-in-law, John Rastell attended the Inns of Court in London, where training in the common law was complemented – for the sons of gentlemen, at least – by schooling in social accomplishments: debating, dancing, music, theatrical revels.[10] Middle Temple records of 1502 list Rastell as an 'utter Barrister' (i.e. next in seniority to the benchers). Earlier than this, in 1499, he was associated in providing securities for a loan with John and Thomas More. By 1504 he was married to Elizabeth More. In 1506 he succeeded his father as coroner in Coventry and presided over the Court of Statute Merchant, adjudicating matters of mercantile law, until 1509, when he resigned.

By 1510 Rastell had started a printing business and produced Thomas More's *Life* of Pico della Mirandola. Setting up must have involved buying a press and type (his black-letter type has been traced to the foundry of Wolfgang Hopyl in Paris), finding at least two skilled men to set type and work the press, and acquiring premises on the south side of St Paul's churchyard.[11] By 1512 he had entered the service of Sir Edward Belknap, one of Henry VIII's privy councillors, and he is mentioned as responsible during the French war of 1512–14 for the transport of artillery and heavy equipment. The association with Belknap brought financial reward. One of Belknap's duties was to assist the Master of Wards, so that it was probably through him that Rastell was granted the revenues of the lands confiscated after the death of Richard Hunne, together with the wardship of Hunne's daughters.

---

[9] A. W. Reed, *Early Tudor Drama* (1926), ch. 1 and Appendices I–VIII.

[10] See Marie Axton, *The Queen's Two Bodies* (Royal Historical Society, 1978), ch. 1.

[11] See A. Hyatt King, 'The Significance of John Rastell in Early Music Printing', *Library*, 5th ser. 26 (1971), 195–214; Roger Coleman, ed. *The Four Elements as performed at the University Printing House* (Cambridge, 1971), pp. 8–13.

This windfall of 1515 proved a mixed blessing when London took up the 'heretical' Hunne's cause against the clergy in the 1520s, so that Rastell was involved in litigation for many years. At the time it may have helped float some ambitious printing projects. In these first years he printed the first dictionary of law terms, and a book of assizes and of pleas of the crown. The greatest undertaking was an edition of *La Graunde Abbregement de le Ley* made by Anthony Fitzherbert (among his many offices a recorder of Coventry, and so presumably known to Rastell for some time previous). In 1516 Rastell brought out the three large folios with Latin, French, and English texts printed in parallel columns. For the next fifteen years Rastell's press continued to produce and revise the law text books that were the backbone of England's administration and legal education.

With the printing business launched, a country house leased and modernised, his children's upbringing provided for in an agreement with Sir John More, his father-in-law, Rastell turned to a risky trading venture to the New World. The failure of this voyage of 1517 is happily documented in the legal proceedings which Rastell started on returning to London and in his play *Four Elements*. On 5 March 1517 the king granted letters of recommendation to John Rastell and two other London citizens intending to go on the king's business 'ad longiques mundi partes'. (This was a customary procedure since 1497, when Henry VII had given his approval to John Cabot's voyage of exploration.) Some of the money needed for the enterprise may have been advanced by the royal treasury, to which in 1521 Rastell and John More still owed 250 marks.

Independent evidence of an expedition in the year 1517 says that it was organised by Sebastian Cabot and Sir Thomas Sperte, 'whose faynt heart was the cause that the viage took none effect'.[12] Sperte, who had a contract with Thomas Howard, the Lord High Admiral, for balasting ships in the Thames in the summer of 1517, seems not to have accompanied the voyage. Two ships were chartered by the London consortium: the *Barbara* (with John Richards as master), and the *Mary Barking*, whose owner John Ravyn was also engaged by Rastell as purser to provision the *Barbara*. Ravyn and Richards are the principal agents against whom Rastell later brought successful proceedings in the Court of Requests, and who caused him to abandon the voyage and lose goods worth a hundred pounds. Sperte and Howard appear to have connived at the abortion of the voyage and it is easy to see that the Lord

---

[12] Richarde Eden's dedicatory preface to Sebastian Münster's *Cosmographie* (1553), cited by Reed, p. 187. My account is based on Reed's transcription of the Proceedings in his Appendix I.

High Admiral would not have wanted to allow these two well-proved ships away from home waters for an indefinite period.

Ravyn's technique was to delay the departure of the ships until the easterly Atlantic winds of early summer (which had made possible Cabot's speedy trip to Newfoundland) gave way to westerlies, so that the trip would have to be postponed until the following year, either January or May (the times of the bi-annual fishing expeditions from Normandy to Labrador). He seems to have been a past-master at fermenting dissent among the crew and in cheating over matters of provisioning. There were delays at Gravesend, at Sandwich, where the *Barbara* went aground; at Dartmouth Ravyn claimed that he still lacked a brick hearth, a kettle, a grindstone, and other gear. At Plymouth, Rastell alleged, Ravyn deliberately spiked the ship and delayed for caulking. At Falmouth Ravyn and Richards disappeared for a week to buy tin 'for their own profit'. They also took on board a professional agitator called Coo, a ringleader in the recent 'Ill May Day' revolt of apprentices. They tried to persuade Rastell to sail to Bordeaux to sell his trade goods. The *Mary Barking* reached Cork harbour, at which point the captain merchant William Hotyng was locked in his cabin, while the master and mariners sailed the ship back to the Thames. Ravyn and Richards made further efforts to urge Rastell 'to gyff up his viage and to fall to robbyng uppon the sea', a course, they assured him, more profitable than 'his fysshyng in the new lands'. When Rastell put ashore at Waterford he was told of Hotyng's treatment and threatened with the same. Understandably he stayed on dry land, eventually agreeing under pressure that the ships should go to Falmouth and thence to Bordeaux to realise the money tied up in cargo, on the understanding that the voyage go forward the following year. The hundred pounds credit never materialised and the money raised from the sale of bales of cloth at Bordeaux and La Rochelle was divided among the mariners. It looks as if Rastell stayed for a while in Ireland ('that holesome ground' of *Four Elements*, 714) before returning to London and filing his bill of complaint. Supposing that the hundred pounds were eventually paid to him, this can hardly have recompensed the outlay for such an expedition.

The geographical knowledge that Rastell had gleaned from reading, from studying ocean maps, from talking to seamen and merchant venturers, he put to use in writing *Four Elements* and in constructing the *figura* that is the play's central property. This 'figure' or model seems to be a huge terrestrial globe. Much of the information conveyed in the exposition of the *figura* was readily available on the giant *Carta Marina*, designed and printed by Martin Waldseemüller in 1516 and measuring, when its twelve sheets are stuck together, about eight feet by five. Since Rastell's shop sold (and probably printed) maps it is very likely he saw Waldseemüller's *Carta Marina*; about a thousand were printed and Rastell may have owned one.[13]

It is no wonder, in view of the hijacked expedition of 1517, that Rastell felt moved to digress in his account of the 'new landes' to speak angrily for the 'venturers' in cursing the 'maryners, / Fals of promys and dissemblers, / That falsly them betrayed' and to warn others against the growing practice of 'such kaytyffes'. More surprising is his optimism in urging his fellow Englishmen to 'take possessyon' and extend the king's dominion 'into so farre a grounde'. The labour of instructing savages 'whiche as yet lyve all bestly', is to be rewarded by the promise of wealth. But Rastell offers no exotic treasure, rather, practical commodities: coniferous timber for ships, tar and soap ashes, vast hauls of cod fish. In his account of the New World one can hear the same sober, practical voice of the man who, in later years, together with Thomas Cromwell, acquired mining rights on Dartmoor.

By 1520 Rastell's engineering skill was known at court, and he was summoned to Guisnes, where preparations involving three thousand men were going forward for the Field of the Cloth of Gold, to take charge of making and decorating the roofs of the banquet halls.[14] In 1522 he was authorised by the Aldermen of London to spend £15 erecting a pageant at the 'lytel conduit' in Cheapside, almost opposite his printing shop, to celebrate the visit of the Emperor Charles V and Henry VIII to St Paul's: 'there was builded a place like heaven, curiously painted with cloudes, orbes, starres and hierarchies of angels'. It was a prodigy of 'cosmography' and mechanical skill:

> Also att the Stockys ther dyd stand a pageaunte off an ylonde betokenyng the Ile of englond compassede all abowte with water made in silver and byce lyke to waves off the see and rockys ioynyng therto watelde abowte with roddys off silver and golde and wythyn them champion contrey mountayns and wooddys where were dyvers bestes goyng abowte the mountayns by vyces and dyvers maner off trees herbys and flowres . . .[15]

---

[13] See further the notes on F.708–876. Martin Waldseemüller's *Carta Marina* of 1516 is printed in facsimile by J. Fischer and Fr.R.v.Wieser, *The Oldest Map With The Name America* (Innsbruck, 1903). The stock of Rastell's shop after his death included 110 'mappis of Europa' at a penny apiece (R. J. Roberts, 'John Rastell's Inventory of 1538', *Library* 6th ser. 1 (1979), 34–42).

[14] Reed, pp. 165–6.

[15] Sydney Anglo, *Spectacle Pageantry and Early Tudor Policy* (Oxford, 1969), p. 197.

For the entertainment of the French ambassadors at Greenwich in the summer of 1527 Rastell devised a pageant called 'the Father of Heaven', staged, it seems, under the astrological roof of the inner banquet chamber, which portrayed the 'hole earth environed with the Sea, like a very Mappe or Carte'. He also wrote a dialogue of *Love and Riches*.[16]

It is tempting to follow A. W. Reed in his perception that these separate spectacles were the transformation of a single image: a model of the cosmos.[17] It is an image traceable to a civic pageant in Rastell's native Coventry, where at Jourdain Well in 1510 Henry VIII viewed 'the nine orders of Angells'. A variation of the image appears in the printer's woodcut device first used by Rastell in his *Liber assisarum et placitorum corone* (1513–14) and re-used throughout his printing career: above, Christ in majesty over the sun, moon and planets; below, the four elements, a semi-circle of earth, surrounded by water, air, and fire. The merman and mermaid rising from creation like a secular Adam and Eve refer directly to the sign of the mermaid used on Rastell's printing shops. This image of the world is embodied in the *figura* of *Four Elements* expounded by Natura Naturata (lines 161–8). It is a convenient emblem of Rastell's secularity, of his attempt to make the stage physically embody man's world.

When, in 1524, Rastell began work building himself a house in Finsbury Fields, he also built a stage; it was constructed of board, timber, lath, nail, sprig, and daubing, to the value of fifty shillings.[18] The players' garments used there were sewn by Mrs Rastell and a servant. During one of Rastell's absences in France, his servant Walton hired them out to other players. The loss and deterioration of the costumes (some of which seem to have been made originally for the Greenwich occasion) in the course of sixty or eighty alleged hirings were the substance of a law suit brought against Walton. Two of Rastell's witnesses were regular members of the king's players of interludes.[19] The fortunes of theatrical properties make a fascinating underplot to the history of play texts.

The sequence of Rastell's publications may eventually be determined accurately by close typographical study. Whether the printing of *Four Elements* belongs early or late in the 1520s makes little difference to one

---

[16] Anglo, pp. 217–18.
[17] Reed, pp. 18–20.
[18] Details from 'Pleadings in a Theatrical Lawsuit, John Rastell v. Henry Walton' in *Fifteenth-Century Prose and Verse*, ed. A. W. Pollard (1903), pp. 307–21.
[19] E. K. Chambers, *The Elizabethan Stage* (4 vols., Oxford, 1923), II, 80–1.

fact that has embarrassed historians of type. The song, 'Tyme to pas', appears in musical score, the earliest printed score at present known, and was set in movable type at a single impression.[20] Wherever it was that Rastell acquired this type, it is certain that he was abreast of a great technical innovation and may, indeed, have engaged in some sharp practice to achieve his 'first'. The play's topical interest is an argument in favour of printing close to 1520.[21] During this decade the stream of editorial compilations continued; year books, books of statutes and abridgements in English and Latin, revision of the dictionary of law terms were interspersed with more popular works: *Calisto*, *Gentleness*, *A Hundred Merry Tales*, the *Book of a Hundred Riddles*, *Twelve Merry Jests of Widow Edyth*, a 'boke of new cardys' to make English composition and spelling enjoyable, a play of *Christmas or Good Order* (now lost), a big illustrated book of popular history, *The Pastime of People*.[22]

The printing of More's *Dialogue of Images* (1529) and the writing and publication of *A New Book of Purgatory* (1530) heralded an inevitable engagement in religious controversy that was to lead to the strenuous and sadly unrewarding last phase of John Rastell's career. His son William, who had helped with printing during the previous three or four years, in 1530 set up on his own, while Rastell *père* devoted more and more energy to public life. Around 1529 he was working as a lawyer in Chancery, under Wolsey. In that year he visited France, Reed hazards, to seek academic support for the divorce. The same year he became member of parliament for the Cornish borough of Duneveden and sat in the Reformation Parliament. According to John Bale's brief biographical note, Frith's reply to Rastell's *Book of Purgatory* converted him to the reformers' cause. He devoted himself to Cromwell's service.[23] With the death of John More in 1530 family ties were weakened and relations with Thomas More must have been made difficult if not impossible by their opposed positions during the 1530s (More was put to death in 1535). In 1532 Rastell was involved with Cromwell in a premature plan to secularise the Priory of Holy Trinity in Aldgate, and was to have been its first governor. In 1534 he carried messages between the Bishop of Coventry, who was dealing with social

---

[20] A. Hyatt King, in *Library* (1971), 195–214; Coleman, pp. 17–18.

[21] A. Hyatt King, p. 208.

[22] See P. G. Morrison, *Index of Printers, Publishers and Booksellers in STC, 1475–1640* (Charlottesville, Virginia, 1950), p. 61 for a complete list of Rastell's publications (now in need of updating); also Ray Nash, 'Rastell Fragments at Dartmouth', *Library* 4th ser., 24 (1943), 66–73.

[23] Reed, p. 28; Anglo, pp. 262–3.
J. Bale, *Scriptorum Illustrium Maioris Brytannie* (Basle, 1557; facs. repr. Gregg, 1971), p. 659.

unrest on the Welsh borders, and Cromwell. The same year Rastell sent Cromwell plans for a far-reaching campaign of reformatory propaganda against the Pope. A *Book of the Charge* to be printed by Rastell was to be sent as from the king to all judges and stewards, enjoining them to ignore the Pope's opinion and instruct the people likewise. Further polemics were to urge that priests should be free to marry, that images should not be honoured, that prayers for the dead have no efficacy, that the common law and court of chancery should be reformed. But the time was not ripe for these sweeping reforms.

In 1534 Rastell lost his long suit against the descendants of William Hunne from whose death and 'martyrdom' he had benefited financially. The next year he was imprisoned for his opposition to the royal proclamation which settled that old dispute about tithes and offerings. He wrote pathetically to Cromwell for relief. On 20 April 1536 he made his will. In June he died.

As Rastell spent his last two wretched months in prison the Atlantic easterlies were blowing his son John, gentleman of the Inns of Court, to Labrador. Young Rastell got further than his father but fared even worse, entangled in a nightmarish saga of starvation, cannibalism, and piracy. In London his brother William continued practising law and set about his greatest life work, collecting and editing the works of Thomas More. John Heywood collected a royal pension and continued to devise dramatic entertainments for Cromwell; in 1544 he faced hanging but survived to write 'pleasant and harmless verses' for Protestant and Catholic monarchs alike. An inventory of 1538 shows that at Rastell's death he had 370 unsold copies of 'the play of melebea', 289 of 'the play of good order', 80 of 'the play of gentilnes & nobilite' and 8 of 'the second part of the play of Epicure'.[24] One would like to think that he had sold every copy of his own *Four Elements*.

Four Elements

The biographical interest of *Four Elements* has already been discussed, together with reasons for dating its publication around 1520. Rastell's authorship is attested by John Bale in his catalogue of British writers; Rastell is described as *cosmographus* and is said to have 'put together' (*composuit* in the earlier version, *editit* in the revision) as the first of his works 'a very long and learned comedy to be accompanied by

---

[24] The text of the inventory is transcribed by R. J. Roberts in *Library* (1979), pp. 34–42. I am grateful to Mr Roberts for bringing this information to my notice.

instruments and models' (*ingeniosissimam ac longissimam comoediam primum editit, cum instrumentis & figuris*). Bale calls it by the name of the first of the cast *Naturam naturatam* and mentions its description of the three parts of the world.[25] Rastell's own lengthy advertisement offers the play as 'A new interlude and a mery' to readers who appreciate the delight and novelty of scientific fact: 'proper poyntys of phylosophy naturall', 'dyvers straunge landys' and 'dyvers straunge effectis and causis'. It has been argued that Rastell consulted late medieval encyclopædias of scientific lore (e.g. Bartholomaeus Anglicus, *De Proprietatibus Rerum*, of which Wynken de Worde had printed an English translation in 1495), as well as more up-to-date ones (Gregorius Reisch, *Margarita Philosophica Nova*, Argentine, 1512 and 1517), cosmological treatises (Sacrobosco's thirteenth-century *Textus De Sphaera*, printed 1507) and cosmographies (M. Waldseemüller's *Cosmographie Introductio*, 1507).[26] It is possible and likely that Rastell knew these books. But *Four Elements* itself is not esoteric; it offers the plainest kind of popular instruction in science, in the style of Caxton's *Mirrour of the World*. When Caxton printed his own translation from the French *Miroir* in 1480 (the first of three editions), he advertised his contents like this:

> Of the fourme of the firmament.
> How the foure elementes ben sette.
> How the erthe holdeth hym ryght in the myddle of the world . . .
> What the Roundenesse of the erthe is . . .
> How clowdes, haylles, tempestes, thondres, lightnynges . . .[27]

Rastell's closely similar list of 'points' was a way of setting himself in a great tradition. He offers to instruct not scholars (who have always known the earth is round) but ordinary men.

In the interlude the 'sad' (serious) matter is 'made merry'. Rastell's Messenger articulates the aesthetic and moral principle:

> But because some folke be lyttyll disposyd
> To sadnes, but more to myrth and sport,
> This phylosophycal work is myxyd
> With mery conseytis, to gyve men comfort
> And occasyon to cause them to resort
> To here this matter, wherto yf they take hede
> Some lernynge to them therof may procede.
>
> (134–40)

[25] Bale, *Scriptorum* (1557), pp. 659–60.
[26] J. Parr, 'Rastell's Geographical Knowledge of America', *Philological Quarterly*, 27 (1948), 229–40.
[27] *Caxton's Mirrour of the World*, ed. Oliver H. Prior (EETS, 1913), pp. 2–3.

By suggesting that playing time can be cut from an hour-and-a-half to three-quarters of an hour Rastell recognises the needs of acting troupes beyond his immediate control. The text is available for playing and he suggests that it may also be extended if 'ye may brynge in a dysgysynge' (as indeed happens when Sensual Appetite brings in dancers). The proportions half-and-half, 'sad' and merry, describe the extant text quite accurately.

The play's form resembles a geography lecture with practical demonstrations. Its loose, open-ended construction, seeming to depend on improvisation, is typical of late medieval morality plays. The dramatic purpose is to clarify rather than represent experience. Plot exists only at an abstract level, so that Humanity's progress from initiation (instruction in virtue) through temptation and fall to recognition and repentance traces an archetypal pattern. This verbal instruction of Humanity is not inherently dramatic. Indeed, the only thing that Humanity *does* is to choose his company (as happens in *Nature*, *Youth*, and *Magnificence*). The conflict necessary to drama is created from the alternative to serious learning that is offered to Humanity by Sensual Appetite in the tavern. These 'merry' scenes take the form of interruption of and distraction from the serious lesson.

After the first lesson (physics) (148–500), Humanity is lured away from Studious Desire by Sensual Appetite. The second lesson (geography) continues in his absence with Experience telling Studious Desire about the world (659–878). The two parties then clash; Experience denounces Sensual Appetite and persuades Humanity to learn more (971–1030). In the third lesson Experience adduces more proofs of the earth's rotundity (1031–1134, where the text breaks off). In the missing section it seems that Humanity grows weary of instruction and rejoins Sensual Appetite; their revels grow violent under the rule of Ignorance, who is lording it when the text resumes (1135–50). Humanity, rescued from prostration by Sensual Appetite and Ignorance, makes clear his preference for the tavern wine and women (1150–1289). This triumph over hero and audience is signalled by Sensual Appetite's bringing dancers into the hall (1289–1368). The orderly pleasures of song and dance are then parodied in Ignorance's nonsense ballad (1369–1419). Finally, Nature returns to admonish Humanity for his bestial life (1420–43). The end of the play is missing, but all that the plot requires is for Ignorance to be banished and Humanity to repent so he can be reinstated with his former tutor Studious Desire.

The 'myxyd' nature of the construction is visible on a smaller scale in the verse forms and language. Like all early English drama *Four Elements* is composed in stanzaic verse (a few lines of prose are used for

12

the first time in Medwall's *Nature*, c.1495). The stanza is a mnemonic aid to actors, and the rhythmic lines carry across a noisy crowd better than prose speech. The making of verse also demonstrates the playwright's craft. But Rastell eschews the elaborate stanza schemes developed by the playwrights of the Wakefield cycle, of *Castle of Perseverance*, *Mankind*, and *Mary Magdalene*, preferring the simpler tail-rhyme stanza, staple of popular romance and of popular drama, particularly in East Anglia, and the 'literary' 7-line rhyme royal stanza used by Chaucer and Lydgate. The principles of early Tudor versification are even less certain than those of Chaucerian poetry. The long line used for the rhyme royal stanzas averages ten syllables and some read like the familiar iambic pentameters of later English poetry; but many lines more naturally have four stresses, two balanced each side of a central caesura –

> Thaboúndant gráce of the pówer devýne
>
> (1)

– approximating to the principle of stress in Middle English alliterative verse.

The 7-line stanzas (rhyming ababbcc) are used for the dignified opening lines 1–390, except for odd 8-line stanzas (281–8, 317–32, 340–7, 382–90). The bulk of the play is composed in 6-line stanzas (tail rhyme or *rime couée*). The normal form is $aa_4b_3cc_4b_3$ but larger combinations of three-line units occur, and the stanzas are expanded by occasional couplets or by the addition of extra rhyming lines. It has been suggested that these excrescences on the basic pattern are lines added to a literary text for performance. But not all can be so explained, and some deviations seem deliberately aimed at doggerel effect. The basic metre of popular ballad ($a_4b_3c_4b_3$) is just discernible in the nonsense rhyme of lines 1396–1419. The words of 1319–24 and 1335–45 follow the musical structure of the songs.

In his prologue Rastell claims to tell the 'matter'

> Without great eloquence in ryme rudely
> Because the compyler is but small lernyd.
>
> (128–9)

He thinks of himself as 'compiler' not poet. But there is also the question of decorum:

> This worke with rethoryk is not adournyd,
> For perhappis in this matter muche eloquence
> Sholde make it tedyous or hurt the sentence.
>
> (130–3)

Some rhetorical habits, however, were inherent in the literary language of Rastell's models, associated particularly with the weighty rhyme royal stanza used by Chaucer, Lydgate, and Stephen Hawes, so that *Four Elements* is not quite as plain as is claimed (e.g. the first stanza, with its reminiscences of pageant-play God the Father's Latinate and Frenchified vocabulary, its adjectival inversions and polysyllabic rhyming). Nevertheless, most of the Latinity in Rastell's vocabulary is technical and belongs to the scientific matters treated (*corrupcyons, generacyons, ponderosyte, insensate, adnychelate* – reduced to nothing). The author's great theme, that 'our tonge is now suffycyent / To expoun any hard sentence evydent', asks that language be functional; the success of education lies in clarification. Rastell is at his best making the abstract concrete, even if the images are well worn. Thus air and fire are described:

> About the yerth and water joyntly they go
> And compasse them everywhere orbycularly
> As the whyte aboute the yolke of an egg doth lye.
>
> (248–50)

This plainness is also evident in the swifter, short-line stanzas used to expound the globe. Sensual Appetite's disruptive vigour is indicated by colloquial rapidity, a loose string of idiomatic expressions and song-like formulae, often accompanied by physical activity on stage:

> Make rome, syrs, and let us be mery,
> With huffa, galand, synge tyrll on the bery,
>   And let the wyde worlde wynde!
>
> (416–18)

Sense is finally disrupted completely in Ignorance's ballad of Robin Hood, a jumbled patchwork of broadsheet ballad and nursery rhyme:

> He start up to a thystell top
> And cut hym downe a holyn clobe,
> He stroke the wren betwene the hornys
> That fyre sprange out of the pyggys tayle.
>
> (1406–6)

The moral point is obvious. But the technique is a little unfair to the audience. It is a consequence of the dramatic necessity of equating learning with 'sadness' that 'myrth and sport' are the domain of vice. It is the 'vice', Sensual Appetite, self-appointed 'marshal of these revels', who brings in the dancers and who leads the singing of a song whose composition is attributed elsewhere to Henry VIII. The play's larger strategy of making us feel guilty about 'Tyme to pas with goodly sport' is broadly in line with other cultural changes that were happening on

14

the eve of the English Reformation and which were to leave their imprint on the national character.

Calisto and Melebea

The printing of this 'new commodye in Englysh in maner of an enterlude' was done in about 1525. John Rastell's cosmic device appears, together with the legend 'Johēs rastell me imprimi fecit', which may mean that he had the actual printing done by sub-contract (possibly by John Skot, some of whose printing ornaments also are used in the book).[28] The circumstances of the composition of the play are not known for sure. Since it is a landmark of Anglo-Spanish literary relations, it has been associated with the Spanish humanist Vivés, at once time tutor to Princess Mary, a friend of More's and a visitor to England six times between 1523 and 1528.[29] Vivés's pupil Richard Hyrd tutored More's daughters. Vivés and Hyrd are the only contemporaries in England known to have referred to La Celestina.

Fernando de Rojas's novel-in-dialogue came to be known as La Celestina by virtue of the immense vitality of the old bawd Celestina. The first version appeared in 1499, followed by an expanded version, La tragicomedia de Calisto y Melibea, in 1500. Success was so startling and immediate that the profusion of subsequent editions and pirated versions remains a bibliographical cause célèbre.[30] The book was soon translated into Italian, French, and Hebrew. The anonymous English playwright worked from the Spanish only, even though his understanding was often imperfect – and it is likely that copies would have been owned by members of Queen Catherine's circle at court.

Vivés refers twice to La Celestina.[31] In his De causis corruptarum artium of 1531 he praises its bitter moral ending (presumably the death

[28] STC 20721. The Interlude of Calisto and Melebea, ed. W. W. Greg (MSR, Oxford, 1908), p. v.
[29] G. Ungerer, Anglo-Spanish Relations in Tudor Literature (Schweizer Anglistische Arbeiten 38, Berne, 1956), pp. 9–41; Henry de Vocht, 'Vivés and his Visits to England' in Monumenta Humanistica Lovaniensia (Louvain, 1934), pp. 1–60; G. J. Brault, 'English Translations of the Celestina in the Sixteenth Century', Hispanic Review, 27 (1960), 301–12.
[30] Before 1600 there were at least 187 editions. See J. Homer Herriott, Towards a Critical Edition of the 'Celestina' (Madison and Milwaukee, 1964), pp. 3–13; J. J. Norton, Printing in Spain 1501–20 (Sandars Lecture in Bibliography, Cambridge, 1963); A. S. Mandel, ed. La Celestina Studies (Metuchen, N. J., 1971).
[31] Ungerer, pp. 14–15.

of the lovers). Earlier, in his *De institutione foeminae Christianae*, dedicated to Queen Catherine and Princess Mary in 1524, he includes *La Celestina* with *Tristan* in his list *de pestiferis libris*. The erotic intrigue and hard violence of a brothel underworld could scarcely suit the syllabus he planned for the instruction of a Christian woman (Vivés's tone veers uneasily between the shrill harshness of *Hali Maedenhed* and the sickly piety of Ruskin's *Of Queens' Gardens*). Vivés's Latin was translated by Richard Hyrd, who refers briefly to 'those ungracious bokes, such as be in my countre in Spayne: Amadise . . . Celestina, the baude, mother of noughtynes'.[32] This slender evidence, together with Vivés's influence at court, his friendship with More and his two-and-a-half years spent in England, Hyrd's tutoring of More's daughters, Rastell's connections with the More family and at court, provide at least an ambience for the English version of *La Celestina*. The circumstances support what is clear from a comparison of the Spanish and English: that the interlude, intended to show 'the bewte and good propertes of women . . . with a morall conclusion and exhortacyon to virtue', was partly an attempt to chasten and domesticate an international best-seller for a refined, morally-minded audience. It was a project that appealed to Rastell.

That the printed title makes no mention of the Spanish source is not surprising, since the play is not a translation but an adaptation. Moreover, by the time of printing relations with Spain had become strained. The originality of making a play out of the first European prose novel is concealed by offering the interlude in familiar terms of vice and virtue. Only the words 'new commodye' hint at the parentage and look like a humanist ploy to align the native 'interlude' with the vogue for Terentian revivals and imitations that was sweeping the continent.[33] *La tragicomedia* is composed in twenty-one acts and cast entirely in dialogue; though it was intended for private reading, it seems to invite adaptation for the stage.

[32] R. Hyrde, *The very fruteful and plesant boke called the Instruction of a Christen Woman*, 1541, sig. E4.
[33] In a poem prefatory to the 1501 (Seville) edition of the *Comedía de Calisto y Melíbe* the author claims originality by rejecting the accusation that he used a Terentian model. The woodcuts in a Toledo edition of *La Comedia de Calisto* (1523) derive from an earlier Grüninger edition of Terence's plays. In England Terence had been printed in Latin during the fifteenth century. An interlinear Latin/English text of *Andria*, c.1520, once thought to be by Rastell, is now thought to have been printed in Paris (*STC* 23894). On the Terentian stage revival see T. E. Lawrenson and Helen Purkis, 'Les Éditions Illustrées de Térence dans l'Histoire du Théâtre' in *Le lieu théâtral à la Renaissance*, ed. J. Jacquot & Elie Konigson (Paris, 1969), pp. 1–23.

In fact, the English adapter could use little of his Spanish treasure.[34] He translated, compressed, and rearranged parts of the Prologue, Acts 1, 2, and 4, adding a few isolated speeches from Acts 5 and 6. His interlude is concerned only with Calisto's wooing of Melebea by means of the skilful arguments of Celestina, and so it ends at the point where Melebea gives up her belt and the old bawd carries it off to Calisto, rejoicing in a symbolic victory of lust over chastity. In the Spanish, the tragedy of a passionate illicit love sustained for a while by a vicious underworld accelerates into a nightmare of violence. Celestina and her agents die at one another's hands, Calisto falls from a ladder at Melebea's window, and she jumps to her death from the house top before her father's eyes. All this is omitted. The English provides an original ending in which Melebea begs her father's forgiveness for a sin committed only by the will.

The Spanish cast of fourteen is reduced in English to six, an appropriate number for playing interludes, by leaving out Melebea's mother and maid, two of Calisto's servants, two of Celestina's girls, a lecher, and a pimp. The thematic interest of *La Celestina* is drastically pruned by excision of the philosophical digressions habitual to de Rojas, in the manner of Jean de Meun's *Roman de la Rose*, and by avoiding the gross humour (e.g. a jest about God's sodomy with the angels) and seamy detail that seventeenth-century English audiences so enjoyed after William Mabbe's full-blooded translation of *Celestine* appeared in 1631.

The effect of these changes was to 'make a wild horse tame', to avert tragedy, substituting satirical comedy. Interest focuses on the wooing, viewed morally as the temptation and fall of Melebea leading to her recognition and repentance, her forgiveness, and a moral exhortation. In making this pattern the English playwright allowed himself to be guided by a native tradition at least two hundred years old – in particular by a formulaic wooing play of the medieval secular repertory. Two versions of the model are known: the fabliau-play of *Dame Sirith and the Weeping Bitch*, and the fragmentary *Interludium de Clerico et Puella*.[35] From this popular tradition the playwright of *Calisto* adapted the 'weeping bitch' motif to provide his denouement. The line running from *interludium* to *enterlude* is long but unbroken.

A simple principle of dramatic construction keeps the audience informed of the plot's progress. There are three almost equal 'acts'

---

[34] See H. D. Purcell, 'The *Celestina* and the *Interlude of Calisto and Melibea*', *Bulletin of Hispanic Studies*, 44 (1967), 1–15.

[35] R. Axton, 'Folk Play in Tudor Interludes', in *English Drama: Forms and Development*, ed. M. Axton and R. Williams (Cambridge, 1977), pp. 15–18.

(1–309, 310–632, 633–919) and an epilogue (920–1087); the divisions fall when the acting place is empty and they may have been intended as pauses in performance, perhaps for refreshment. Each 'act' begins with a solo entry (Melebea at 1, Celestina at 310, Melebea at 633); other characters enter and leave, and the stage is occupied until the end of the act is marked by a solo character taking leave of the audience (Calisto at 310, Parmeno at 629 ff., Celestina at 912 ff.). The 'maner of an enterlude' demands a respectful but playful attentiveness towards the audience; and this is written into the dialogue. Celestina showers them with pious blessings, apologises for her abrupt entrance, and regales them with a 'prety game' – a farcical anecdote from the bawdy house. Sempronio mocks his lovelorn master in an aside. Melebea is afraid to enter a hall where there are so many men; later, outraged by Celestina's proposal, she turns to the audience for help: 'Som good bodi take this old thefe fro me!' (791). The audience are to assist (in the French sense) at the play.

The satire has two principal objects – romantic love and spurious piety. Both targets were traditional in medieval secular drama; the lover-clerk, the would-be-virtuous girl and the sanctimonious bawd are already stereotypes in the early English *interludium*. The English poet tunes in to the 'pious' language of the original and amplifies it. The debate about reformation which was growing louder in England towards 1529 gives a new critical edge to Celestina's oaths and ostentatious Mariolatry, her duping of the young virgin into yielding her girdle as a wonder-working relic, her insistence on 'works of pyte' (mercy). Similarly, Calisto's bold preference of Pythagorean metempsychosis to Christian purgatory has 'a spyce of heresye'. Dramatic licence in airing these matters is underlined when Calisto's servant apologises to the audience, 'Hys sayeng in this none can controll'. The author's own position is not radical – he is no John Bale – but it is made clear at the end by Melebea's father that the heroine has been saved from 'actuall dede of shame' by saying her daily prayers.

This moral conclusion, original in the English, forms a bridge to the final exhortation, in which all John Rastell's familiar hobby-horses are trotted out. The fatherly Danio addresses 'ye faders, moders, and other which be / Rulers of yong folkis', telling them to train the young people to be usefully occupied, and urging men in authority to make good laws and execute them strictly. This is the only realistic 'reformyng'. The 'heavy' epilogue helps to establish the satirical intention in the presentation of Calisto earlier in the play; this idle Petrarchan mooncalf, with his exclamations on Fortune and his fashionable courtly melancholy, belongs in a world that John Rastell had little time for.

The play is composed entirely in 7-line rhyme royal stanzas, except

18

for an isolated, epigrammatic couplet (71–2). The lines usually have four stresses and a variable number of unstressed syllables:

> Now sóry, now sád, now jóyous, now pénsyfe!
>
> (12)

Metrically, *Calisto* is similar to the rhyme royal sections of *Four Elements* (from line 1025 to the end the vocabulary and phraseology are indistinguishable from much of *Four Elements*), and quite distinct from John Heywood's practice.[36]

The title boasts that the play is 'ryght elygant and full of craft of rethoryk', a term which covers formulae of apostrophe and alliterative devices –

> O what fortune is egall unto myne?
> O what wofull wyght with me may compare?
>
> (101–2)

attempts at 'dark' figurative usage –

> The thurst of sorow is my myxyd wyne,
> Which dayly I drynk wyth deepe draughtys of care.
>
> (103–4)

and also more extended topoi. Calisto's rhapsodic description of Melebea, carefully itemised from top to toe, which he calls 'rehersyng my style' (226 ff.), keeps close to the models set down in the medieval *artes poeticae* and is worked through like an exercise. Sempronio's catalogue of women's wiles is peppered with proverbial maxims and *sententiae* (178 ff.). Celestina enumerates *exempla* from the bestiary (759 ff.) and her first exchange with Melebea soon slips into a proverbial dialogue of Age and Youth.

> *Celestina* Fayre damesell, who can shew all the hurtys of age?
> His werynes, feblenes, his discontentynge,
> His chyldishnes, frowardnes of his rage,
> Wrynkelyng in the face, lak of syght and heryng . . .
>
> (661–4)

The English poet has a liking for proverbs, adding to those he finds in the Spanish and developing allusive dialogue from them in a way that Heywood was to make his own (see below, p. 25). One proverb is of particular interest and structural importance. As Celestina leaves the stage clutching the precious belt she is confident of victory because,

> Now know ye by the half tale what the hole doth meane.
>
> (910)

---

[36] J. E. Bernard, *The Prosody of the Tudor Interlude* (New Haven, 1939), pp. 51–2.

The poet has truncated the story of his source and prides himself on his English understatement.

For much that is 'crafty' the rhetorical prose of the Spanish provides a model which involves the English poet in difficulties. Some, at least, of the crabbedness of his syntax is due to the effort of translation. Sometimes his meaning is cloudy (e.g. 64–6). Misunderstandings as well as garblings of the Spanish are quite common, as in the classic howler of lines 119–20, where Nero burns in love for the Tarpean rock.

In general the English poet is most successful when he completely recasts the original, as in the monologue of Celestina (320–73) where a little comedy-within-a-comedy is brilliantly evoked in the rapid cut and thrust of speech reported and mimicked:

> Cryto in my chamber above that was hyddyn
> I thynk lay not easyly and began to romble.
> Sempronio hard that and askyd who was within
> Above in the chamber that so dyd jomble.
> 'Who?' quod she, 'a lover of myne'. 'May hap ye stomble',
> Quod he, 'on the trewth, as many one doth.'
> 'Go up,' quod she, 'and loke whether it be soth.'
>
> 'Well,' quod he, 'I go'. Nay, thought I, not so,
> I sayd, 'Com Sempronio, let this foole alone . . .'
>
> (353–61)

It is a pity Rastell died with 370 copies of the play unsold. Language like this deserves to have made more impact on the English drama.

Gentleness and Nobility

Like *Calisto*, the play was printed c.1525, by which time William Rastell may have been helping his father.[37] Its date of composition, circumstances of performance, and authorship can only be guessed from internal evidence. From a thorough study of the background and sources, K. W. Cameron concluded cautiously in favour of John Heywood.[38] I agree with this judgement, and also with Cameron's view that the play's epilogue, written in rhyme royal to be spoken by 'a Philosopher', is Rastell's addition. The mixture of stage directions (Latin and English) points also to collaboration or revision.

---

[37] *STC* 20723. *Gentleness and Nobility*, ed. F. P. Wilson and A. C. Partridge (MSR, Oxford, 1950), p. v.

[38] K. W. Cameron, *Authorship and Sources of 'Gentleness and Nobility'* (Raleigh, N.C., 1941). Wilson and Partridge, pp. v–vii, review the external evidence for authorship.

John Heywood (born c.1497) is variously described in contemporary documents as 'gentleman', 'servant of the King', 'member of the Mercers company', 'a singinge man' and 'pleyar of the virginals'.[39] From 1519–28 he received a salary of at least £20 a year which is recorded in the King's Book of Payments; after this he had an annual royal pension. In 1523 he received the Freedom of the City and took up residence in London. It was probably at about this time that he married Joan Rastell. Some time before 1529/30 he had become a member of the Stationers' Company, perhaps through Rastell's influence.[40] As we have seen already, Rastell was associated with court entertainments in 1520, 1522, and 1527. *Gentleness* cannot be pushed closer to the court than this. Clearly its satirical jibes against knights and merchants would be most appreciated by an audience from those classes. The possibility of some actual social rivalry between 'gentylman' Heywood and his father-in-law (or prospective father-in-law) adds spice to the play's interest, and may in part explain the discrepancy between the dismissive ironies of Heywood's work and the earnest optimism which contradicts the tenor of the dialogue in Rastell the philosopher's conclusion. One is on firmer ground observing that the play's concerns are exclusively social; the three estates represented are all secular, and there is no clergy. This is unlikely to have been the case if the play had been composed during the period 1524–30, when clergy were openly attacked. The Plowman's dark reference to 'A tyme tyll our governours may intend / Of all enormytees the reformacyon / And bryng in theyr handis the rod of coreccyon' (997–9) sounds as if it was written in a period of long recess, in anticipation of the parliament of 1523.

The play is advertised as 'a dyaloge betwen the Marchaunt, the Knyght and the Plowman dysputyng who is a verey gentylman and who is noble and how men shuld come to auctoryte'. The central issues are of two kinds: the relation between social rank and inner worth; and the relative merit of the different 'estates' of society. These related matters are the subject of an immense literature in the later Middle Ages and early Renaissance. Chaucer stands at the head of the English tradition; he uses the word *gentilesse* to define ethical values he has distilled from his masters – Guillaume de Lorris, Jean de Meun, and Dante. Chaucer is clear in his moral balade *Gentilesse* that 'unto vertu longeth dignitee, / And noght the revers', and the old hag of the *Wyf of Bath's Tale* educates her arrogant young knight by citing Dante, Valerius, Seneca, and Boethius to prove 'he is gentil that dooth gentil dedis'. Gentle deeds

---

[39] Reed, p. 37; J. Stevens, *Music and Poetry in the Early Tudor Court* (1961), p. 319; R. de la Bère, *John Heywood, Entertainer* (1937), p. 24.

[40] Reed, pp. 45–6.

are not defined; for Chaucer, *gentilesse* is above all a lack of self-interest, a moral generosity of spirit. It is not a question of economics.

Chaucer's contemporaries Langland and Gower were more concerned with the conflict of the economic estates, with winning and wasting. But eventually the solutions adumbrated in *Piers Plowman* are spiritual ones, not economic reforms. The thrust of Langland's satire is against corrupt clergy of all sorts. The play *Gentleness* adopts the traditional tripartite division of the estates, but in a secularized form, replacing clergy by the middle estate of merchants. (This is also the case in Christine de Pisan's *Body of Polycye*, printed in English by John Skot in 1521.) The rapid growth of a well-educated and wealthy middle class towards the end of the fifteenth century eclipsed the importance of 'clergy' in social thinking and challenged the 'gentle' class. There was competition for places at the universities, at the inns of court, and for public office. The *Great Chronicle of London* for 1509 speaks disparagingly of those of 'grete byrth & gentylnesse of blood' who join the scramble to advance themselves, arrogantly possessing few good 'condicions' and no 'points of virtue'.[41]

Insistence that true nobility depends on inner virtue and active merit became a commonplace of humanist writing. The same criteria discussed in the play are found in contemporary works: property, ancestry, intelligence, work, virtue, freedom from compulsion. So too are the views put forward about the abuse of authority, the exploitation of labour, man's difference from the beasts, the true nature of wealth, and the golden age. Cameron's study of sources cites analogues to the play from Erasmus (*Institutio Principi Christiani*, 1516, *Colloquia*, *Encomium Morae*), More (*Dialogue of Comfort*, *Utopia*), Christine de Pisan (*Body of Polycye*), Elyot (*The Governour*), an anonymous *Dyaloge betwene a Gentillman and a Husbandman*, French and Spanish versions of the *Disputation of the Ass*, Lydgate's *Debate of the Horse, Goose, and Sheep*, and more popular sources. The arguments, Cameron rightly insists, are commonplace to educated people of the time.

The way in which the arguments are deployed is another matter. The play exaggerates opposing social views for humorous effect, dispelling conflict in critical mirth rather than channelling it into reformatory proposals. In this it follows the sophisticated debate initiated on the English stage by Henry Medwall's *Fulgens and Lucrece* (c.1495). Where Medwall's Florentine Latin source left open the conclusion, Medwall makes his heroine decide in favour of plebeian virtue while at the same time upholding the principle of aristocratic superiority. Any offen-

---

[41] Quoted by Cameron, p. 21. See also J. Hexter, 'The Education of the Aristocracy in the Renaissance' in *Reappraisals in History* (1961), pp. 45–70.

siveness to the 'gentle' audience (Cardinal Morton's household) is forestalled by the witty commentary of the foolish servants A and B ('What? Wyll they afferme that a chorles son / Sholde be more noble than a gentilman borne?').[42] *Fulgens*, composed at about the time of Heywood's birth, was printed by Rastell before 1516. Like *Gentleness* it is in two parts, but there is little similarity of structure or content (*Gentleness* has no story line). If Heywood is indebted to the earlier play then it is perhaps to the spirit of disruptive humour provided by the 'low' characters A and B, who play about the edge of the serious centre. In *Gentleness* the play's centre is filled by the bulk of the obstreperous Plowman.

The Plowman's intellectual vigour and self-confidence are in part a literary inheritance. Behind him stands a Christian tradition of satirical *complaint*, in particular, of course, *Piers the Plowman* and its progeny: *Pierce the Ploughman's Crede*, the pseudo-Chaucerian *Plowman's Tale*, *Jack Upland*. The honest plowman was a touchstone against pretension, a licensed spokesman against exploitation by landlords, clergy, and the 'kyngis purviours'.[43] Similarly, the pauper in the influential dialogue of *Dives and Pauper* (printed by Pynson in 1493) has the intellectual authority of patient poverty grounded on biblical texts and teaching. Other ancestors of the dialogue Plowman trod the medieval stage as shepherds, that other dominant type of the simple good Christian. The concern with practical affairs, the satirical wit and quick deflation of pretence by coarseness are all found in the Wakefield shepherds; it is in those plays that explicit social commentary was most fully developed (Mak's pretence that he is a yeoman causes a celebrated exchange).[44] Another, more sinister, ancestor is the Wakefield plowman Cain, social rebel and black humorist, quick with scatological imprecations and blows for those who cross him. The roles of various popular stereotypes are less fully scripted: 'rude upplandissche people' complained about their wives in a 'disguysing' composed by Lydgate for Henry VI in 1426;[45] the traditional dramatic 'games' of English ploughlads offered respectful service to their overlords and also indulged in festive folly.[46]

[42] *Fulgens and Lucres*, ed. F. S. Boas and A. W. Reed (Oxford, 1926) and forthcoming in *The Plays of Henry Medwall*, ed. Alan H. Nelson (Tudor Interludes, Ipswich) Part I, lines 130–1.
[43] 'God spede the plough' in *Piers the Ploughman's Crede*, ed. W. W. Skeat (EETS, 1867), p. 70.
[44] *The Wakefield Pageants in the Towneley Cycle*, ed. A. C. Cawley (Manchester, 1958), 4.201 ff.
[45] John Lydgate, *Minor Poems*, ed. H. MacCracken, Part II (EETS, 1934), p. 539.
[46] Axton, 'Folk Play', p. 4.

The Plowman of *Gentleness* has something of all these traditions; he is Christian moralist and pungent proverbial satirist, bully, and fool.

For the purpose of the dramatic conflict the 'questyon movyd at the begynnyng' provides the grounds for triangular dispute:

> whych of us all three
> Coud prove hym selfe most gentylman to be.
>
> (857–8)

The mode of argument is a simple and ancient one, used in medieval debate poems since before the *Owl and the Nightingale*: self-recommendation, and criticism or abuse of one's adversaries. Without preamble the Merchant sets up as 'king of the castle':

> O what a gret welth and prosperyte
> It is to any reme where marchauntes be . . .
> I am magnyfyed and gretly regardyd,
> And for a wyse and noble man estemyd.
>
> (1–10)

The printed text is divided in two parts, each having a long, three-cornered dispute (175–463, 473–982). Dialogue between the Merchant and Knight forms a prelude (1–74) and postlude (1014–99) to this symmetry. The balance is weighted at the end by the Philosopher's epilogue (1100–76). The Plowman's dramatic authority comes partly from the fact that he speaks almost as many lines as the other two taken together (527 whole lines, to the Knight's 300 and Merchant's 272). He also holds the stage alone for 30 lines before his final exit (983–1013). His professional vigour, both menacing and comic, is implied when he 'commith in with a short whyp in hys hand' and is manifest in the beating he gives the Knight at line 193. The stage direction and some of the dialogue here are repeated verbatim at 714. This shaping of formulaic verbal conflict into periodic physical bouts is also characteristic of Heywood's *John John* and the *Pardoner and Friar*.

The 'manner of an interlude' requires solicitous awareness of the audience's presence and tastes, so that a breach of decorum is itself seen as a cause of merriment:

> *Merchaunt* Kepe the peace, masters, hold your handys, for shame!
> To make thys besynes ye be gretely to blame.
> Ye wyll dysturb all thys hole company.
> *Plowman* Nay, mary, it is a cause to make them mery,
> To walke [i.e. beat] such a proude foole is but sport
>   and game.
>
> (715–19)

The metrical principles of the dialogue are hard to establish. The line

24

is roughly decasyllabic, varying from eight to twelve syllables. But many lines more happily take four stresses than five, e.g.:

Thou aŕt not hónest, I téll the pláynly

(198)

though some lines are regular pentameters:

Sīr, hóld yŏur tóng, yŏur wórdis bĕ nóthyñg góod.

(722)

The dialogue is arranged in couplets, with two triplets (193–5, 278–80); the epilogue is in 7-line rhyme royal stanzas. Rhyme serves to smooth out the sense of uneven staves in a bundle. Much of the rhyme is light and imperfect (thys/lyffys, unto/*eterno*, body/worthy, nakyd/wrechyd, etc.) and, in the rhyme royal stanzas, rather repetitive. Metre and rhyme of the couplets match Heywood's practice in other plays; the rhyme royal stanzas are consistent with Rastell's metrical practice in *Four Elements*. Forty-four couplets and 3 single lines are divided between speakers (as is often the case in Heywood's work), most effectively where the Plowman catechises the Knight in the seven deadly sins and their remedies (882–91).

The language is mostly plain, the vocabulary concrete, and the syntax unforced. What rhetorical patterning there is is mostly scholastic (e.g. the Plowman's syllogism: 'For musyke makyth one a musycyon, / Grammer to be a good gramareon' 871–2). Colloquial and vulgar exclamations abound ('Straw for thi councell, torde, a fart! 419). Proverbs are liberally used, not for their idiomatic flavour so much as for their pithy aptness as authorities in a drama of ideas. The much-quoted verses,

For when Adam dolf and Eve span,
Who was then a gentylman?

(485–6)

were current before the Peasants' Revolt of 1382. In the interlude they come not as the rallying cry of a new social revolution but as ideas, subject to ironic qualification.

There is much to be mocked in all the estates, but little in the end to be done. The Plowman leaves the 'reformation of enormities' to 'our governours':

For exortacyons, techyng, and prechyng,
Gestyng, and raylyng, they mend no thyng.

(1002–3)

25

As for changing other men's opinions,

> In effect it shall no more avayle
> Than wyth a whyp to dryfe forth a snayle.
>
> (992–3)

The nature of proverbs is to be both fatalistic and reversible (a quality Heywood was brilliantly to explore for his debate of youth and age concerning marriage in the *Dialogue of Proverbs*, 1546).[47] The proverb, so loved by Erasmus and the humanist wits, is the most succinct and urbane and demotic form of irony. The Philosopher's epilogue is lacking in proverbial language. Indeed, it somewhat flat-footedly contradicts the Plowman by asserting that the best way

> To convert the people by exhortacyon
> Ys to perswade them by naturall reason.
>
> (1132–4)

The knights and merchants of the audience cannot all have been complacently amused by the interlude. Some of them were men working towards the English Reformation. Father Rastell, for one, disguised as the Philosopher, cannot forbear to correct the logical errors in the earlier argument and to remind the audience soberingly that many a true word is spoken in jest.

---

[47] *Heywood's Dialogue of Proverbs*, ed. R. E. Habenicht (Berkeley, Cal., 1963).

Adams, R. P. *The Better Part of Valor; More, Erasmus, Colet, and Vivés, on Humanism, War, and Peace, 1496–1535*, Seattle, 1962.

Anglo, Sydney. *Spectacle Pageantry, and Early Tudor Policy*, Oxford, 1969.

Barber, C. *Early Modern English*, London, 1976.

Bennett, H. S. *English Books and Readers, 1475–1557*, 2nd edn., Cambridge, 1969.

Bernard, J. E. *The Prosody of the Tudor Interlude*, New Haven, 1939.

Bevington, D. M. *From Mankind to Marlowe*, Cambridge, Mass., 1962.
Tudor Drama and Politics, Cambridge, Mass., 1968.

Cameron, K. W. *Authorship and Sources of 'Gentleness and Nobility'*, Raleigh, N.C., 1941.

Chambers, E. K. *The Medieval Stage*, 2 vols., Oxford, 1903.
The Elizabethan Stage, 4 vols., Oxford, 1923.

Craik, T. W. *The Tudor Interlude*, Leicester, 1958.

de la Bére, R. *John Heywood, Entertainer*, London, 1937.

Dickens, A. G. *The English Reformation*, London, 1964.

Harbage, A. B. *Annals of English Drama, 975–1700*, revised by S. Schoenbaum, London, 1966.

Mason, H. A. *Humanism and Poetry in the Early Tudor Period*, London, 1959.

Maxwell, Ian. *French Farce and John Heywood*, London, 1946.

Potter, R. *The English Morality Play*, London, 1975.

Reed, A. W. *Early Tudor Drama*, London, 1926.

Southern, R. *The Staging of Plays Before Shakespeare*, London, 1973.

Stevens, John. *Music and Poetry in the Early Tudor Court*, London, 1961.

Wickham, Glynne. *Early English Stages, 1377–1660*, vol. 1, London, 1958 (revised edn. 1963).

Wilson, F. P. *The English Drama, 1485–1585*, Oxford, 1969.

The editor's aim has been to reproduce the spelling of the original texts, free from the merely typographical conventions of early Tudor printing. Thus, u and v, i and j are regularised, and capitals are used sparingly, according to modern practice. Although Rastell's printing house has a distinct style, irregular spelling is a typical feature of work of the period; no attempt has been made to standardise word forms, except where speakers' names have been supplied by the editor. Abbreviations and contractions are expanded to the forms most commonly used in each text. In the case of the plural ending ꝯ, expansion to the forms *es*, *ys*, or *is* depends on which form of the plural occurs most frequently in the text. Doubtful readings or expansions are noted. Roman numerals are given in words, or, in cases of large numbers, in Arabic figures.

The word separation of early Tudor English was not consistent, even within the same printing house (e.g. *with out*, *there for*, *a nother*, *in dede*, etc.). Words have been run together or separated by the editor according to two criteria: if they appear in the normal modern form at some point in the original, and also if unfamiliar spacing might impede comprehension.

Wherever possible the original readings are retained. Editorial additions are placed in square brackets and original readings recorded in the Notes. Minor printing errors, such as transposed or inverted type, are silently emended.

All punctuation is editorial. Rastell's compositors used, very sparingly, the bar (/) and point (.), and the force of these marks has been taken into account. Editorial punctuation has been kept as light as was possible to prevent misunderstanding of the syntax. The use of the semicolon proved necessary to present long, paratactic sentences without suggesting either staccato or breathlessness in the original Tudor verse. The apostrophe has been introduced by the editor only for the common expression *quoth'a* or *quod'a* ('said he' or 'says he', spoken in a mocking tone).

The beginning of a new speech or a new rhyme royal stanza is normally indicated by Rastell's printers by the use of a paragraph sign. The text of this edition is therefore laid out to make apparent the regularly stanzaic nature of most of the play's dialogue.

Editorial additions to the stage directions are placed in square brackets.

FOUR ELEMENTS

The players' names

The Messenger	Sensual Appetite
Nature	Taverner
Humanity	Experience
Studious Desire	Ignorance

Singers and Dancers

A NEW INTERLUDE AND A MERY,
OF THE NATURE OF THE FOUR ELEMENTIS,

declarynge many proper poyntys of phylosophy naturall, and of dyvers straunge
landys, and of dyvers straunge effectis and causis; whiche interlude, yf the hole
matter be playde, wyl conteyne the space of an hour and a halfe; but yf ye lyst ye
may leve out muche of the sad mater, as the messengers parte, and some of Naturys
parte and some of Experyens parte, and yet the matter wyl depend convenyently,
and than it wyll not be paste thre quarters of an hour of length.

Here folow the namys of the pleyers:

The Messengere, Nature Naturate, Humanyte, Studyous Desire, Sensuall
Appetyte, the Taverner, Experyence, Yngnoraunce. Also yf ye lyst ye may brynge
in a dysgysynge.

Here folow dyvers matters whiche be in this interlude conteynyd:

Of the sytuacyon of the four elementis, that is to sey, the yerth, the water, the
ayre, and fyre, and of theyr qualytese and propertese, and of the generacyon and
corrupcyon of thyngys made of the commyxion of them.
Of certeyn conclusions provynge that the yerth must nedis be rounde and that it
hengyth in the myddys of the fyrmament, and that it is in circumference above
21,000 myle.
Of certeyn conclusions provynge that the see lyeth rounde uppon the yerth.
Of certeyne poyntys of cosmography, as how and where the see coveryth the yerth,
and of dyvers straunge regyons and landys and whiche wey they lye, and of the new
founde landys and the maner of the people.
Of the generacyon and cause of stone and metall, and of plantis and herbys.
Of the generacyon and cause of well spryngys and ryvers, and of the cause of hote
fumys that come out of the yerth, and of the cause of the bathys of water in the yerth
whiche be perpetually hote.
Of the cause of the ebbe and flode of the see.
Of the cause of rayne, snowe and hayle.
Of the cause of the wyndys and thonder.
Of the cause of the lyghtnynge of blasyng sterrys and flamys fleynge in the ayre.

Thaboundant grace of the power devyne,
Whiche doth illumyne the worlde invyron,
Preserve this audyence and cause them to inclyne
To charyte, this is my petycyon.
For by your pacyens and supportacyon   5
A lytyll interlude, late made and preparyd,
Before your presence here shall be declaryd,

Which of a few conclusyons is contrivyd,
And poyntys of phylosophy naturall.
But though the matter be not so well declaryd   10
As a great clerke coude do, nor so substancyall,
Yet the auctour hereof requiryth you all,
Though he be yngnorant and can lytyll skyll,
To regarde his only intent and good wyll,

Whiche in his mynde hath oft tymes ponderyd   15
What nombre of bokys in our tonge maternall
Of toyes and tryfellys be made and impryntyd,
And few of them of matter substancyall.
For though many make bokys yet unneth ye shall
In our englyshe tonge fynde any warkys   20
Of connynge that is regardyd by clerkys.

The grekys, the romayns, with many other mo,
In their moder tonge wrot warkys excellent;
Than yf clerkys in this realme wolde take payn so,
Consyderyng that our tonge is now suffycyent   25   A2ᵛ
To expoun any hard sentence evydent,
They myght, yf they wolde, in our englyshe tonge
Wryte workys of gravyte somtyme amonge.

For dyvers prengnaunt wyttes be in this lande,
As well of noble men as of meane estate,   30
Whiche nothynge but englyshe can understande.
Than yf connynge laten bokys were translate
Into englyshe, wel correct and approbate,
All subtell sciens in englyshe myght be lernyd
As well as other people in their owne tonges dyd.   35

But now so it is that in our englyshe tonge
Many one there is, that can but rede and wryte,
For his pleasure wyll oft presume amonge
New bokys to compyle and balates to indyte:
Some of love or other matter not worth a myte;   40
Some to opteyn favour wyll flatter and glose,
Some wryte curyous termys nothyng to purpose.

31

Thus every man after his fantesye
Wyll wryte his conseyte, be it never so rude,
Be it vertuous, vycyous, wysedome or foly.   45
Wherfore to my purpose, thus I conclude:
Why shold not than the auctour of this interlude
Utter his owne fantesy and conseyte also,
As well as dyvers other nowadayes do?

For wysedome and foly is as it is takyn,   50
For that one callyth wysedome, another callyth foly;   A3
Yet amonge moste folke that man is holdyn
Moste wyse, whiche to be ryche studyeth only;
But he that for a commyn welth bysyly
Studyeth and laboryth and lyvyth by Goddys law,   55
Except he wax ryche, men count hym but a daw.

So he that is ryche is ever honouryd,
All though he have got it never so falsely;
The pore beynge never so wyse is reprovyd.
This is the oppynyon moste commynly   60
Thorowe out the worlde, and yet no reason why.
Therfore in my mynde, whan that all suche dawis
Have babelyd what they can, no force of two strawis.

For every man in reason thus ought to do,
To labour for his owne necessary lyvynge,   65
And than for the welth of his neyghbour also.
But what dyvylish mynde have they which, musing
And labouryng all their lyffys, do no nother thyng
But bringe ryches to their owne possessyon,
Nothyng regardinge their neyghbours distruccion.   70

Yet all the ryches in the worlde that is
Rysyth of the grounde by Goddys sendynge,
And by the labour of pore mennys handys,
And though thou, ryche man, have therof the
    kepynge,
Yet is not this ryches of thy gettynge,   75
Nor oughtyst not in reason to be preysyd the more
For by other mennys labour it is got before.   A3

A great wytted man may sone be enrychyd,
That laboryth and studyeth for ryches only,
But how shall his conscyens than be discharged?   80
For all clerkys afferme that that man presysely,
Whiche studyeth for his owne welth pryncypally,
Of God shall deserve but lytyll rewarde,
Except he the commyn welth somwhat regarde.

32

So they sey that that man occupyed is   85
For a commyn welth, whiche is ever laborynge
To releve pore people with temporall goodys,
And that it is a commyn good act to brynge
People from vyce and to use good lyvynge.
Lykewyse for a commyn welth occupyed is he   90
That bryngyth them to knowlege that yngnorant be.

But man to knowe God is a dyffyculte,
Except by a meane he hym selfe inure,
Whiche is to knowe Goddys creaturys that be:
As furst them that be of grosyst nature,   95
And than to know them that be more pure,
And so by lytyll and lytyll ascendynge
To know Goddys creaturys and mervelous werkinge.

And this wyse man at the last shall come to
The knowlege of God and his hye mageste,   100
And so to lerne to do his dewte, and also
To deserve of his goodnes partener to be.
Wherfore in this work declaryd shall ye see
Furst of the elementis the sytuacyon,   A4
And of their effectis the cause and generacyon.   105

And though some men thynke this matter to hye
And not mete for an audyence unlernyd,
Me thynke for man nothynge more necessary
Than this to know, though it be not usyd,
Nor a matter more lowe can not be arguyd.   110
For though the elementis Goddys creaturis be,
Yet they be most grose and lowyst in degre.

How dare men presume to be callyd clerkys,
Dysputynge of hye creaturis celestyall,
As thyngys invysyble and Goddys hye warkys,   115
And know not these vysyble thyngys inferyall?
So they wolde know hye thyngys and know
        nothinge at all
Of the yerth here wheron they dayly be,
Nother the nature, forme nor quantyte.

Wherfore it semyth nothynge convenyent   120
A man to study and his tyme to bestowe
Furst for the knowlege of hye thyngys excellent,
And of lyght matters beneth nothynge to know –
As of these four elementis here below,
Whose effectis dayly appere here at eye.   125
Such thingys to know furst were most mete study.

33

Whiche matter before your presence shortly
In this interlude here shall be declaryd
Without great eloquence, in ryme rudely,
Because the compyler is but small lernyd. 130
This worke with rethoryk is not adournyd, A4ᵛ
For perhappis in this matter muche eloquence
Sholde make it tedyous or hurt the sentence.

But because some folke be lytyll disposyd
To sadnes, but more to myrth and sport, 135
This phylosophycall work is myxyd
With mery conseytis, to gyve men comfort
And occasyon to cause them to resort
To here this matter, wherto yf they take hede
Some lernynge to them therof may procede. 140

But they that shall nowe this matter declare
Openly here unto this audyence –
Beholde I prey you, see where they are!
The pleyers begyn to appere in presence;
I se well it is tyme for me to go hens 145
And so I wyll do. Therfore now shortly
To God I commyt all this hole company.

[Exit the Messenger]

Hic intrat Natura Naturata, Humanyte
et Studyous Desire portans figuram.

Natura Naturata   The hye, myghty, most excellent of all,
The fountayn of goodnes, verteu, and connyng,
Whiche is eterne of power most potencyall, 150
The perfeccyon and furst cause of every thynge –
I meane that only hye nature naturynge –
Lo, he by his goodnes hath ordeynyd and create A5
Me here his mynyster, callyd Nature Naturate.

Wherfore I am the verey naturate nature, 155
The inmedyate mynyster for the preservacyon
Of every thynge in his kynde to endure,
And cause of generacyon and corrupcyon.
Of that thynge that is brought to distruccyon
Another thynge styll I brynge forth agayne. 160
Thus wondersly I worke and never in vayne.

34

The great worlde beholde, lo, devydyd wondersly
In to two regyons, wherof on I call
The etheriall region with the hevyns hye,
Conteynynge the planettys, sterris and speris all;   165
The lower region callyd the elementall
Conteynynge these four elementis beloo:
The fyre, the ayre, the water, and yerth also.

But yet the elementis and other bodyes all
Beneth take theyr effectys and operacyons   170
Of the bodyes in the region ethereall.
By theyr influens and constellacyons
They cause here corrupcyons and generacyons;
For yf the movyngys above sholde onys cease,   175
Beneth sholde be nother increse nor decrese.

These elementis of them selfe so syngle be
Unto dyvers formys can not be devydyd,
Yet they commyx togyder dayly ye see,
Wherof dyvers kyndes of thyngys be ingenderyd,   A5ᵛ
Whiche thyngys eftsonys whan they be corruptyd   180
Yche element I reduce to his furst estate,
So that nothynge can be utterly adnychelate.

For though the forme and facyon of any thyng
That is a corporall body be distroyed,
Yet every matter remaynyth in his beynge,   185
Wherof it was furst made and formyd;
For corrupcyon of a body commyxyd
Ys but the resolucyon by tyme and space
Of every element to his owne place.

For who that wyll take any body corporall   190
And do what he can it to distroy,
To breke it or grynde it into pouder small,
To washe, to drown, to bren it or to dry,
Yet the ayre and fyre therof naturally
To their owne proper places wyll ascende,   195
The water to the water, the yerth to the yerth tende.

For yf hete or moysture of any thynge certayne
By fyre or be water be consumyd,
Yet yerth or asshes on yerth wyll remayne,
So the elementis can never be distroyed.   200
For essencyally ther is now at this tyde
As muche fyre, ayre, water, yerth, as was
Ever before this tyme, nether more nor las.

35

Wherfore thou man – now I speke to the –
Remembre that thou art compound and create   205   A6
Of these elementis, as other creaturis be,
Yet they have not all lyke noble estate,
For plantis and herbys growe and be insensate,
Brute bestis have memory and their wyttes fyve,
But thou hast all those and soule intellectyve.   210

So by reason of thyne understandynge
Thou hast domynyon of other bestis all,
And naturally thou sholdyst desire connynge
To knowe straunge effectis and causys naturall,
For he that studyeth for the lyfe bestyall,   215
As voluptuous pleasure and bodely rest,
I account hym never better than a best.

Humanyte   O excellent prynce, and great lorde Nature,
I am thyne owne chylde and formyd instrument!
I beseche thy grace, take me to thy cure,   220
And teche me suche scyens thou thinkyst expedyent.
Nature   Than syth thou art so humble and benevolent,
That thynge that is mete for thy capasyte
And good for thy knowlege I shall instructe the.

Furst of all, thou must consyder and see   225
These elementis, which do yche other penetrate,
And by contynuall alteracyon they be
Of them selfe dayly corruptyd and generate.
The yerth as a poynt or center is sytuate   A6ᵛ
In the myddys of the worlde, with the water joyned,   230
With the ayre and fyre rounde and hole invyronyd.

The yerth of it selfe is ponderous and hevy,
Colde and dry of his owne nature proper;
Some parte lyeth dry contynually
And parte therof coveryd over with water,   235
Some with the salt see, some with freshe ryver.
Whiche yerth and the water togyder with all
So joynyd make a rounde fygure sperycall.

So the water whiche is colde and moyst is founde
In and uppon the yerth, fyllynge the holones   240
In dyvers partis, liynge with the yerth rounde,
Yet the hyllys and mounteyns of the yerth excesse
Take nothynge of hit a way the roundnes,
In comparyson bycause they be so small,
No more than the prikkys do that be on a gall.   245

36

The ayre whiche is hote and moyst also,
And the fyre whiche is ever hote and dry,
About the yerth and water joyntly they go
And compasse them everywhere orbycularly,
As the whyte aboute the yolke of an egg doth lye.   250
But the ayre in the lower parte moste remaynyth;
The fyre naturally to the hyer tendyth.

The etheryall region, whiche conteynyth
The sterrys and planettys and every spere,
About the elementis dayly movyth   255   A7
And coveryth them rounde about every where.
Every sterre and spere in straunge maner
Uppon his owne poles movyth dyversly,
Whiche now to declare were to longe to tary.

The fyre and the ayre of their naturys be lyght,   260
Therfore they move by naturall provydence.
The water, bycause it is ponderous in weyght,
Movyth not naturally but by vyolence
Of the sterris and planettys, by whose influence
The see is compellyd to ebbe and flowe dayly,   265
And freshe waters to sprynge contynually.

And though that the water be grose and hevy
Yet nothynge so grose as the yerth iwys,
Therfore by hete it is vaporyd up lyghtly
And in the ayre makyth cloudys and mystys,   270
But as sone as ever that it grosely is
Gederyd togyder, it descendyth agayne
And causyth uppon the yerth hayle, snow and rayne.

The yerth, because of his ponderosyte,
Avoydyth equally the movynges great   275
Of all extremytes and sperys that be,
And tendyth to the place that is most quiet;
So in the myddys of all the sperys is set
Formast, abject from all maner movynge,
Where naturally he restyth and movyth nothynge.   280

Marke well now how I have the shewyd and tolde   A7v
Of every element the very sytuacyon
And qualyte; wherfore this fygure beholde
For a more manyfest demonstracyon.
And by cause thou sholdyst not put to oblyvyon   285
My doctryne, this man callyd Studyous Desire
With the shall have contynuall habytacyon,
The styll to exhort more scyens to adquire.

37

For the more that thou desyrest to know any thynge,
Therin thou semyst the more a man to be;   290
For that man that desireth no maner connynge,
All that wyle no better than a best is he.
Why ben the eyes made, but only to see,
The leggys, to bere the body of a creature?
So every thynge is made to do his nature.   295

So lykewyse reason, wit, and understondyng
Ys gyven to the, man, for that thou sholdyst in dede
Knowe thy maker and cause of thyne owne beynge,
And what the worlde is, and wherof thou doest
    procede.
Wherfore it behovyth the of verey nede   300
The cause of thyngys furst for to lerne,
And than to knowe and laude the hye God eterne.

Humanyte
O gloryous lorde and prynce moste plesant,
Greatly am I now holdyn unto the
So to illumyne my mynde that was yngnorant   305
With soch noble doctryne as thou hast here
    shewed me!   A8
Wherfore I promyse uppon my fydelyte
My dylygence to do to kepe in memory,
And the for to honour styll perpetually.

Studyous Desire
And syth it hath pleasyd thy grace to admyt   310
Me uppon this man to gyve attendaunce,
With thy doctryne here shewyd I shall quikkyn
    his wyt
And dayly put hym in remembraunce.
His courage and desyre I shall also inhaunce,
So that his felycyte shall be most of all   315
To study and to serche for causys naturall.

Nature
Well than, for a season I wyll departe,
Levynge you togyder here both twayne.
What I haue shewid, man, prynt well in thyne hert
And marke well this fygure that here shall remayne,   320
Wherby thou maist perceyve many thynges more playn
Concernynge the matter I spake of before.
And whan that I shall resort here agayne
Of hye poyntys of connynge I shall shew the[e] more.

[Exit Nature]

38

Studyous Desire	Now, Humanyte, call to your memory 325
	The connynge poyntys that Nature hath declaryd,
	And though he have shewed dyvers pointys and many
	Of the elementis so wondersly formed,
	Yet many other causys there are wolde be lernyd, A8ᵛ
	As to knowe the generacyon of thyngys all 330
	Here in the yerth, how they be ingendryd
	As herbys, plantys, well spryngys, ston and metall.
Humanyte	Those thyngys to knowe for me be full expedient,
	But yet in those poyntys whiche Nature late shewyd me,
	My mynde in them as yet is not content, 335
	For I can no maner wyse parceyve nor see,
	Nor prove by reason why the yerth sholde be
	In the myddys of the fyrmament hengyng so small
	And the yerth with the water be rounde with all.
Studyous Desire	Me thynkyth my selfe, as to some of those pointys, 340
	I coude gyve a suffycyent solucyon.
	For furst of all thou must nedys graunt this,
	That the yerth is so depe, and botom hath non,
	Or els there is some grose thyng hit stondyth upon,
	Or els that it hangyth, thou must nedys consent, 345
	Evyn in the myddys of the fyrmament.
Humanyte	What than? go forth with thyne argument.
Studyous Desire	Than marke well, in the day or in a wynters nyght,
	The sone and mone and sterris celestyall
	In the est furst they do apere to thy syght, 350
	A[nd] after in the west they do downe fall, B1
	A[nd] agayne in the morowe next of all
	Wi[thi]n twenty four houres they be come just
	To [th]est pointys again where thou sawist them furst.
	Than yf the erthe shulde be of endles depnes 355
	Or shulde stande upon any other grose thynge,
	It shulde be an impedyment dowtles
	To the sone, mone, and sterris in theyr movynge;
	They shulde not so in the est agayne sprynge.
	Therfore in reason it semyth moste convenyent 360
	The yerth to hange in the myddys of the fyrmament.
Humanyte	Thyne argument in that poynt doth me confounde,
	That thou hast made, but yet it provyth not ryght
	That the yerth by reason shulde be rounde.
	For though the fyrmament with his sterris bryght 365
	Compas aboute the yerth eche day and nyght,
	Yet the yerthe may be playne, peradventure,
	Quadrant, triangle, or some other fygure.

Studyous Desire	That it can not be playne I shall well prove the,	
	Because the sterris that aryse in the oryent	370
	Appere more soner to them that there be,	
	Than to the other dwellynge in the occident.	
	The eclypse is therof a playne experymente	B1ᵛ
	Of the sone or mone which, whane it dothe fu[ll],	
	Is never one tyme of the day in placys all.	375

Yet the eclyps generally is alwaye
In the hole worlde as one tyme beynge;
But whan we that dwell here see it in the mydday,
They in the west partis see it in the mornynge,
And they in the est beholde it in the evenyng.   380
And why that sholde so be, no cause can be found
But onely by reason that the yerthe is rownde.

Humanyte	That reason proveth the yerth, at the lest	
	One wayes to be rownde, I cannot gayne say,	
	As for to accompt frome the est to the west;	385
	But yet not withstondynge all that, it may	
	Lese hys rowndenesse by some other waye.	
Studyous Desyre	Na, no dowte yt is rownde everywhere,	
	Which I coulde prove, thou shoudest not say nay,	
	Yf I had therto any tyme and leser.	390

But I knowe a man callyd Experyens,
Of dyvers instrumentys is never without,
Cowde prove all these poyntys, and yet by his scyens   395   B2
Can tell how many myle the erthe is abowte,
And many other straunge conclusions, no dowte.
Thys instrumentys cowde shew them so certayn
That every rude carter shold them persayve playn.

Humanyte	Now wolde to God I had that man now here	
	For the contembtacyon of my mynde!	
Studyous Desyre	Yf ye wyll, I shall for hym enquere	400
	And brynge hym heder yf I can hym fynde.	
Humanyte	Then myght I say ye were to me ryght kynde.	
Studyous Desyre	I shall assay by God that me dere bought,	
	For cunnyng is the thynge that wolde be sought.	

[Studious Desire starts to leave, but Sensual Appetite
comes in running and knocks him down.]

Sensuall Apetyte	Well hyet! quod Hykman, when that he smot	405
	Hys wyffe on the buttockys with a bere pott.	
	Aha! now, god evyn, fole, god evyn!	
	It is even the, knave, that I mene.	
	Hast thou done thy babelyng?	

Studyous Desyre	Ye, peradventure, what than?	410
Sensuall Apetyte	Than hold downe thy hede lyke a prety man	
	And take my blyssyng	411a
	Benedicite! I graunt to the this pardon	B2ᵛ
	And gyve the[e] absolucion;	
	For thy soth saws, stande up, Jack daw!	
	I beshrew thy faders sone!	415

Make rome, syrs, and let us be mery,
With huffa, galand, synge tyrll on the bery,
      And let the wyde worlde wynde!
Synge fryska joly, with hey troly loly,
For I se well it is but a foly   420
      For to have a sad mynd.

For rather than I wolde use suche foly
To pray, to study or be pope holy,
      I had as lyf be ded.
By Goggys body, I tell you trew,   425
I speke as I thynke, now els I beshrew
      Evyn my next felowes hed.

Master Humanyte, syr, be your leve,
I were ryght loth you to greve
      Though I do hym dyspyse,   430
For yf ye knewe hym as well as I,
Ye wolde not use his company
      Nor love hym in no wyse.

Humanyte	Syr, he loketh lyke an honest man,	
	Therfore I merveyll that ye can	435
	This wyse hym deprave.	B3
Sensuall Appetyte	Though he loke never so well,	
	I promyse you he hath a shrewde smell.	
Humanyte	Why so? I prey you tell.	
Sensuall Appetyte	For he saveryth lyke a knave.	440

Studyous Desire	Holde your pease, syr, ye mystake me.	
	What, I trowe that ye wolde make me	
	Lyke to one of your kyn.	
Sensuall Appetyte	Harke, syrs, here ye not how boldly	
	He callyth me knave agayne by polycy?	445
	The devyll pull of his skyn!	

I wolde he were hangyd by the throte,
For by the messe I love hym not;
 We two can never agre.
I am content, syr, with you to tary,   450
And I am for you so necessary
 Ye can not lyve without me.

Humanyte   Why syr, I say, what man be ye?

Sensuall Appetyte I am callyd Sensuall Apetyte,
All craturs in me delyte;   455
 I comforte the wyttys fyve
The tastyng, smellyng, and herynge.
I refresh the syght and felynge
 To all creaturs alyve.

For whan the body wexith hongry   460 B3ᵛ
For lacke of fode, or ellys thursty,
 Than with drynkes plesaund
I restore hym out of payne,
And oft refresshe nature agayne
 With delycate vyand·   465

With plesaunde sound of armonye
The herynge alwaye I satysfy –
 I dare this well reporte;
The smellynge, with swete odour,
And the syght with plesaunte fygour   470
 And colours I comforte.

The felynge that is so plesaunte
Of every member, fote or hande,
 What pleasure therin can be
By the towchynge of soft and harde,   475
Of hote or colde, nought in regarde,
 Excepte it come by me.

Humanyte   Than I cannot see the contrary
But ye are for me full necessary
 And ryght convenyent.   480
Studyous Desire   Ye, syr, beware yet what ye do
For yf you forsake my company so
 Lorde Nature wyll not be contente.

Of hym ye shall never lerne good thyng   B4
Nother vertu nor no other connynge,   485
 This dare I well say.
Sensuall Appetyte Mary, avaunt, knave! I the defye!
Dyde Nature forbyde hym my company?
What sayst thou therto? Speke openly.
Humanyte   As for that I know well nay.   490

Sensuall Appetyte	No by God, I am ryght sure, For he knoweth well no creature Without me can lyve one day.	

Humanyte	Syr, I pray you be contente.
	It is not utterly myne intente
	    Your company to exyle,
	But onely to have communycacyon
	And a pastyme of recreacyon
	    With this man for a whyle.
		495

Studyous Desire *Sensuall Appetyte*	Well for your pleasure I wyll departe. Now go, knave, go! I beshrew thy hart! The devyll sende the forwarde!	*[Exit]* 500

	Now by my trouth I mervell gretly
	That ever ye wolde use the company
	    So myche of suche a knave.
	For yf ye do no nother thynge
	But ever study and to be musynge
	As he wolde have you, it wyll you brynge
	    At the last unto your grave.
		505
		
		B4ᵛ

	Ye shulde ever study pryncypall
	For to comfort your lyfe naturall
	    With metis and drynkes dilycate,
	And other pastymes and pleasures amonge,
	Daunsynge, laughynge or plesaunt songe;
	    This is mete for your estate.
		510
		
		515

Humanyte	Because ye sey so, I you promyse
	That I have musyd and studyed such wyse,
	    Me thynketh my wyttes wery.
	My nature desyreth some refresshynge,
	And also I have ben so longe fastynge
	    That I am somwhat hongry.
		520

Sensuall Appetyte
 	
Humanyte
	Well than, wyll ye go with me
	To a taverne where ye shall se
	Good pastaunce, and at your lyberte
	    Have what so ever ye wyll?
	I am content so for to do
	Yf that ye wyll not from me go
	    But kepe me company styll.
		525

Sensuall Appetyte
 	
Humanyte
	Company, quod'a! Ye, that I shall, poynt devyse,
	And also do you good and trew servyce,
	    And therto I plyght my trouthe.
	And yf that I ever forsake you,
	I pray God the devyl take you!
	    Mary, I thanke you for that othe.
		530
		
		B5

Sensuall Appetyte	A myschyfe on it! my tonge, loo, 535
	Wyll tryp somtyme, what so ever I do –
	But ye wot what I mene well.
Humanyte	Ye, no force! let this matter passe.
	But seydest evin now thou knewyst where was
	A good taverne to make solas? 540
	Where is that, I prey the, tell?
Sensuall Appetyte	Mary, at the dore, evyn here by.
	Yf we call any thynge on hye
	The taverner wyll answere.
Humanyte	I prey the, than, call for hym nowe. 545
Sensuall Appetyte	Mary, I wyll. How, taverner, how!
	Why doste thou not appere?

[Enter Taverner]

Taverner	Who is that calleth so hastely?
	I shrew thyne hert, speke softely!
	I tell the I am not here. 550
Sensuall Appetyte	Than I beshrew the[e], page, of thyne age!
	Come hyther, knave, for thyne avauntage.
	Why makyst thou hit so tow?
Taverner	For myne avauntage, mary, than I come.
	Beware, syrs! how! let me have rome! 555
	Lo, here I am! What seyst thou?
Sensuall Appetyte	Mary, thus: here is a gentylman, I say, B5ᵛ
	That nother ete nor dranke this day;
	Therfor tell me, I the praye
	Yf thou have any good wyne. 560
Taverner	Ye shall have spayneshe wyne and gascoyn,
	Rose coloure, whyt, claret, rampyon,
	Tyre, capryck, and malvesyne,
	Sak, raspyce, alycaunt, rumney
	Greke ipocrase, new made clary, 565
	Suche as ye never had.
	For yf ye drynke a draught or too,
	Yt wyll make you or ye thens go,
	By Goggys body, starke madde.
Sensuall Appetyte	I wot thou art not without good wyne. 570
	But here is a gentylman hath lyst to dyne –
	Canst thou get hym any good mete?

Taverner	What mete, mayster, wolde ye have?
Humanyte	I care not, so God me save,
	So that it be holsome to ete. 575

    I wolde we had a good stewyd capon.

Sensuall Appetyte As for capons ye can gette none,
    The kyngys taker toke up eche one.
      I wot well there is none to get.

Taverner Though all capons be gone, what than?   580 B6
    Yet I can get you a stewed hen
      That is redy dyght.
Humanyte Yf she be fat yt wyll do well.
Taverner Fat or lene I cannot tell,
    But as for this, I wot well   585
      She lay at the stewes all nyght.

Humanyte Thou art a mad gest, be this lyght!

Sensuall Appetyte Ye, syr, it is a felow that never faylys.
    But canst get my mayster a dyshe of quales,
    Smal byrdes, swalowes, or wagtayles –   590
    They be lyght of dygestyon.

Taverner Lyght of dygestyon, for what reason?

Sensuall Appetyte For physyk puttyth this reason therto:
    Bycause those byrdes fle to and fro
      And be contynuall movynge.   595

Taverner Then know I a lyghter mete than that.
Humanyte I pray the, tell me what.

Taverner Yf ye wyll nedys know at short and longe
    It is evyn a womans tounge,
      For that is ever sterynge.   600
Humanyte Syr, I pray the, let suche fanteses be.
    And come heder nere and harke to me,
      And do after my byddynge.

    Goo purvey us a dyner evyn of the moste,   B6ᵛ
    Of all maner dysshes both sod and roste   605
    That thou canst get, spare for no coste
      Yf thou make thre course.
Taverner Than ye get nother gose nor swane,
    But a dyshe of dreggys, a dyshe of brane,
    A dysshe of draffe, and I trowe than   610
      Ye can not get thre worse.

Humanyte	What, horson! woldyst thou purvey	
	Bran, draffe and stynkynge dreggys, I sey?	
	I holde the mad, I trowe.	
Taverner	Gogges passyon! sayd ye not thus,	615
	That I shulde purvey you thre course dysshes,	
	And these be course inowe.	

Humanyte	Thre course dysshes, quod'a!	
	What, mad fole! thou mystakest me clene	
	I se well thou wotest not what I mene,	620
	And understandyst amys.	
	I mene this wyse: I wolde have the	
	To purvey mete so great plente	
	That thou sholdyst of necessyte	
	Serve them at thre coursys.	625

	That is to understande, at one worde,	
	Thou shuldest brynge them unto the borde	
	At thre severall tymes.	B7

Taverner	What than, I se well ye wyll make a feste.	
Humanyte	Ye, by the rode, evyn with the gretest.	630
Sensuall Appetyte	By my trouth, than do ye best	
	Evyn after my mynde.	
	But ye must have more company.	
Humanyte	That is trewe and so wolde I gladly	
	If I knewe any to fynde.	635

Sensuall Appetyte	Why, wyll ye folowe my counsell?	
Humanyte	Ye.	
Sensuall Appetyte	Than we wyll have lytell Nell,	
	A proper wenche, she daunsith well,	
	And Jane with the blacke lace;	
	We wyll have bounsynge Besse also,	640
	And two or thre proper wenchis mo,	
	Ryght feyr and smotter of face.	

Humanyte	Now be it so, thou art saunce pere.	
Taverner	Than I perceyve ye wyll make gode chere.	
Humanyte	Why, what shulde I els do?	645
Taverner	If ye thynke so best, than wyll I	
	Go before and make all thynge redy	
	Agayne ye come therto.	

Humanyte	Mary, I prey the do so.	

46

Taverner	Than farewell syrs for I am gone. *[Exit]*	650
Humanyte	And we shall folow the anon	B7ᵛ
	Without any taryyng.	

Sensuall Appetyte	Then it is best, syr, ye make hast,	
	For ye shall spende here but tyme in wast	
	And do no nother thynge.	655
Humanyte	Yf ye wyll, let us goo by and by.	
Sensuall Appetyte	I pray you be it, for I am redy,	
	No man better wyllynge.	

Exeat Sensuall Apetyte et Humanyte,
Intrat Experiens et Studyous Desire

Studyous Desire	Now, cosyn Experyens, as I may say,	
	Ye are ryght welcom to this contrey,	660
	Without any faynyng.	
Experiens	Syr, I thanke you therof hertely,	
	And I am as glad of your company	
	As any man lyvynge.	

Studyous Desire	Syr, I understonde that ye have be	665
	In many a straunge countree,	
	And have had grete fylycyte,	
	Straunge causes to seke and fynde.	
Experiens	Ryght farr, syr, I have rydden and gone,	
	And seen straunge thynges many one,	670
	In Affryk, Europe, and Ynde,	

	Both est and west I have ben farre,	
	North also, and seen the sowth sterre,	
	Bothe by see and lande,	B8
	And ben in sondry nacyons	675
	With peple of dyvers condycyons,	
	Marvelous to understonde.	

Studyous Desire	Syr, yf a man have suche corage	
	Or devocyon in pylgrymage	
	Jheruzalem unto,	680
	For to accompt the nexte way,	
	How many myle is it I you pray	
	From hens theder to goo?	

Experiens	Syr, as for all suche questyons	
	Of townes to know the sytuacyon,	685
	How ferre they be asunder,	
	And other poyntes of cosmogryfy,	
	Ye shall never lerne then more surely	
	Then by that fygure yonder.	

	For who that fygure dyd fyrst devyse,	690
	It semeth well he was wyse	
	And perfyte in this scyens,	
	For bothe the se and lande also	
	Lye trew and just as the sholde do,	
	I know by experyens.	695

Studyous Desire   Who thynke you brought here this fygure?
Experiens   I wot not.
Studyous Desire   Certes, lorde Nature   B8ᵛ
Hym selfe not longe agone,
Whiche was here personally
Declarynge hye phylosophy,   700
And lafte this fygure purposely
For Humanytes instruccyon

Experiens   Dowtles ryght nobly done.

Studyous Desire   Syr, this realme ye know is callid Englande,
Somtyme Brettayne, I understonde,   705
Therfore I prey you point with your hande
In what place it shulde lye.

Experiens   Syr, this is Ynglande lyenge here,
And this is Skotlande that joyneth hym nere,
Compassyd aboute every where   710
With the occian see rownde.
And next from them westwardly
Here by hymselfe alone doth ly
Irelande, that holsome grounde.

Here than is the narowe seey,   715
To Calyce and Boleyne the next wey,
And Flaunders in this parte.
Here lyeth Fraunce next hym joynynge,
And Spaynn, southwarde from them standynge,
And Portyngale in this quart.   720

This contrey is callyd Italye—   Cⁱ
Beholde where Rome in the myddys doth ly,
And Naples here beyonde;
And this lytell see, that here is,
Is callyd the Gulfe of Venys,   725
And here Venys doth stande.

48

As for Almayne lyeth this way.
Here lyeth Denmarke and Norway,
    And northwarde on this syde
There lyeth Iselonde, where men do fyshe,   730
But beyonde that so colde it is,
    No man may there abyde.

This See is called the great Occyan,
So great it is that never man
Coude tell it sith the worlde began,   735
    Tyll nowe, within this twenty yere,
Westwarde be founde new landes
That we never harde tell of before this
By wrytynge nor other meanys,
    Yet many nowe have ben there.   740

And that contrey is so large of rome,
Muche lenger than all cristendome,
    Without fable or gyle;
For dyvers maryners haue it tryed
And sayled streyght by the coste syde   745
    Above fyve thousand myle.

But what commodytes be within,   Cl^V
No man can tell nor well imagin.
    But yet not longe ago
Some men of this contrey went,   750
By the kynges noble consent,
It for to serche to that entent
    And coude not be brought therto.

But they that were the venteres
Have cause to curse their maryners,   755
Fals of promys and dissemblers,
    That falsly them betrayed,
Whiche wolde take no paine to saile farther
Than their owne lyst and pleasure.
Wherfore that vyage and dyvers other   760
    Suche kaytyffes have distroyed.

O, what a thynge had be than,
Yf that they that be englyshe men
    Myght have ben the furst of all
That there shulde have take possessyon   765
And made furst buyldynge and habytacion,
    A memory perpetuall!

49

And also what an honorable thynge,
Bothe to the realme and to the kynge,
To have had his domynyon extendynge 770
    There into so farre a grounde,
Whiche the noble kynge of late memory,
The moste wyse prynce the seventh Herry, C2
    Causyd furst for to be founde.

And what a great meritoryouse dede 775
It were to have the people instructed
    To lyve more vertuously,
And to lerne to knowe of men the maner,
And also to knowe God theyr maker,
    Whiche as yet lyve all bestly. 780

For they nother knowe God nor the devell,
Nor never harde tell of hevyn nor hell,
    Wrytynge nor other scripture.
But yet, in the stede of God almyght,
The[y] honour the sone for his great lyght, 785
    For that doth them great pleasure.

Buyldynge nor house they have non at all,
But wodes, cotes, and cavys small;
    No merveyle though it be so,
For they use no maner of yron 790
Nother in tole nor other wepon,
    That shulde helpe them therto.

Copper they have, whiche is founde
In dyvers places above the grounde,
    Yet they dyg not therfore; 795
For, as I sayd, they have non yryn,
Wherby they shuld in the yerth myne,
    To serche for any wore.

Great haboundaunce of woddys ther be, C2ᵛ
Moste parte vyr and pyne aple tre; 800
    Great ryches myght come therby,
Both pyche and tarre and sope asshys,
As they make in the eest landes
    By brynnynge therof only.

Fyshe they have so great plente, 805
That in havyns take and slayne they be
    With stavys withouten fayle.
Nowe Frenchemen and other have founde the trade,
That yerely of fyshe there they lade
    Above an hundred sayl. 810

But in the south parte of that contrey
The people there go nakyd alway,
    The lande is of so great hete;
And in the north parte all the clothes
That they were is but bestis skynnes,   815
    They have no nother fete.

But howe the people furst began
In that contrey or whens they cam,
    For clerkes it is a questyon.
Other thynges mo I have in store   820
That I coude tel therof, but now no more
    Tyll another season.

Studyous Desire   Than at your pleasure shew some other thinge.
Yt lyketh me so wel your commyninge,
    Ye can not talke amys.   825   C3
Experiens   Than wyl I torne agayne to my matter
Of Cosmogryfy where I was err.
    Beholde, take hede to this.

Loo, estwarde beyonde the great occyan
Here entereth the see callyd Mediterran,   830
    Of two thousand myle of lengthe.
The Soudans contrey lyeth here by,
The great Turke on the north syde doth ly,
    A man of merveylous strengthe.

This sayde north parte is callyd Europa,   835
And this south parte callyd Affrica,
    This eest parte is callyd Ynde,
But this newe landys founde lately
Ben callyd America by cause only
    Americus dyd furst them fynde.   840

Loo, Jherusalem lyeth in this contrey,
And this beyonde is the Red See,
    That Moyses maketh of mencyon.
This quarter is India Minor
And this quarter India Maior,   845
    The lande of Prester Johnn.

But northwarde this way, as ye se,
Many other straunge regions ther be
    And people that we not knowe.
But est warde on the see syde   850
A prynce there is that rulyth wyde,   C3^v
    Callyd the Cane of Catowe.

51

And this is called the great eest see,
Whiche goth all alonge this wey
    Towardes the newe landis agayne;   855
But whether that see go thyther dyrectly
Or if any wyldernes bytwene them do ly,
    No man knoweth for certeyne.

But these newe landis, by all cosmografye,
Frome the Cane of Catous lande can not lye   860
    Lytell paste a thousande myle;
But from those new landis men may sayle playne
Estwarde, and com to Englande againe,
    Where we began ere whyle.

Lo, all this parte of the yerth whiche I   865
Have here discryvyd openly
    The north parte we do it call.
But the south parte on the other syde
Ys as large as this full, and as wyde,
    Whiche we knowe nothynge at all.   870

Nor whether the moste parte be lande or see,
Nor whether the people that there be
    Be bestyall or connynge,
Nor whether they knowe God or no,
Nor howe they beleve nor what they do,   875
    Of this we knowe nothynge.

Lo, is not this a thynge wonderfull,   C4
How that –
        Et subito Studyouse Desire dicat:

Studyous Desire   Pese, syr, no more of this matter!
Beholde where Humanyte commeth here.   880

    *[Studious Desire and Experience withdraw.
Re-enter Humanity and Sensual Appetite.]*

Sensuall Appetyte   How sey you, maister Humanyte,
I prey you have ye not be mere
    And had good recreacyon?
Humanyte   Yes, I thanke the therof every dell,
For we have faryd mervelously well   885
    And had good communycacyon.
        [Enter Taverner.]

52

Taverner	What, how, maister, where be ye now?
Sensuall Appetyte	What! I shrewe the! what haste hast thou
	That thou spekyst so hye?
Taverner	So hye, quod'a! I trow ye be mad, by Saynt Gyle! 890
	For dyd ye not ere whyle
	Make poyntment openly
	To come agayne all to supper,
	There as ye were to day at dyner?
	And yet ye poynted not playne 895
	What mete that ye wyll have drest
	Nor what delycatys ye love best.
	Me thynke you farre oversayne.
Humanyte	As for myne owne parte, I care not.
	Dresse what mete thou lovest, spare not 900
	What so ever thou doest best thynke.
Taverner	Now, if ye put it to my lyberte, C4^v
	Of all metis in the worlde that be,
	By this lyght, I love best drynke.
Sensuall Appetyte	It semyth by thy face so to do. 905
	But my maister wyll have mete also,
	What so ever it cost.
Taverner	By God, syr, than ye must tell what.
Humanyte	At thy discressyon I force nat
	Whether it be soden or rost. 910
Taverner	Well syr, than care not, let me alone.
	Ye shall se that all thynge shall be done
	And ordeyned well and fyne.
Humanyte	So I require the hertely,
	And in any wyse specyally 915
	Let us have a cuppe of newe wyne.
Taverner	Ye shall have wyne as newe as can be,
	For I may tell you in pryvyte
	Hit was brued but yester nyght.
Humanyte	But that is nothynge for my delyte. 920
Taverner	But than I have for your apetyte
	A cup of wyne of olde claret,
	There is no better by this lyght.
Humanyte	Well I trust the well inowe.
Taverner	But on thynge, if it please you nowe, 925
	Ye se well I take muche payne for you;
	I trust ye wyll se to me.
Humanyte	Ye, I promyse the. Get the[e] hens, C5
	And in this matter do thy dylygence,
	And I shall well rewarde the. 930

	By cause thou lokyst for a rewarde,	
	One thynge for the I have prepared	
	That here I shall the gyffe.	
	Thou shalte have a knavys skyn	
	For to put thy body therin,	935
	For terme of thy lyfe.	
Taverner	Now gramercy, my gentyll brother,	
	And therfore thou shalt have nother	
	For voydynge of stryfe.	
Sensuall Appetyte	Nowe farewell, gentyll Johnn.	940
Taverner	Than farewell, fole, for I am gone.	
Sensuall Appetyte	Abyde, torne ones agayne! harke what I sey!	
	Yet there is another thynge	
	Wolde do well at our maisters wasshynge.	
Humanyte	What thynge is that, I the prey?	945
Sensuall Appetyte	Mary, thus: canst thou tell us yet	
	Where is any rose water to get?	
Taverner	Ye, that I can well purvey,	
	As good as ever you put to your nose,	
	For there is a feyre wenche callyd Rose	950
	Dystylleth a quarte every day.	

Sensuall Appetyte	By God, I wolde a pynt of that	
	Were powryd evyn upon thy pate	
	Before all this presence.	C5ᵛ
Taverner	Yet I had lever she and I	955
	Where both togyther secretly	
	In some corner in the spence.	

For by God, it is a prety gyrle!
It is a worlde to se her whyrle,
    Daunsynge in a rounde.   960
O lorde God, how she wyll tryp!
She wyll bounce it, she wyll whyp,
    Ye, clene above the grounde!

Humanyte	Well, let all suche matters passe, I sey,	
	And get the[e] hens, and goo thy way	965
	Aboute this other matter.	
Taverner	Than I goo streyght, lo, fare ye well.	
Sensuall Appetyte	But loke yet thou remembre everydell	
	That I spake of full ere.	
Taverner	Yes, I warrant you, do not fere.	970

Exeat Taverner. [Re-enter Studious Desire and Experience.]

Humanyte	Goddis lorde, seist not who is here now?	
	What, Studyous Desire, what newis with you?	
Studyous Desire	Ye shall knowe, syr, or I go.	
Sensuall Appetyte	What, art thou here? I se well, I,	
	The mo knavys the worse company.	975
Studyous Desire	Thy lewde condycyons thou doest styll occupy,	
	As thou art wont to do.	

Humanyte	But I say, who is this here in presence?	
Studyous Desire	Syr, this is the man callyd Experiens	C6
	That I spake of before.	980
Humanyte	Experyens! Why, is this he?	
	Syr, ye ar ryght welcome unto me,	
	And shall be ever more.	

Experience	Syr, I thanke you therof hertely,	
	But I assure you feythfully	985
	I have small courage here to tary,	
	As longe as this man is here.	
Sensuall Appetyte	Why, horson, what eylyst at me?	
Experience	For thou hast ever so leude a properte	
	Science to dispyse, and yet thou art he	990
	That nought canst nor nought wylt lere.	

Sensuall Appetyte	Mary, avaunt, knave! I make God avowe,	
	I thynke my selfe as connynge as thou,	
	And that shall I prove shortly.	
	I shall put the a questyon now, come nere,	995
	Let me se how well thou canst answere.	
	How spellest this worde Tom Couper	
	In trewe artografye?	

Experyence	Tom Couper, quod'a! a wyse questyon, herdly!	

Sensuall Appetyte	Ye, I tel the agayn yet:	1000
	Tom Couper, how spellyst it?	[1000a]
	Lo, he hath forgotten, ye may se,	
	The furste worde of his ABC.	
	Harke, fole, harke! I wyll teche the.	
	P – A, pa, T – E – R, ter,	
	Do togyther Tom Couper.	[1004a]
	Ys not this a sore matter?	1005 C6ᵛ
	Loo, here ye may se hym provyd a fole!	
	He had more nede to go to scole	
	Than to come hyther to clatter.	

Studyous Desire	Certeyne this is a solucyon	1010
	Mete for suche a boyes questyon.	

55

Humanyte	Sensuall Apetyte, I prey the,
	Let passe all suche tryfles and vanyte
	For a wyle – it shall not longe be –
	And depart, I the require.
	For I wolde talke a worde or two 1015
	With this man here or he hens go,
	For to satysfy my desyre.
Sensuall Appetyte	Why, Goggis soule, wyll ye so shortly
	Breke poyntment with yonder company
	Where ye shulde come to supper? 1020
	I trust ye wyll not breke promys so.
Humanyte	I care not greatly yf I do,
	Yt is but a taverne matter.
Sensuall Appetyte	Than wyll I go shew them what ye sey.
Humanyte	Spare not, if thou wylt go thy wey, 1025
	For I wyll here tary.
Sensuall Appetyte	Than adew for a whyle, I tel you playne,
	But I promyse you whan I come agayne
	I shall make yonder knavys twayne
	To repent and be sory. 1030

[Exit Sensual Appetite]

Experyence	Nowe I am full glad that he is gone.
Studyous Desire	So am I, for good wyll he do none
	To no man lyvynge.
	But this is the man with whome ye shall
	I trust be well content with all, 1035
	And glad of his commynge.
	For he hath expownyd connyngly
	Dyvers poyntes of cosmogryfy,
	In fewe wordes and shorte clause.
Humanyte	So I understande he hath gode science 1040
	And that he hath by playne experience
	Lernyd many a straunge cause.
Studyous Desire	Ye, syr, and I say for my parte
	He is the connyngest man in that arte
	That ever I coude fynde. 1045
	For aske what questyon ye wyll do,
	Howe the yerth is rounde or other mo,
	He wyll satysfye your mynde.
Experyence	Why, what doute have ye therin founde?
	Thynke ye the yerth shulde not be rounde, 1050
	Or elles howe suppose ye?

C7

56

Humanyte	One wey it is rounde, I must consent,
	For this man provyd it evydent;
	Towarde the eest and occydent
	It must nedis rounde be. 1055
Experyence	And lykewyse from the south to north.
Humanyte	That poynt to prove were sum thanke worth. C7ᵛ
Experyence	Yes, that I can well prove,
	For this ye knowe as well as I,
	Ye se the north starre in the skye, 1060
	Marke well, ye shall unethe it spye
	That ever it doth remove.

But this I assure you, if you go
Northwarde an hundreth myle or two,
    Ye shall thynke it ryseth, 1065
And how that it is nere aproched
The poynt over the top of your hed,
    Whiche is callyd your zenyth.

Yet yf ye go the other wey,
Southwarde ten or twelve dayes jorney, 1070
    Ye shall then thynke anon
It discended, and come more nye
The sercle partynge the yerth and skye,
As ye loke streyght with your eye, 1075
    Whiche is callyd your oryson.

But ye may go southwarde so farre
That at the last that same starre
    Wyll seme so farre downe ryght,
Clere underneth your oryson,
That syght therof can you have non, 1080
    The yerth wyll stop your syght.

	This provyth of necessyte
	That the yerth must nedis rounde be, C8
	This conclusyon doth it trye.
Humanyte	Nowe that is the properist conclusyon 1085
	That ever I herde, for by reason
	No man may hit denye.
	But, sir, if that a man sayle farre
	Upon the see, wyll than that starre
	Do there as on the grounde? 1090
Experyence	Ye, doutles. Sayle northwarde, ryse it wyl,
	And sayle southwarde, it falleth styl,
	And that provyth the see rounde.

57

Studyous Desire	So dothe it in myne oppynyon.	
	But knowe you any other conclusyon	1095
	To prove it rounde, save that alone?	
Experyence	Ye, that I knowe ryght well,	
	As thus: marke well whan the see is clere	
	That no storme nor wawe theron doth pere —	
	This maryners can tell —	1100

Than if a fyre be made on nyght
Upon the shore, that gyveth great lyght,
 And a shyp in the see farre,
They in the toppe the fyre se shall
And they on hache nothynge at all,   1105
 Yet they on haches be nerre.

Also, on the see where men be saylynge
Farre from lande, they se nothynge
 But the water and the skye;   C8ᵛ
Yet whan they drawe the lande more nere,   1110
Than the hyll toppes begyn to apere,
 Styll the nere more hye and hye,

As though they were styll growynge faste
Out of the see, tyll at laste,
 Whan they come the shore to,   1115
They se the hyll, toppe, fote, and all;
Whiche thynge so coude not befall
 But the see lay rounde also.

Humanyte	Me thynketh your argument somwhat hard.	
Experyence	Than ye shall have it more playnly declared,	1120
	If ye have great desyre;	
	For here, loo, by myne instrumentis	
	I can shew the[e] playne experimentis	
Humanyte	Therto I you requyre.	

Experyence	With all my herte it shall be done.	1125
	But for the furst conclusyon,	
	That I spake of the fyre,	

Be this the seey that is so rounde,
And this the fyre upon the grounde,
 And this the shyp that is here.   1130
Ye knowe well that a mannes syght
Can never be but in a lyne ryght.

Humanyte	Just you say, that is clere.

Experyence	Marke well, than. May not that mannis eye . . .	1134

[There is a gap of eight leaves (D1–8) in the copy. About 360 lines are lost, during which Experience demonstrates to Humanity the earth's roundness, using the globe, a candle flame, and a telescope, and tells him of the earth's physical properties. Apparently Humanity grows weary of instruction and rejoins Sensual Appetite. When their revels grow violent he hides, but his legs are still visible. Ignorance speaks:]

[Yngnoraunce]	With argyng here theyr folyshe [sawes] That is not worth thre strawes.	[1135]	E1

	I love not this horeson losophers,
	Nor this great connyng extromers,
	That tell how far it is to the sterres;
	    I hate all maner connyng.
	I wolde ye knew it, I am Ignorance,
	A lorde I am of gretter pusans
	Than the kynge of Yngland or Fraunce,
	    Ye, the grettyst lord lyvyng.
		1140	

	I have servauntes at my retynew That longe to me, I assure you, Here within Ynglande, That with me, Yngnorance, dwell styll And terme of lyfe contynew wyll — Above fyve hundred thowsand.	1145 1150	

[Enter Sensual Appetite.]

Sensuall Appetyte	Goggys naylys, I have payed som of them, I tro!	
Yngnoraunce	Why man, what eylyth the so to blow?	
Sensuall Appetyte	For I was at a shrewd fray	
Yngoraunce	Hast thou any of them slayn than?	
Sensuall Appetyte	Ye, I have slayn them every man, Save them that ran away.	1155
Yngnoraunce	Why, is any of them skapyd and gone?	
Sensuall Appetyte	Ye, by Goggys body, everychone, All that ever were there.	
Yngnoraunce	Why than, they be not all slayne.	1160 E1ᵛ
Sensuall Appetyte	No, but I have put some to payne, For one horeson there was that torned again And streyght I cut of his ere.	
Yngoraunce	Than thou hast made hym a cut purs.	
Sensuall Appetyte	Ye, but yet I servyd another wors: I smot of his legge by the hard ars, As sone as I met hym there.	1165

Yngnoraunce	By my trouth, that was a mad dede.
	Thou sholdest have smyt of his hed,
	Than he sholde never have troublid the more. 1170
Sensuall Appetyte	Tushe, than I had ben but mad,
	For there was another man that had
	Smyt of his hed before.
Yngnoraunce	Than thou hast quyt the lyke a tal knyght.
Sensuall Appetyte	Ye, that I have, by this lyght. 1175
	But, I sey, can you tell me ryght
	Where becam my maister?
Yngnoraunce	What, he that you call Humanyte?
Sensuall Appetyte	Ye.
Yngnoraunce	I wot never except he be
	Hyd here in some corner. 1180
Sensuall Appetyte	Goggys body! and trew ye sey,
	For yonder, lo, beholde ye may
	Se where the mad fole doth ly.

[Humanity is discovered, prostrate, his head hidden]

Yngnoraunce	Now, on my feyth and treuth [iwys],	E2
	Hit were evyn great almys 1185	
	To smyte his hed from his body.	
Sensuall Appetyte	Nay God forbed ye sholde do so.	
	For he is but an innocent, lo,	
	In maner of a fole.	
	For as sone as I speke to hym agayne, 1190	
	I shall torne his mynde clene	
	And make hym folowe my skole.	
Yngnoraunce	Than byd hym ryse, let us here hym speke.	
Sensuall Appetyte	Now ryse up, maister Huddy Peke,	
	Your tayle totyth out behynde. 1195	
	Fere not, man, stande up by and by;	
	I warrant you, ryse up boldly!	
	Here is non but is your frynde.	

[Humanity gets up]

Humanyte	I cry you mercy, maister dere.
Yngnoraunce	Why, what is cause thou hydest the here? 1200
Humanyte	For I was almoste for fere
	Evyn clene out of my mynde.

Sensuall Appetyte	Nay, it is the study that ye have had		
	In this folyshe losophy hath made you mad,		
	And no nother thynge iwys.	1205	
Yngnoraunce	That is as trewe as the gospell.		
	Therfor I have great mervell		
	That ever thou wylt folowe the counsell		
	Of yonder two knavys.		

Humanyte	O syr, ye know ryght well this,	1210	E2ᵛ
	That when any man is		
	In other mens company,		
	He must nedis folow the app[et]yte		
	Of such thyngys as they delyte		
	Som tyme amonge, perdy.	1215	

Yngnoraunce	But such knaves wold alway have the		
	To put all thy mynde and felicite		
	In this folysh connyng to study,		
	Which, if thou do, wyll make the mad		
	And alway to be pensyf and sad;	1220	
	Thou shalt never be mery.		

Sensuall Appetyte	Mery quod'a! No, I make God avow!		
	But I pray the, mayster, hark! On word now,		
	And aunswere this thyng:		
	Whether thought you it better chere	1225	
	At the taverne where we were ere,		
	Or ellys to clatter with these knaves here		
	Of theyr folysh cunnynge?		

Humanyte	Nay, I can not say the contrary		
	But that I had mych myryer company	1230	
	At the taverne than in this place.		
Sensuall Appetyte	Than yf ye have any wyt or brayn,		
	Let us go to the taverne agayn		
	And make some mery solace.		

Yngnoraunce	Yf he wyll do so, than doth he wysely.	1235	
Humanyte	By my troth, I care not gretely,		E3
	For I am indyfferent to all company,		
	Whether it be here or there.		

Sensuall Appetyte	Then I shall tell you what we wyll do;		
	Mayster Yngnorans, you and he also	1240	
	Shall tary both styll here,		
	And I wyll go fet hyther a company,		
	That ye shall here them syng as swetly		
	As they were angellys clere.		

And yet I shall bryng hydyr another sort   1245
Of lusty bluddys to make dysport,
    That shall both daunce and spryng,
And torne clene above the ground
With fryscas and with gambawdes round,
    That all the hall shall ryng.   1250

And that done, within an howre or twayn,
I shall at the towne agayne
    Prepare for you a banket
Of metys that be most delycate,
And most plesaunt drynkes and wynes therate,   1255
    That is possyble to get;

Which shall be in a chamber feyre,
Replete with sote and fragrant eyre,
    Preparyd poynt devyse,
With damaske water made so well   1260
That all the howse therof shall smell
    As it were pardyse.   E3ᵛ

And after that, if ye wyll touche
A feyre wenche nakyd in a couche
    Of a soft bed of downe,   1265
For to satisfye your wanton lust,
I shall apoynt you a trull of trust,
    Not a feyrer in this towne.

And whan ye have taken your delyte,
And thus satisfyed the appetyte   1270
    Of your wyttis fyve,
Ye may sey than I am a servaunt
For you so necessary and plesaunt,
    I trowe non suche a lyve.

Humanyte   Nowe, by the wey that God dyd walke,   1275
                    It comforthe myne herte to here the talke,
                        Thy mache was never seyn.
Yngnoraunce   Than go thy wey by and by
                    And brynge in this company,
                    And he and I wyll here tary   1280
                        Tyll thou come agayne.

Humanyte   And I prey the hertely also.
Sensuall Appetyte At your request so shall I do.
                        Lo, I am gone! Nowe, fare well!
                    I shall brynge them in to this hall   1285
                    And come my selfe formast of all
                    And of these revellis be chefe mershall
                        And order all thynge well.   *[Exit]* E4

Yngnoraunce	Nowe set thy hert on a mery pyn	
	Agayns these lusty bluddys come in,	1290
	And dryve fantesys awey!	
Humanyte	And so I wyll, by hevyn kynge,	
	If they other daunce or synge,	
	Have amonge them, by this day!	

Yngnoraunce	Than thou takyst good and wyse weys,	1295
	And so shalt thou best please	
	All this hole company.	
	For the folyshe arguynge that thou hast had	
	With that knave Experiens, that hath made	
	All these folke therof wery.	1300

	For all they that be nowe in this hall,	
	They be the most parte my servauntes all,	
	And love pryncypally	
	Disportis, as daunsynge, syngynge,	
	Toys, tryfuls, laughynge, gestynge;	1305
	For connynge they set not by.	

Humanyte	I se well suche company ever more,	
	As Sensuell Appetyte is gone fore,	
	Wyll please well this audyens.	
Yngnoraunce	Ye, that I suppose they wyll.	1310
	But pease! harke! I prey the be styll.	
	I wene they be not far hens.	E4^v

Then the daunsers without the hall syng this wyse
and they within answer or ellys they may say it for nede.

The Daunsers and Sensuall Appetyte [off]
      Pease, syrs, pease! Now pease, syrs all!
Humanyte and Yngnorans
      Why, who is that so hye doth call?

The Daunsers	Sylence, I say, be you among.	1315
	For we be dysposyd to syng a song.	

Humanyte and Yngnorans
      Come in then boldely among this presens,
      For here ye shall have good audyens.

[The Dancers and Sensual Appetite enter and sing:]

Tyme to pas with goodly sport,	
our sprytys to revyve and comfort,	1320
to pipe, to singe,	
to daunce, to spring,	
with plesure and delyte,	
folowing sensual appetyte.	

Yngnoraunce   I can you thank, that is done well.   1325 E6ᵛ
                 It is pyte ye had not a mynstrell
                     For to augment your solas.

Sensuall Appetyte As for mynstrell, it maketh no force,
                   Ye shall se me daunce a cours
                   Without a mynstrell, be it better or wors.   1330
                       Folow all, I wyll lede a trace.
Humanyte   Now have amonge you, by this lyght!
Yngnoraunce   That is well sayd, be God almyght.
                       Make rome, syrs, and gyf them place!

                   Than he syngyth this song and daun[c]yth with all
                   and evermore maketh countenaunce accordyng to the
                   mater and all the other aunswer lyke wyse:

[Sensuall Appetyte] Daunce we, daunce we.
[All]   *Praunce we, praunce we.*   1335
[Sensuall Appetyte] So merely let us daunce, ey!   *[All]   So merely etc.*
                   And I can daunce it gyngerly,
                   And I can fote it by and by,
                   And I can pranke it properly,
                   And I can countenaunse comely,   1340
                   And I can kroke it curtesly,
                   And I can lepe it lustly,
                   And I can torn it trymly,
                   And I can fryske it freshly,
                   And I can loke it lordly.   1345

65

Yngnoraunce	I can the thanke, Sensuall Apetyte.
	That is the best daunce without a pype
	That I saw this seven yere.
Humanyte	This daunce wold do mych better yet
	Yf we had a kyt or taberet,
	But alas ther is none here.

1350

Sensuall Appetyte	Then let us go to the taverne agayne,
	There shall we be sure of one or twayn
	Of mynstrellys that can well play.
Yngnoraunce	Then go, I pray ye, by and by,
	And purvey some mynstrell redy,
	And he and I wyll folow shortly
	As fast as ever we may.

1355

Humanyte	Therwith I am ryght well content.
Sensuall Appetyte	Then wyll I go incontynent
	And prepare every thyng
	That is metely to be done.
	And, for lacke of mynstrellys, the mean season
	Now wyll we begyn to syng.

1360

[Sensual Appetite and the Dancers sing:]

Now we wyll here begyn to syng,   1365
For daunce can we nomore,
For mynstrellys here be all lackyng,
To the taverne we wyll therfore.

Et exeunt cantando, etc.

Humanyte	Now yf that Sensuall Appetyte can fynd
	Any good mynstrellys after hys mynd,
	Dowt not we shall have good sport.
Yngnoraunce	And so shall we have for a suerte;
	But what shall we do now, tell me,
	The meane whyle for our comfort?

1370

Humanyte	Then let us some lusty balet syng.
Yngnoraunce	Nay, syr, by the hevyn kyng,
	For me thynkyth it servyth for no thyng
	All suche pevysh prykyeryd song.
Humanyte	Pes, man, pryksong may not be dispysyd,
	For therwith God is well plesyd,
	Honowryd, praysyd, and servyd,
	In the churche oft tymes among.

1375

1380

Yngnoraunce	Is God well pleasyd, trowst thou, therby?
	Nay, nay, for there is no reason why.
	For is it not as good to say playnly 1385
	'Gyf me a spade'
	As, 'Gyf me a spa – ve–va–ve–va–ve–vade'?
	But yf thou wylt have a song that is good,
	I have one of Robyn Hode,
	The best that ever was made. 1390

Humanyte	Then, a feleshyp, let us here it.		
Yngnoraunce	But there is a bordon, thou must bere it,		
	Or ellys it wyll not be.		
Humanyte	Than begyn and care not fo[r me].	*[sings]*	E8
	Downe, downe, downe, downe, etc.	1395	

Yngnoraunce

Robyn Hode in Barnysdale stode
And lent hym tyl a mapyll thystyll,
Than cam our lady and swete Saynt Andrewe,
Slepyst thou, wakyst thou Geffrey Coke?

A hundred wynter the water was depe,   1400
I can not tell you how brode,
He toke a gose nek in his hande
And over the water he went.

He start up to a thystell top
And cut hym downe a holyn clobe,   1405
He stroke the wren betwene the hornys
That fyre sprange out of the pyggys tayle.

Jak boy, is thy bowe ibroke,
Or hath any man done the wryguldy wrage?
He plukkyd muskyllys out of a wyllowe   1410
And put them in to his sachell.

Wylkyn was an archer good
And well coude handell a spade,
He toke his bend bowe in his hand
And set hym downe by the fyre.   1415

He toke with hym threscore bowes and ten,
A pese of befe, another of baken,
Of all the byrdes in mery Englond
So merely pypys the mery botell.

[Enter Nature.]

Nature	Well, Humanyte, now I see playnly	1420	E8
	That thou hast usyd muche foly,		
	The whyle I have ben absent.		
Humanyte	Syr, I trust I have done nothynge		
	That shold be contrary to your pleasynge,		
	Nor never was myne intent.	1425	

For I have folowed the counsell clere,
As ye me bad of Studyouse Desire,
    And for necessyte amonge
Somtyme Sensuall Appetytes counsell,
For without hym, ye knowe ryght well,   1430
    My lyfe can not endure longe.

Nature Though it be for the full necessary
For thy comfort somtyme to satysfy
    Thy sensuall appetyte,
Yet it is not convenyent for the   1435
To put therin thy felycyte
    And all thy hole delyte.

For if thou wylt lerne no sciens,
Nother by study nor experiens,
    I shall the never avaunce,   1440
But in the worlde thou shalt dure than,
Dyspysed of every wyse man,
    Lyke this rude best Ygnoraunce.

[The rest of the play is lost.
See Introduction, p. 12]

CALISTO AND MELEBEA

The players' names

Melebea
Calisto
Sempronio his servant
Celestina the bawd
Parmeno, servant of Calisto
Danio, Melebea's father

A NEW COMMODYE IN ENGLYSH IN MANER OF AN ENTERLUDE, A1
*ryght elygant and full of craft of rethoryk, wherein is shewd and dyscrybyd as well
the bewte and good propertes of women, as theyr vycys and evyll condicions, with
a morall conclusion and exhortacyon to vertew.*

Melebea	Franciscus Petrarcus the poet lawreate
	Sayth that Nature, whych is mother of all thing,
	Without stryff can gyve lyfe to nothing create;
	And Eraclito the wyse clerk, in his wrytyng
	Sayth in all thyngis create, stryff is theyre workyng,

Franciscus Petrarcus the poet lawreate
Sayth that Nature, whych is mother of all thing,
Without stryff can gyve lyfe to nothing create;
And Eraclito the wyse clerk, in his wrytyng
Sayth in all thyngis create, stryff is theyre workyng, 5
And ther is no thing under the firmament
With any other in all poyntes equivalent.

And accordyng to theyre dictys rehersyd as thus,
All thyngis are create in maner of stryfe.
These folysh lovers then, that be so amerous, 10
From pleasure to displeasure how lede they theyr lyfe,
Now sory, now sad, now joyous, now pensyfe!
Alas, I, pore mayden, than what shall I do,
Combryd by dotage of one Calisto?

I know that nature hath gyvyn me bewte, 15
With sanguynyous compleccyon, favour and fayrenes;
The more to God ought I to do fewte
With wyll, lyfe, laud, and love of perfytnes.
I deny not but Calisto is of grete worthynes,
But what of that? For all hys hygh estate, 20 A1v
Hys desyre I defy and utterly shall hate.

O, his saynges and sutes so importune,
That of my lyfe he makyth me almost wery!
O, hys lamentacyons and exclamacyons on Fortune
With similytude maner as one that shuld dy! 25
But who shall pyte thys? In fayth not I.
Shall I accomplysh hys carnall desyre?
Nay, yet at a stake rather bren in a fyre!

Of trouth I am sory for hys troble
To stryve wyth hym self thus for love of me, 30
But though hys sorows, I assure you, shuld doble,
Out of his daunger wyll I be at lyberte.
What, a mys woman? Now Cristes benedicite!
Nay, nay, he shall never that day see
Hys voluptuous appetyte consentyd by me. 35

Wyst he now that I were present here,
I assure you shortely he wold seke me;
And without dout he doth now inquere
Wether I am gone or where I shuld be.   *[Enter Calisto.]*
Se! Is he not now come? I report me!   40
Alas, of thys man I can never be ryd!
Wold to Cryst I wyst where I myght be hyd.

Calisto	By you feyre Melebea may be sene
	The grace, the gyftes, the gretnes of God.
Melebea	Where in?
Calisto	In takyng effect of dame Naturys strene, 45

Nor yerthly, but angellyke of lykelyhode,
In bewte so passyng the kinde of womanhod.
O God, I myght in your presens be able
To manyfest my dolours incomperable!

Greter were that reward than the grace   50
Hevyn to optayn by workys of pyte.
Not so gloryous be the saintes that se Goddes face,
Ne joy not so moch as I do you to see;
Yet dyfferens there is bytwene theym and me,   55
For they gloryfy by his assuryd presens
And I in torment because of your absens.

Melebea	Why, thynkyst thou that so grete a reward?
Calisto	Ye, more greter than yf God wold set me
	In hevyn above all seyntes and more in regard,
	And thynk it a more hyer felycyte. 60
Melebea	Yet more gretter thy reward shalbe
	Yf thou fle from the determynacyon
	Of thy consent of mynd by such temptacion.

I perseyve the entent of thy wordys all   A2
As of the wyt of hym that wold have the vertew   65
Of me such a woman to become thrall.
Go thy wey wyth sorow! I wold thou knew
I have foule skorn of the, I tell the trew,
Or any humayn creature with me shuld begyn
Any communycacyon perteynyng to syn.   70

And I promyse the, where thou art present,
Whyle I lyff, by my wyll I wyll be absent.   *Et exeat.*

Calisto	Lo, out of all joy I am fallyn in wo,
	Uppon whom advers Fortune hath cast her chauns
	Of cruell hate, whych causyth now away to go 75
	The keper of my joy and all my pleasauns.
	Alas, alas, now to me what noyauns!

[Enter Sempronio.]

Sempronio	Dew gard my lordys, and God be in this place!
Calisto	Sempronio!
Sempronio	Ye, syr.
Calisto	A, syr, I shrew thy face!

	Why hast thou bene from me so long absent?	80
Sempronio	For I have bene about your bysynes	
	To order such thyngis as were convenient:	
	Your house and horse and all thyng was to dress.	
Calisto	O, Sempronio, have pyte on my dystres,	
	For of all creaturys I am the wofullest.	85
Sempronio	How so, what is the cause of your unrest?	

Calisto	For I serve in love to the goodlyest thyng	
	That is or ever was.	
Sempronio	What is she?	
[Calisto]	It is one which is all other excedyng—	
	The picture of angellys yf thou her see;	90
	Phebus or Phebe no comparyson may be	
	To her.	
Sempronio	What hyght she?	
Calisto	Melebea is her name.	
Sempronio	Mary, syr, this wold make a wyld hors tame!	

Calisto	I pray the Sempronio, goo fet me my lute,	
	And bryng some chayre or stole with the,	95
	The argumentys of love that I may dispute;	
	[Wyth] scyens. I fynd [thou] arte without pyte—	
	Hy the, Sempronio, hy the I pray the!	
Sempronio	Syr, shortly I assure you it shalbe done. *[Exit]*	
Calisto	Then farewell. Cryst send the agayn sone!	100

	O what fortune is egall unto myne?	
	O what wofull wyght with me may compare?	
	The thurst of sorow is my myxyd wyne,	
	Which dayly I drynk wyth deepe draughtys of care.	
	[Re-enter Sempronio.]	
Sempronio	Tush, syr, be mery! let pas awey the mare!	105
	How sey you, have I not hyed me lyghtly?	
	Here is your chayre and lute to make you mery.	A2ᵛ

Calisto	Myry, quod'a! nay, that wyll not be.	
	But I must nedys syt for very feblenes.	
	Gyve me my lute and thou shalt see	110
	How I shall syng myne unhappynes.	
	Thys lute is out of tune now as I ges.	
	Alas! in tune how shuld I set it,	
	When all armony to me discordith yche whyt	

72

	As he to whos wyll reson is unruly?	115
	For I fele sharp nedyls within my brest,	
	Peas, warr, truth, haterad, and injury,	
	Hope and suspect, and all in one chest.	
Sempronio	Behold Nero in the love of Tapaya oprest,	
	Rome how he brent; old and yong wept	120
	But she toke no thought nor never the less slept.	

Calisto	Gretter is my fyre and less pyte shewd me.	
Sempronio	I wyll not mok – this foule is a lover. *[Aside]*	
Calisto	What sayst thou?	
Sempronio	I say, how can that fyre be,	125
	That tormentyth but one lyvyng man, gretter	
	Than that fyre that brennyth a hole cyty here	
	And all the people therin?	
Calisto	Mary, for the fyre ys grettyst	
	That brennyth verey sore and lastyth lengyst.	

	And gretter is the fyre that brennyth one soule	
	Than that whych brennyth an hundred bodyes.	130
Sempronio	Hys sayeng in this none can controll.	
Calisto	None but such as lyst to make lyes.	
	And yf the fyre of purgatory bren in such wyse,	
	I had lever my spirete in brute bestys shuld be	
	Than to go thyder and than to the deyte.	135

Sempronio	Mary, syr, that is a spyce of heryse.	
Calisto	Why so?	
Sempronio	For ye speke lyke no crystyn man.	
[Calisto]	I wold thou knewyst, Melebea worshyp I,	
	In her I beleve and her I love.	
Sempronio	A ha, than	
	Wyth the Melebea is a grete woman!	140
	I know on whych fote thou dost halt on;	
	I shall shortly hele the, my lyff theruppon.	

Calisto	An uncredable thyng thou dost promyse me.	
Sempronio	Nay, nay, it is easy inough to do.	
	But furst for to hele a man knowlege must be	145
	Of the seknes; than to gyff counsell therto.	
Calisto	What counsell can rule hym, Sempronio,	
	That kepyth in hym no order of counsell?	
Sempronio	A! is this Calisto his fyre? Now I know well	

	How that love over hym hath cast her net,	150
	In whose perseverans is all inconstans.	A3
Calisto	Why, is not Eliceas love and thyn met?	
Sempronio	What than?	
Calisto	Why reprovest me than of ignorans?	
Sempronio	For thou settyst mannis dignite in obeysauns	
	To the imperfeccion of the weke woman.	155
Calisto	A woman! Nay, a god of goddesses.	
Sempronio	Belevyst that than?	

Calisto	Ye, and as a goddes I here confesse	
	And I beleve there is no such sufferayn	
	In hevyn though she be in yerth.	
Sempronio	Peas, peas!	
	A woman a god? Nay, to God a vyllayn.	160
	Of your sayeng ye may be sory.	
Calisto	It is playn.	
Sempronio	Why so?	
Calisto	Because I love her, and thynk surely	
	To obteyn my desyre I am unworthy.	

Sempronio	O ferfull hart, why comparyst thou with Nembroth	
	Or Alexander – of this world not lordys onely,	165
	But worthy to subdew hevyn, as sayeng goth –	
	And thou reputyst thy self more hye	
	Then them both, and dyspayryst so cowardly	
	To wyn a woman, of whom hath ben so many	
	Gotten and ungotten – never hardys[t] of any?	170

	It is resytyd in the fest of Seynt Jhonn,	
	'Thys is the woman of auncyoun malyce';	
	Of whom but of a woman was it long on	
	That Adam was expulsyd from paradyse?	
	She put man to payn whom Ely dyd dispyse.	175
Calisto	Than syth Adam gaff hym to theyre governaunce,	
	Am I gretter than Adam my self to avaunce?	

Sempronio	Nay, but of those men, it were wysedome,	
	That overcame them, to seke remedy,	
	And not of those that they dyd overcome.	180
	Fle from theyre beginnynges, eschew theyre foly.	
	Thou knowyst they do evyll thyngis many:	
	They kepe no meane, but rygour of intencyon,	
	Be it fayre, foule, wylfull without reason.	

Kepe them never so close, they wylbe shewyd,   185
Gyff tokyns of love by many subtell ways,
Semyng to be shepe, and serpently shrewd,
Craft in them renewyng, that never decays –
Theyre seyenges, sightynges, provokynges, theyr plays!
O what payn is to fulfyll theyre appetytys   190
And to accomplysh theyre wanton delytis.

It is a wonder to se theyre dyssemblyng,
Theyre flatteryng countenaunce, theyr ingratytude,
Inconstaunce, fals witnese, faynyd wepyng,
There vayn glory and how they can delude,   195   A3ᵛ
Theyre folyshnes, theyre janglyng not mewde,
Theyre lecherous lust and wylenes therfore,
Whychcraftys and charmys to make men to theyre lore;

Theyre enbawmyng and theyre unshamfastnes,
Theyre bawdry, theyre suttelte, and fresh attyryng,   200
What trimmyng, what payntyng to make fayrnes,
Theyre fals intentys and flykkeryng smylyng!
Therfore, lo, yt is an old sayeng
That women be the dyvellys nettys and hed of syn,
And mannys mysery in paradyse dyd begyn.   205

Calisto   But what thynkyst thou by me yet for all this?
Sempronio   Mary, syr, ye were a man of clere wyt,
                   Whom nature hath indewyd with the best gyftes,
                   As bewte and gretnes of membres perfyt,
                   Strenght, lyghtnes, and beyond this yche whyt 210
                   Fortune hath partyd with you of her influens,
                   For to be able of lyberall expens.

                   For wythout goodys, wherof Fortune is lady,
                   No man can have welth; therfore by conjecture
                   Yow shuld be belovyd of every body.   215
Calisto   But not of Melebea now I am sure,
                   And though thou hadst praysyd me without mesure
                   And comparyd me without comparison,
                   Yet she is above in every condicion.

                   Behold her noblenes, her auncyon lynage,   220
                   Her gret patrymony, her excellent wyt,
                   Her resplendent verteu, hye portly corage,
                   Her godly grace, her suffereyn bewte perfyte!
                   No tong is able well to expresse it,
                   But yet, I pray the, let me speke a whyle,   225
                   My selff to refresh in rehersyng of my style.

	I begyn at her herr which is so goodly,	
	Crispyd to her helys, tyed with fyne lase,	
	Farr shynyng beyond fyne gold of Araby;	
	I trow the son coler to hyt may gyff place,	230
	That who to behold it myght have the grace,	
	Wold say in comparison nothyng countervaylys.	
Sempronio	Then is it not lyke here of asse tayles?	

	O, what foule comparison this felow raylys!	
Calisto	Her gay glasyng eyen so fayre and bryght,	235
	Her browes, her nose in a meane no fassyon faylys,	
	Her mouth proper and feate, her teeth small and whyght,	
	Her lyppis ruddy, her body streyght upryght,	
	Her lyttyll tetys to the eye is a pleasure.	A4
	O what joy it is to se such a fygure!	240

Her skyn of whytnes endarkyth the snow,
Wyth rose colour ennewyd – I the ensure –
Her lyttyll handys in meane maner – this is no trow –
Her fyngers small and long, with naylys ruddy most pure,
Of proporcyon none such in purtrayture,   245
Without pere, worthy to have for fayrenes
The apple that Parys gave Venus the goddes.

Sempronio	Sir, have ye all done?	
Calisto	Ye, mary, what than?	
Sempronio	I put case all this ye have sayd be trew;	
	Yet are ye more noble syth ye be a man.	250
Calisto	Wherin?	
Sempronio	She is unperfyte, I wold ye knew,	
	As all women be, and of lesse valew.	
	Phylozophers say the matter is less worthy	
	Than the forme; so is woman to man surely.	

Calisto	I love not to here this altercacion	255
	Betwene Melebea and me her lover.	
Sempronio	Possyble it is in every condicyon	
	To abbor her as mych as you do love her.	
	In the wynnyng, begilyng is the daunger —	
	That ye shall see here after wyth eyen fre.	260
Calisto	With what eyen?	
Sempronio	With clere eyen, trust me.	

Calisto	Why, wyth what eyen do I se now?	
Sempronio	Wyth dyme eyen whych shew a lytyl thyng much.	
	But for ye shall not dispayre, I assure you	
	No labour nor dylygens in me shall gruch.	265
	So trusty and fryndely ye shall fynd me such	
	In all thyngis possyble, that ye can adquire	
	The thyng to accomplysh to your desyre.	

Calisto	God bryng that to pase, so glad it is to me	
	To here the thus, though I hope not in thy doyng.	270
Sempronio	Yet I shall do yt, trust me, for a surete.	
Calisto	God reward the for thy gentyll intendyng;	
	I gyff the this chayn of gold in rewardyng.	
Sempronio	Sir, God reward you, and send us good sped.	
	I dout not but I shall performe it in dede;	275

But wythout rewardes it is hard to work well.

Calisto	I am content so thou be not neclygent.
Sempronio	Nay, be not you; for it passyth a mervell,
	The master slow, the servant to be dylygent.
Calisto	How thynkyst it can be? Shew me thyne intent.
Sempronio	Sir, I have a neyghbour, a moder of bawdry,
	That can provoke the hard rokkys to lechery.

Calisto — line 280

In all evyll dedys she is perfet wyse.   A4ᵛ
I trow more than a thousand vyrgyns
Have bene distroyed by her subtell devyse,   285
For she never faylyth where she begynnis.
All onely by thys craft her lyffyng she wynnis.
Maydes, wyffys, wydows and everychone —
If she ones meddyll, ther skapyth none.

Calisto	How myght I speke wyth her, Sempronio?	290
Sempronio	I shall bryng her hydyr unto this place,	
	But ye must in any wyse let rewardis go,	
	And shew her your grevys in every case.	
Calisto	Ellys were I not worthy to attayn grace.	
	But alas, Sempronio, thou taryest to long.	295
Sempronio	Syr, God be with you.	
Calisto	Cryst make the strong!	

[Exit Sempronio]

The myghty and perdurable God be his gyde,
As he gydyd the thre kyngis in to Bedleme
From the est by the starr, and agayn dyd provyde
As theyre conduct to retorn to theyre own reame;   300
So spede my Sempronio to quench the leme
Of this fyre which my hart doth wast and spende,
And that I may com to my desyryd ende.

To pas the tyme now wyll I walk
Up and down within myne orchard,   305
And to myself go comyn and talke,
And pray that Fortune to me be not hard.
Longyng to here, whether made or mard,
My message shall return by my servaunt Sempronio.
Thus farewell, my lordys, for a whyle I wyll go.   310

[Exit Calisto. Enter Celestina.]

Celestina	Now the blessyng that Our Lady gave her sone,
	That same blessyng I gyve now to you all!
	That I com thus homely, I pray you of pardon.
	I am sought and send fore as a woman universall;
	Celestina, of trewth, my name is to call.
	Sempronio for me about doth inquere,
	And it was told me I shuld have found hym here.

Now the blessyng that Our Lady gave her sone,
That same blessyng I gyve now to you all!
That I com thus homely, I pray you of pardon.
I am sought and send fore as a woman universall;
Celestina, of trewth, my name is to call.   315
Sempronio for me about doth inquere,
And it was told me I shuld have found hym here.

I am sure he wyll com hyther anone,
But the whylyst I shall tell you a pretty game.
I have a wench of Sempronio's, a pretty one,   320
That sojornyth with me – Elecea is her name.
But the last day we were both ny a stark shame,
For Sempronio wold have her to hymself severell,
And she lovyth one Cryto better or as well.

Thys Cryto and Elicea sat drynkyng   325
In my hous, and I also makyng mery,
And as the devyll wold, farr from our thynkyng,   A5
Sempronio almost cam on us sodenly.
But then wrought I my craft of bawdery;
I had Cryto go up and make hym self rome   330
To hyde hym in my chamber among the brome.

Then made I Elicea syt doun a sowyng,
And I wyth my rok began for to spyn,
As who seyth of Sempronio we had no knowyng.
He knokkyd at the dore and I lete hym in,   335
And for a countenaunce I dyd begyn
To catch hym in myne armys, and seyd, 'See, see
Who kyssyth me, Elicea, and wyll not kys the.'

Elicea for a countenaunce made her grevyd,
And wold not speke but styll dyd sowe,   340
'Why speke ye not?' quod Sempronio, 'be ye mevyd?'
'Have I not a cause?' quod she. 'No', quod he, 'I trow.'
'A! traytour!' quod she, 'full well dost thou know!
Where hast thou ben these thre days fro me?
That the inpostume and evyll deth take the!'   345

'Pease, myne Elicea,' quod he, 'why say ye thus?
Alas, why put you your self in this wo?
The hote fyre of love so brennyth betwene us
That my hart is wyth yours where ever I go,
And for thre days absens to say to me so,   350
In fayth me thynkyth ye be to blame.'
But now hark well, for here begynnyth the game.

78

Cryto in my chamber above that was hyddyn,
I thynk lay not easyly, and began to romble;
Sempronio hard that, and askyd who was within,   355
Above in the chamber, that so dyd jomble.
'Who?' quod she, 'a lover of myne.' 'May hap ye stomble'
Quod he, 'on the trewth, as many one doth.'
'Go up,' quod she, 'and loke whether it be soth.'

'Well,' quod he, 'I go.' Nay, thought I, not so.   360
I sayd, 'Com Sempronio, let this foole alone;
For of thy long absens she is in such wo,
And half besyde her self, and her wyt ny gone.'
'Well,' quod he, 'above yet ther is one.'
'Wylt thou know?' quod I. 'Ye,' quod he, 'I the requere.' 365
'It is a wench,' quod I, 'sent me by a frere.'

'What frere?' quod he. 'Wilt thou nedis know?' quod
    I than,
'It is the f[   ]   368
'O,' quod he, 'what a lode hath that woman
To bere hym,' 'Ye,' quod I, 'though women per case   370
Bere hevy full oft, yet they gall in no place.'   A5ᵛ
Then he laught. 'Ye,' quod I, 'no mo wordes of this,
For this tyme to long we spend here amys.'
                            Intrat Sempronio.

Sempronio   O moder Celestyne, I pray God prosper the.
Celestina   My son Sempronio, I am glad of our metyng,   375
             And, as I here say, ye go aboute to seke me?
Sempronio   Of trouth, to seke you was myne hyther commyng.
             Mother ley aperte now all other thyng,
             And all only tend to me, and imagyn
             In that that I purpose now to begyn.   380

             Calisto in the love of fayre Melebea
             Burnyth, wherfore of the he hath grete nede.
Celestina   Thou seyst well. Knowyst not me Celestina?
             I have the end of the matter, and for more spede
             Thou shalte wade no ferther; for of this dede   385
             I am as glad as ever was the surgyon
             For salvys for broke hedys to make provysyon.

             And so intend I to do to Calisto,
             To gyff hym hope and assure hym remedy;
             For long hope to the hart mych troble wyll do,   390
             Wherfore to the effect therof I wyll hye.
Sempronio   Peas, for me thynkyth Calisto is nye.
                        Intrat Calisto et Parmeno

Calisto   Parmeno.
Parmeno   What sey you?
Calisto   Wottyst who is here?
             Sempronio that revyvyth my chere.

Parmeno	It is Sempronio with that old berdyd hore.	395
	Be ye they my maister so sore for doth long?	
Calisto	Peas, I sey, Parmeno, or go out of the dore.	
	Commyst thou to hinder me? then dost thou me wrong.	
	I pray the help for to make me more strong	
	To wyn this woman, ellys Goddes forbod.	400
	She hath equall power of my lyff under God.	

Parmeno	Wherfore to her do ye make such sorow?	
	Thynk ye in her [e]ars ther is any shame?	
	The contrary who tellyth you, be never his borrow;	
	For as much she gloryfyeth her in her name,	405
	To be callyd an old hore, as ye wold of fame.	
	Doggys in the strete and chyldren at every dore	
	Bark and cry out, "There goth an old hore!"	

Calisto	How knowyst all this, dost thou know her?	
Parmeno	Ye, that [ ] day agone	410
	For a fals hore, the devyll over throw her!	
	My moder when she dyed gave me to her alone,	
	And a sterker baud was ther never none.	A6
	For that I know I dare well se[y],	
	Let se the contrary who can ley.	415

	I have bene at her hows and sene her trynkettys	
	For payntyng, thyngis innumerable,	
	Squalmys and balmys. I wonder where she gettys	
	The thyngis that she hath with folkis for to fable,	
	And to all baudry ever agreable.	420
	Yet wors then that, whych wyl never be laft,	
	Not only a baud, but a wych by her craft.	

Celestina	Say what thow wylt, son, spare not me.	
Sempronio	I pray the, Permeno, lefe thy malycyous envy.	
Parmeno	Hark hydyr, Sempronyo, here is but we thre;	425
	In that I have sayd canst thou denye?	
Calisto	Com hens Permeno, I love not thys, I;	
	And good mother, greve you not, I you pray.	
	My mynde I shall shew, now hark what I say.	

	O notable woman, O auncyent vertew!	430
	O gloryous hope of my desyryd intent!	
	Thende of my delectable hope to renew,	
	My regeneracion to this lyfe present,	
	Resurreccon from deth: so excellent	
	Thou art above other. I desyre humbly	435
	To kys thy handes, wherin lyeth my remedy.	

80

	But myne unworthines makyth resystence.	
	Yet worship I the ground that thou gost on,	
	Beseching the, good woman, with most reverens	
	On my payn with thy pyte to loke uppon.	440
	Without thy comfort my lyfe is gone;	
	To revyve my dede sprytys thou mayst preferr me,	
	With the wordes of thy mouth to make or marr me.	

Celestina	Sempronio, can I lyff with these bonys	
	That thy master gyffyth me here for to ete?	445
	Wordes are but wynd; therfore attons	
	Byd hym close his mouth and to his purs get,	
	For money makyth marchaunt that must jet.	
	I have herd his wordes, but where be his dedes?	
	For without money with me no thyng spedys.	450

Calisto	What seyth she, Sempronio? Alas, my hart bledes	
	That I wyth you, good woman, mystrust shuld be.	
Sempronio	Syr, she thynkyth that money all thyng fedys.	
[Calisto]	Then come on, Sempronio, I pray the, wyth me;	
	And tary here, moder, a whyle I pray the.	455
	For where of mystrust ye have me appelyd,	
	Have here my cloke, tyll your dout be assoylid.	A6ᵛ

Sempronio	Now do ye well, for wedes among corn,	
	Nor suspecious with fryndes, dyd never well;	
	Or faythfulnes of wordes tornyd to a skorn	460
	Makyth myndes doutfull, good reason doth tell.	
Calisto	Come on, Sempronio, thou gyffyst me good counsell.	
Sempronio	Go ye before and I shall wayt you uppon.	
	Farewell, mother, we wyll come agayn anon.	
	[Exit Calisto and Sempronio.]	

Parmeno	How sey ye, my lordis, se ye not this smoke	*[Aside]* 465
	In my maisters eyes that they do cast?	
	The one hath his chayn, the other his cloke,	
	And I am sure they wyll have all at last.	
	Ensample may be by this that is past,	
	How servauntis be dissaytfull in theyr maisters foly.	470
	Nothyng but for lucre is all theyr bawdry.	

Celestina	It pleasyth me, Parmeno, that we togedyr	
	May speke, wherby thou maist se I love the,	
	Yet undeservyd now thou commyst hydyr;	
	Wherof I care not, but vertew warnyth me	475
	To fle temptacyon and folow charyte,	
	To do good agayns yll, and so I rede the.	
	Sempronio and I wyll helpe thy necessyte.	

81

	And in tokyn now that it shall so be,	
	I pray the among us let us have a song,	480
	For where armony is ther is amyte.	
Parmeno	What, a old woman syng?	
Celestina	Why not among?	
	I pray the no lenger the tyme prolong.	
Parmeno	Go to, when thou wylt, I am redy.	
Celestina	Shall I begyn?	
Parmeno	Ye, but take not to hye.	485

Et cantant.

[Celestina]	How sey ye now by this, lytyll yong fole?	
	For the thyrd parte Sempronio we must get.	
	After that, thy maister shall come to skole	
	To syng the fourth parte, that his purs shall swet,	
	For I so craftely the song can set,	490
	Though thy maister be hors, his purs shal syng clere,	
	And taught to solf that womans flesh is dere.	

	How seyst to this, thou praty Parmeno?	
	Thou knowyst not the world nor no delytis therin;	
	Dost understand me? In feyth, I tro no.	495
	Thou art yong inough the game to begyn.	
	Thy maister hath wadyd hym self so farr in	
	And to bryng hym out lyeth not in me, old pore.	
Parmeno	Thou shuldyst sey, 'it lyeth not in me, old hore.'	

Celestina	A, horeson, a shame take such a knave!	500
	How darst thou wyth me, thou boy, be so bold?	B1
[Parmeno]	Because such knolege of the I have.	
Celestina	Why, who art?	
Parmeno	Parmeno, son to Albert the old.	
	I dwelt with the by the ryver, where wyne was sold.	
[Celestina]	And thy moder I trow hyght Claudena.	505
[Parmeno]	That a wyld fyre bren the, Celestena!	

Celestina	But thy moder was as olde a hore as I!	
	Come hydyr, thou lytyll fole, let me see the.	
	A! it is even he, by our blyssyd lady!	
	What, lytyll urchyn, hast forgotyn me?	510
	When thou layst at my beddys fete how mery were we!	
Parmeno	A, thou old matrone, it were almys thou were ded!	
	How woldest thou pluk me up to thy beddys hed	

	And inbrace me hard unto thy bely,	
	And for thou smellydyst oldly, I ran from the.	515
Celestina	A! shameful horeson, fy uppon the, fy, fy!	
	Come hyther, and now shortly I charge the,	
	That all this folysh spekyng thou let be.	
	Leve wantonnes of youth, than shalt thou do well;	
	Folow the doctryne of thy elders and counsell,	520

To whom thy parentis, on whos soulis God have mercy,
In payn of cursyng bad the be obedyent.
In payn wherof I command the straytly,
To much in mastership put not thyne intent;
No trust is in theym, if thyne owen be spent.   525
Maysters nowadays coveyt to bryng about
All for theym self, and let theyre servantes go without.

Thy maister, men sey, and as I thynk he be –
But lyght, karych not who come to his servyce!
Faire wordes shall not lak, but smal rewardis, trust me!   530
Make Sempronio thy frynd in any wyse,
For he can handle hym in the best gyse.
Kepe thys and for thy profet tell it to none,
But loke that Sempronio and thou be one.

Parmeno   Moder Celestyne, I wot not what ye meane.   535
Calisto is my mayster and so I wyll take hym,
And as for ryches I defye it clene.
For who so ever with wrong rych doth make hym,
Soner than he gat it, it wyll forsake hym.
I love to lyfe in joyfull poverte   540
And to serve my mayster with trewth and honeste.

Celestina   Troth and honeste be ryches of the name,
But surete of welth is to have ryches,
And after that for to get hym good fame
By report of fryndes; thys is truth dowtles.   545   B1ᵛ
Than no such maner frynd can I expresse
As Sempronyo, for both your profettys to spede;
Whych lyeth in my handys now, yf ye be agreyd.

O Parmeno, what a lyfe may we endure!
Sempronyo lovyth the doughter of Elyso.   550
Parmeno   And who Arusa?
Celestina   Lykyst her?
Parmeno   Peradventure.
[Celestina] I shall get her to the, that shall I do.
Parmeno   Na, moder Celystyne, I purpose not so.
A man shuld be conversant, I here tell,
Wyth them that be yl, and thynk to do well.   555

Sempronyo hys ensample shall not make me
Better nor wors, nor hys fautes wyll I hyde.
But moder Celestyne, a questyon to the:
Is not syn anon in one espyed
That is drownyd in delyte? How shuld he provyde   560
Agayns vertew to save hys honeste?
Celestina   Lyke a chyld without wysdome thou answeryst me.

Without company mirth can have non estate:
Use no slowth; nature abhorryth idelnes,
Whych lesyth delyte to nature appropryate.   565
In sensuall causys delyght is chefe maistres,
Specyally recountyng lovys bysynes;
To say, thus doth she, the tyme thus they pas,
And soch maner they use, and thus they kys and basse,

And thus they mete and enbrase togyther.   570
What spech, what grase, what pleys is betwene theim!
Where is she? there she goth – let us se whyther.
Now pleasyd, now froward, now mume, now hem!
Stryke up, mynstryl, with sawes of love, the old problem!
Syng swete songes, now justes and torney!   575
Of new invencyons what conseytes fynd they!

Now she goth to mas, to morow she commyth owt.
Behold her better; yonder goth a cokold.
I left her alone; she comyth; turn abowt!
– Lo, thus, Permeno, thou mayst behold,   580
Fryndes wyll talk togeder as I have told.
Wherfore perseyve thou that I sey truly,
Never can be delyte without company.

                              [Parmeno retires.]
          Hic iterum intrat Calisto. [Enter Sempronio.]

Calisto	Moder, as I promysed to assoyle thy dowt,
	Here I gyfe the an hundred pesis of gold. 585
Celestina	Syr, I promyse you I shall bryng it about,
	All thyng to purpose, evyn as ye wold.
	For your reward I wyll do as I shuld. B2
	Be mery, fere nothyng, content ye shall be.
[Calisto]	Then moder, fare well, be dylygent I pray the. 590

                              [Exit Celestina.]

	How sayst, Sempronio, have I done well?
Sempronio	Ye, syr, in my mynd, and most accordyng.
Calisto	Then wylt thou do after my councell?
	After this old woman wylt thou be hyeng,
	To remember and hast her in every thyng. 595
Sempronio	Syr, I am content as ye commaund me.
Calisto	Then go, and byd Parmeno come, I pray the.

                              [Exit Sempronio.]

84

Now God be theyre gyddys, the postys of my lyfe,
My relefe fro deth, the imbassades of my welth,
My hope, my hap, my quyetnes, my stryfe,   600
My joy, my sorow, my sekenes, my helth!
The hope of thys old woman my hart telth
That comfort shall come shortly as I intend,
Or els come deth and make of me an end!

[Parmeno comes forward.]

Parmeno	In fayth it makyth no forse nor matter mych.	605
Calisto	What seyst, Parmeno, what sayst to me?	
Parmeno	Mary, I say playnly that yonder old wych	
	And Sempronio togeder wyll undo the.	
Calisto	A! yll tongyd wrech, wyll ye not see?	
	Thynkyst thou, lordeyn, thou handelyst me fayre?	610
	Why, knave, woldest thow put me now in dyspayre?	

Et exeat Calisto.

Parmeno   Lo, syrs, my master ye se is angry
But thys it is, tell folys for theyre proffyt
Or warn theym for theyre welth, it is but foly,
For stryk theym on the hele, and as moch wyt   615
Shall com forth as at theyr forehede to perseyve it.
Go thy way, Calesto, for on my charge
Thy thryft is sealyd up, though thou be at large.

O, how unhappy I am to be trew!
For other men wyn by falsehed and flatery;   620
I lese for my troth, the world doth so ensew,
Troth is put bak and takyn for foly.
Therfore now I wyll chaunge my copy.
If I had done as Celystyne bad me,
Calysto hys mynyon styll wold have had me.   625

Thys gyvyth me warnyng from hens forward
How to dele with hym for all thyng as he wyll:
I will the same forward or bakward.
I will go streyght to hym and folow hym still,
Say as he sayth, be it good or yll.   630
And syth these bawdys get good provokyng lechery,   B2ᵛ
I trust flatery shall spede as well as bawdery.

Hic exeat Parmeno et intret Melebea.

Melebea	I pray you, came this woman here never syn?
	In fayth, to entre here I am half adrad.
	And yet, why so? I may boldly com in; 635
	I am sure from you all I shall not be had.
	But Jesus, Jesus, be these men so mad
	On women as they sey? how shuld it be?
	It is but fables and lyes, ye may trust me.

Intret Celestina.

Celestina	God be here in.
Melebea	Who is ther?
Celestina	Wyl ye bye any thred? 640
Melebea	Ye, mary, good moder, I pray you come in.
Celestina	Cryst save you, fayre mestres, and God be your spede!
	And helth be to you and all your kyn;
	And Mary, Goddes mother, that blessyd vyrgyn,
	Preserve and prosper your womanly personage, 645
	And well to injoy your yough and pusell age.

	For that tyme pleasurys are most eschyvyd;
	And age is the hospytall of all maner sykenes,
	The restyng place of all thought unrelevyd,
	The sporte of tyme past, the ende of all quiknes, 650
	Neybour to deth, a dry stok wythout swetnes;
	Discomforte, disease, all age alowith;
	A tre without sap, that small charge boweth.

Melebea	I mervell moder ye speke so much yll
	Of age, that all folke desyre effectuously. 655
Celestina	They desyre hurt for them self as all of wyll;
	And the cause why they desyre to come therby,
	Is for to lyff, for deth is so lothly.
	He that is sorowfull wold lyff to be soryer
	And he that is old wold lyff to be elder. 660

	Fayre damesell, who can shew all the hurtys of age?
	His werynes, feblenes, his discontentyng,
	His chyldishnes, frowardnes of his rage,
	Wrynkelyng in the face, lak of syght and heryng,
	Holownes of mouth, fall of teth, faynt of goyng; 665
	And, worst of all, possessyd with poverte,
	And the lymmys arestyd with debylite.

Melebea	Moder, ye have takyn grete payn for age;
	Wold ye not retorn to the begynnyng?
Celestina	Folys are they that are past theyre passage 670
	To begyn agayn, which be at the endyng.
	For better is possession than the desyryng.
Melebea	I desyre to lyff lengger; do I well or no?
Celestina	That ye desyre well, I thynk not so,

B3

	For as sone goth to market the lambys fell	675
	As the shyppys. None so old but may lyff a yere,	
	And ther is none so yong but ye wot well	
	May dye in a day. Then no advauntage is here	
	Betwen youth and age, the matter is clere.	
Melebea	Wyth thy fablyng and thy resonyng iwys	680
	I am begylyd; but I have knowen the or thys.	

	Art not Celystyne, that dwellyd by the ryver syde?	
Celestina	Ye for soth.	
Melebea	In dede age hath aray the!	
	That thou art she, now can skant be espyed.	
	Me thynkyth by thy favour thou shuldyst be she.	685
	Thou art sore chaungid, thou mayst beleve me.	
[Celestina]	Fayre maydon, kepe thou well thys tyme of youth	
	But bewte shall passe at the last, thys is truth.	

	Yet I am not so old as ye juge me.	
[Melebea]	Good moder, I joy much of thyne accoyntanaunce,	690
	And thy moderly reasons ryght well please me.	
	And now I thank the here for thy pastaunce.	
	Fare well tyll a nother tyme that hap may chaunce	
	Agayn that we two may mete togedyr.	
	May hap ye have bysynes, I know not whether.	695

Celestina	O angelyk ymage! O perle so precyous!	
	O how thou spekyst, it rejoysyth me to here!	
	Knowist thou not by the devyne mouth gracyous,	
	That agaynst the infernall feend Lucyfere	
	We shuld not only lyf by bred here,	700
	But by our good workys, wher in I take some payn?	
	Yf ye know not my mynd now all is in veyn.	

Melebea	Shew me, moder, hardely all thy nesessite,	
	And yf I can, I shall provyde the remedy.	
Celestina	My necessite! Nay, God wot, it is not for me.	705
	As for myne, I laft it at home surely:	
	To ete when I wyll and drynk when I am dry –	
	And I thank God ever one peny hath be myne	
	To by bred when I lyst, and to have four for wyne.	

	Afore I was wyddow I caryd never for it,	710
	For I had wyne ynough of myne owne to sell	
	And with a tost in wyne by the fyre I coud syt	
	With two dosen soppys the collyk to quell.	
	But now with me it is not so well,	
	For I have nothyng but that is brought me	715
	In a pytcher pot of quartys skant thre.	

87

Thus I pray God help them that be nedy,
For I speke not for my self alone,
But as well for other, how ever spede I,
The infyrmyte is not myne, though that I grone,   720
It is for another that I make mone
And not for my self, it is another way,
But what, I must mone where I dare not say.

Melebea   Say what thou wylt and for whom thou lest.
Celestina   Now gracyous damsell, I thank you than,   725
That to gyf audyens ye be so prest
With lyberall redynes to me, old woman,
Which gyffyth me boldnes to shew what I can
Of one that lyeth in daunger by sekenes,
Remyttyng hys langour to your gentyllnes.   730

Melebea   What meanyst thou, I pray the, good moder?
Go forth with thy demaund as thou hast done.
On the one parte thou provokyst me to anger,
And on the other syde to compassyon.
I know not how thy answere to fassyon;   735
The wordes whych thou spekyst in my presence
Be so mysty, I perseyve not thy sentence.

Celestina   I sayd I laft one in daunger of sekenes
Drawyng to deth for ought that I can se.
Now chose you or no to be murderes,   740
Or revyve hym with a word to come from the.
Melebea   I am happy yf my word be of such necessyte
To help any crystyn man, or ells Goddes forbod!
To do a good dede is lykyng to God,

For good dedys to good men be alowable   745
And specyally to nedy above all other;
And ever to good dedys ye shall fynd me agreable,
Trustyng ye wyll exhort me to non other.
Therfor fere not, spek your peticion, good mother,
For they that may hele seke folk and do refuse theym,   750
Suerly of theyre deth they can not excuse theym.

Celestina   Full well and gracyously the case ye consyder.
For I never belevyd that God in vayn
Wold gyff you such countenaunnce and bewte togedyr
But charyte therwith to releve folke in payn;   755
And as God hath gyvyn you, so gyff hym agayn.
For folkis be not made for them self onely,
For then they shuld lyff lyke bestys all rudely.

88

Among whych bestys yet some be pyteful:
The unicorne humblyth hym self to a mayd; 760
And a dog in all his power yrefull, B4
Let a man fall to ground, his anger is delayd.
Thus by nature pyte is conveyd.
The kok, when he skrapith and happith mete to fynd,
Callith for his hennys; lo, se the gentyll kynde! 765

Shuld humayn creaturys than be of cruelnes,
Shuld not they to theyre neybours shew charyte,
And specyally to them wrappyd in sekenes,
Than they that may hele theym cause the infirmyte?

Melebea   Mother, without delay, for Goddes sake shew me, 770
I pray the, hartly, wythout more prayeng,
Where is the pacient that so is paynyng?

Celestina   Fayre damsell, thou maist well have knowlege herto:
That in this cyte is a yong knyght
And of clere lynage, callyd Calisto, 775
Whose lyfe and body is all in the, I plyght.
The pellycan to shew naturys ryght
Fedyth his byrdys – me thynkyth I shuld not prech the,
Thou wotist what I meane; lo, nature shuld tech the!

Melebea   A ha! is this the entent of thy conclusyon? 780
Tell me no more of this matter, I charge the.
Is thys the dolent for whom thow makyst petycyon?
Art thow come hyther thus to desseyve me?
Thow berdyd dame, shameles thou semest to be!
Is this he that hath the passion of folishnes? 785
Thinkyst, thow rybaud, I am such one of lewdnes?

It is not sayd, 'I se[y] well', in vayn:
The tong of man and woman worst members be.
Thow brut baud, thow gret enmy to honeste, certayn,
Cause of secret errours! Jhesu, Jhesu, b[e]nedicite! 790
Som good bodi take this old thefe fro me,
That thus wold disseyve me with her fals sleyght!
Go owt of my syght now! Get the hens streyght!

Celestina   In an yvyll howre cam I hyther, I may say.
I wold I had brokyn my leggys twayn. 795
Melebea   Go hens, thou brothell, go hens in the dyvyll way!
Bydyst thou yet to increase my payn?
Wylt thow make me of thys fole to be fayn,
To gyve hym lyfe to make hym mery,
And to my self deth, to make me sory? 800

89

Wilt thow bere away profet for my perdicion,
And make me lese the house of my father,
To wyn the howse of such an old matrone
As thow art, shamfullyst of all other?
Thinkist thou that I understand not, thou falls mother,   805 B4ᵛ
Thy hurtfull message, thy fals subtell ways?
Make amendys to God, thou lyffyst to long days!

Celestina   Answere, thou traytres, how darst be so bold?
               The fere of the makyth me so dysmayd
               That the blod of my body is almost cold.   810
               Alas, fayre maydyn, what hast thou sayd
               To me pore wydow? Why am I denayed?
               Here my conclusion, which ys of honeste;
               Without cause ye blame thys gentylman and me.

Melebea   I sey I wyll here no more of that fole.   815
               Was he not here with me evyn now?
               Thow old which, thou bryngyst me in grete dole.
               Ask him what answere he had of me and how
               I toke hys demaund, as now know mayst thou:
               More shewyng is but lost where no mercy can be —   820
               Thus I answerd hym and thus I answer the.

Celestina   The more straunge she makyth, the gladder am I;
               Ther is no tempast that ever doth endure.
Melebea   What seyst thou, what seyst thow, shameful enmy?
               Speke out.
Celestina   So ferd I am of your dyspleasure,   825
               Your anger is so grete, I perseyve it sure,
               And your pacyens is in so gret an hete
               That for wo and fere I both wepe and swete.

Melebea   Lyttyll is the hete in comparyson to say
               To the gret boldnes of thy demeanyng.   830
Celestina   Fayre mayden, yet one word now I you pray:
               Appease with pacyens and here my sayeng.
               It is for a prayer, mestres, my demaundyng,
               That is sayd ye have of Seynt Appolyne,
               For the toth ake, wher of this man is in pyne.   835

               And the gyrdle there thou weryst about the
               So many holy relykys it hath towchyd
               That thys knyght thynkyth his bote thou maist be.
               Therfore let thy pyte now be avouchid,
               For my hart for fere lyke a dog is couchyd.   840
               The delyght of vengennis who so doth use,
               Pyte at theyre nede shall theym refuse.

90

[Melebea]	Yf this be trew that thou seyst to me now,
	Myn hart is lyghtnyd perseyvyng the case.
	I wold be content well yf I wyst how 845
	To bryng this seke knyght unto some solas.
Celestina	Fayre damsell, to the be helth and grace;
	For yf this knyght and ye were aquayntyd both two,
	Ye wold not judge him the man that ye do. C1

By God and by my soule, in him is no malyncoly;   850
With grace indewid, in fredome as Alexandre,
In strenght as Hectour, in countenaunce mery,
Gracious; envy in him reynyd never.
Of noble blod as thou knowyst, and yf ye ever
Saw him armyd, he semeth a Seynt George   855
Rather than to be made in Naturys forge,

An angell thou woldist judge him, I make avow,
The gentyll Narciso was never so fayre,
That was inammoryd on his own shadow;
Wherfore, fayre mayde, let thy pyte repayre,   860
Let mercy be thy mother and thou her heyre.
This knyght, whom I come for, never seasyth
But cryeth out of payn that styll encresyth.

Melebea	How long tyme, I pray the, hath it holdyn hym?
Celestina	I thynk he be four and twenty yeres of age; 865
	I saw hym born and holpe for to fold hym.
Melebea	I demaund the not therof – thyne answer aswage.
	I ask the how long in this paynfull rage
	He hath leyn?
Celestina	Of trewth, fayr maydyn, as he says,
	He hath be in this agony this eight days. 870

	But he semyth he had leyn this seven yere.
Melebea	O how it grevyth me, the il of my pacyent,
	Knowyng his agony and thy innocency here.
	Unto myne anger thou hast made resistens
	Wherfore thy demaund I graunt in recompens. 875
	Have here my gyrdyll; the prayer is not redy;
	To morow it shalbe. Come agayn secretly.

	And moder, of these wordes passyd betwene us
	Shew nothyng therof unto this knyght,
	Lest he wold report me cruell and furyous. 880
	I trust the. Now be trew, for thoughtys be lyght.
Celestina	I mervell gretly thou dost me so atwyght
	Of the dout that thou hast of my secretnes.
	As secret as thy self I shall be dowteles.

And to Calisto with this gyrdle Celestina   885
Shall go, and his ledy hart make hole and lyght.
For Gabriell to our lady with *Ave Maria*
Came never gladder than I shall to this knyght.
Calisto, how wylt thou now syt up ryght!
I have shewid thy water to thy phesycyon;   890
Comfort thy self – the feld is half won.

Melebea   Moder, he is much beholdyn unto the.
Celestina   Fayr maydyn, for the mercy thou hast done to us,   C1ᵛ
                This knyght and I both thy bedfolkis shall be.
Melebea   Moder, yf nede be, I wyll do more than thus.   895
Celestina   It shalbe nedefull to do so, and ryghteous,
                For this thus begon must nedis have an ende,
                Which never can be without ye condescend.

Melebea   Well, mother, to morow is a new day;
                I shall performe that I have you promest.   900
                Shew to this seke knyght in all that I may,
                Byd him be bold, in all thyngis honest,
                And though he to me as yet be but a gest,
                If my word or dede his helth may support,
                I shall not fayle; and thus byd him take comfort.   905

                                    Et exeat Melebea

Celestina   Now Cryst comfort the, and kepe the in thy nede!
                How say you now, is not this matter caryed clene?
                Can not old Celestina her matter spede?
                A thing not well handlyd is not worth a bene.
                Now know ye by the half tale what the hole doth meane; 910
                These women at the furst be angry and furyous;
                Fayre wether comyth after stormys tempestyous.

                And now to Calisto I wyll me dres,
                Which lyeth now languyshyng in grete payn,
                And shew hym that he is not remedyles;   915
                And bere hym this to make hym glad and fayn,
                And handyll hym so that ye shall sey playn
                That I am well worthy to bere the name
                For to be callyd a noble arche dame.

                          [Exit Celestina. Enter]
                          Danio pater Melebee

Danio   O mervelous God, what a dreme had I to nyght!   920
                Most terryble vysyon to report and here!
                I had never none such nor none yerthely wyght.
                Alas, when I thynk theron, I quak for fere.
                It was of Melebea, my doughter dere,
                God send me good tythynges of her shortly,   925
                For, tyll I here from her, I can not be mery.

Melebea	O dere father, nothyng may me more displease,
	Nothyng may do me more anoyans,
	Nothyng may do me gretter disease,
	Than to se you, father, in any perturbans, 930
	For me chefly, or for any other chauns.
	But for me I pray you not to be sad,
	For I have no cause but to be mery and glad.
Danio	O swete Melebea, my doughter dere,
	I am replete with joy and felycyte 935
	For that ye be now in my presens here,
	As I perceyve in joy and prosperite.
	From deth to lyfe me thynkyth it revyvyth me,
	For the ferefull dreme that I had lately.
Melebea	What dreme, syr, was that, I pray you hertely? 940
Danio	Dowtles me though[t] that I was walkyng
	In a fayre orchard where were placys two;
	The one was a hote bath, holsome and pleasyng
	To all people that dyd repayre therto
	To wassh them and clens them from sekenes also; 945
	The other, a pyt of foule stynkyng water;
	Shortely they dyed, all that therin did enter.

C2

<table>
<tr><td></td><td>And unto this holesome bath me thought that ye</td></tr>
<tr><td></td><td>In the ryght path were commyng apase,</td></tr>
<tr><td></td><td>But before that, me thought that I dyd see 950</td></tr>
<tr><td></td><td>A foule rough bych, a prikeryd cur it was</td></tr>
<tr><td></td><td>Whych, strakyng her body along on the gras,</td></tr>
<tr><td></td><td>And with her tayle lykkyd her so that she</td></tr>
<tr><td></td><td>Made her selfe a fayre spaniell to be.</td></tr>
</table>

Thys bych then me thought met you in the way, 955
Leppyng and fawnyng uppon you a pase,
And rownd abowt you dyd renne and play,
Whych made you then dysport and solas,
Whych lykyd you so well that in short space
The way to the hote bath anon ye left it, 960
And toke the streyght way to the foule pyt.

And ever ye lokyd continually
Uppon that same bych and so moch her eyed,
That ye cam to the foule pyt brynk sodeynly,
Lyke to have fallyn in and to have bene dystroyed; 965
Whych when I saw, anon than I cryed,
Stertyng in my slepe, and therwith dyd awake,
That yet for fere me thynk my body doth quake.

Was not this a ferefull dreme and mervelous,
I pray you, doughter, what thynk ye now to this?   970
                    Hic Melebea certo tempore non loquitur
                             sed vultu lamentab[i]li respicit.
Why speke ye not, why be ye now so studious?
Is there any thyng that hath chauncyd you amys?
I am your father: tell me what it is.

Melebea   Alas, now your dreme whych ye have expressyd
                 Hath made me all pensyfe and sore abasshyd.   975

[Danio]   I pray you, dere doughter, now tell me why.
Melebea   Sir, I know the cause of your vision,
                 And what your dredefull dreme doth signyfye.
[Danio]   Therof wold I fayn now have noticion.
Melebea   Alas, dere fader, alas, what have I done?   980   C2
                 Offendyd God as a wrech unworthy.
Danio   Wherein? Dyspayre not; God is full of mercy.

[Melebea]   Than on my knees now I fall downe   *Et genuflectat*
                 And of God chefely askyng forgyfnes,
                 And next of you; for in to oblyvyon   985
                 I have put your doctryne and lessons dowtles.
Danio   Fere not, doughter, I am not merciles.
                 I trust ye have not so gretly offendyd,
                 But that ryght well it may be amendyd.

Melebea   Ye have fosterid me up full lovyngly   990
                 In verteous discyplyne, whych is the ryght path
                 To all grace and vertew, whych doth sygnyfye
                 By your dreme that fayre, plesaunt, holesome bath.
                 The foule pyt whereof ye dremyd, which hath
                 Destroyd so many, betokneth vyse and syn,   995
                 In whych, alas, I had almost fallyn in.

                 The prikeryd curr and the foule bych,
                 Which made her self so smoth and fayre to see,
                 Betokenyth an old quene, a baudy wych,
                 Callyd Celystyne – that wo myght she be!   1000
                 Whych with her fayre wordes ay so perswadyd me,
                 That she had almost brought me here unto,
                 To fulfyll the foule lust of Calisto.

Danio   Alas, dere doughter, I taught you a lesson
                 Whych way ye shuld attayn unto vertew: 1005
                 That was every mornyng to say an orason,
                 Prayeng God for grace all vyce to eschew.
Melebea   O dere fader, that lesson I have kept trew
                 Whych preservyd me. For though I dyd consent
                 In mynd, yet had he never hys intent.   1010

Danio	The verteu of that prayer, I se well on thing,
	Hath preservyd you from the shame of that sin.
	But because ye were somwhat consentyng,
	Ye have offendid God gretly therin.
	Wherefore, doughter, ye must now begyn 1015
	Humbly to besech God of hys mercy
	For to forgyve you your syn and mysery.

Melebea	O blyssid lord and fader celestiall,
	Whose infynite merci no tong can exprese,
	Though I be a sinner, wrech of wrechis all, 1020
	Yet of thy gret merci graunt me forgifnes.
	Full sore I repent, my syn I confese,
	Intendyng hens forth never to offend more. C3
	Now humbly I besech thy mercy therfore.

Danio	Now that is well sayd, myne one fayre doughter. 1025
	Stand up therfore, for I know verely,
	That God is good and mercyfull ever
	To all synners whych wyll ask mercy
	And be repentaunt and in wyll clerely
	To syn no more; he of hys grete goodnes 1030
	Wyll graunt them therfore his grace and forgifnes.

Lo, here ye may see what a thyng it is
To bryng up yong people verteously,
In good custome. For grace doth never mys
To them that use good prayers dayly, 1035
Which hath preservyd thys mayde undoutydly,
And kept her from actuall dede of shame,
Brought her to grace, preservyd her good name.

Wherfore, ye vyrgyns and fayre maydens all,
Unto this example now take good hede; 1040
Serve God dayly, the soner ye shall
To honeste and goodnes no dout procede,
And God shall send you ever his grace at nede
To withstand all evyll temptacions
That shall come to you by any occasions. 1045

And ye faders, moders, and other which be
Rulers of yong folkis, your charge is dowtles
To bryng them up verteously and to see
Them occupied styll in some good bysynes,
Not in idell pastyme or unthryftynes, 1050
But to teche them some art, craft or lernyng,
Whereby to be able to get theyr lyffyng.

The bryngers up of youth in this region
Have done gret harme because of theyr neclygens,
Not puttyng them to lernyng nor occupacyons.   1055
So when they have no craft nor sciens,
And com to mans state, ye see thexperience,
That many of them compellyd be
To beg or stele by very necessite.

But yf there be therfore any remedy,   1060
The hedys and rulers must furst be dylygent
To make good lawes, and execute them straytely,
Uppon such maystres that be neclygent.
Alas, we make no laws but ponyshment
When men have offendyd! But laws evermore   1065
Wold be made to prevent the cause before.

Yf the cause of the myscheffys were seen before,   C
Whych by conjecture to fall be most lykely,
And good laws and ordynauncys made therfore
To put away the cause, that were best remedi.   1070
What is the cause that ther be so many
Theftys and robberies? It is because men be
Dryven therto by nede and poverte.

And what is the verey cause of that nede?
Be cause they labur not for theyr lyffyng,   1075
And trewth is they can not well labour in dede,
Be cause in youth of theyr ydyll upbryngyng.
But this thyng shall never come to reformyng,
But the world contynually shalbe nought,
As long as yong pepyll be evell upbrought.   1080

Wherfore the eternall God, that raynyth on hye,
Send his mercifull grace and influens
To all governours, that they circumspectly
May rule theyr inferiours by such prudence,
To bryng them to vertew and dew obedyens,   1085
And that they and we all, by his grete mercy,
May be parteners of hys blessyd glory.   Amen.

JOHANES RASTELL ME IMPRIMI FECIT
CUM PRIVILEGIO REGALI

GENTLENESS AND NOBILITY

OF GENTYLNES AND NOBYLYTE A DYALOGE BETWEN THE
MARCHAUNT, THE KNYGHT AND THE PLOWMAN, dysputyng who
is a verey gentylman and who is a noble man and how men shuld come to
auctoryte, compilid in maner of an enterlude with divers toys and gestis addyd therto
to make mery pastyme and disport.

The Marchaunt	O what a gret welth and prosperyte
	It is to any reme where marchauntes be,
	Havyng fre lyberte and entercours also
	All marchaundyse to convey to and fro;
	Whych thyng I have usyd and the verey fet found 5
	And thereby gotton many a thousand pownd.
	Wherfore now because of my grete ryches,
	Thoroughowt this land in every place doutles
	I am magnyfyed and gretly regardyd,
	And for a wyse and noble man estemyd. 10

[Enter the Knight]

The Knyght	Maister marchaunt, I here you ryght well.
	But now in presumpsion me thynk ye excell
	To call your self noble in presence here.
	Iwys men know what your auncestours were
	And of what grete stok descendid ye be: 15
	Your fadyr was but a blake smyth, perde.
Marchaunt	Why syr, what than? What be you, I pray you?
Knyght	Mary, I am a gentylman, I wold ye knew,
	And may dyspend yerely five hundred mark land;
	And I am sure all that ye have in hand 20
	Of yerely rent is not worth five markys.
Marchaunt	But I wold thou knewist it, for all thy krakkys,
	I am able to bye now all the land
	That thou hast, and pay for it owt of hand;
	Whych I have got by myn own labour and wit, 25 A1^v
	And that whych thou hast, thyn awncestors left it.
Knyght	Yet art thou but a chorle, and I have skorn
	Thou shuldist compare with me, a gentylman born.
Marchaunt	Why, what callyst thou a gentylman, tel me?

Knyght	Mary, I call them gentylmen that be	30
	Born to grete landys by inherytaunce,	
	As myn auncestours by contynuaunce	
	Have had this five hundred yere, of whom now I	
	Am desendid and commyn lynyally,	
	Beryng the same name and armys also	35
	That they bare this five hundred yere agoo.	
	Myn auncestours also have ever be	
	Lordys, knyghtes, and in grete auctoryte,	
	Capteyns in the warr and governers	
	And also in tyme of pease gret rulers,	40
	And thyn were never but artyfycers,	
	As smythys, masonys, carpenters or wevars.	

Marchaunt	All that is trewth I wyl not denye now,	
	Yet I am more gentylman born than thou,	
	For I call hym a gentylman that gentilly	45
	Doth gyf unto other men lovyngly	
	Such thing as he hath of hys own proper.	
	But he that takith ought away from another,	
	And doth gyf hym no thyng agayn therfore,	
	Owght to be callyd a chorll evermore.	50
	But myn auncestours have giffyn alwey	
	To thyn auncestours such thyng as they	
	By their labours did trewly get and wyn;	
	For myn auncestours bildid howsis wherein	
	Thyne auncestours have had .their dwellyng place.	55
	Also myn auncestours have made tolis	
	To all maner crafti men belongyng,	
	Wherby clothis and every other thyng	
	Whereof thyn auncestours nede have had	
	With the same tolys have ever be made.	60
	So myn auncestours have gyffin their labours	
	Ever to comfort and help thyn auncestours.	

Knyght	I denye that ever thauncestours of thyne	
	Did ever gif to the auncestours of myne	
	At any tyme any thyng except that they	65
	Gaf somewhat therfor, other ware or money.	

Marchaunt	Mary, God a mercy, John, for that now —	
	That is evyn a pyg of our own sow.	
	How can lordys and estatis have ought in store	A2
	Except thartyfycers do get it before?	70
	For all metalls be dyggyd furst by myners	
	And after wrought by the artyfycers.	
	Woll, fell, and every other thyng	
	That is necessary to mannys coveryng	
	And all other thyngis that men use and were	75
	Is alwey made by the artyfycer.	

Knyght	I graunt that the artyfycers do make it,	
	But because comenly they have lytell wyt,	
	Gentylmen that have landys and domynyon	
	Of all such ryches have most possessyon.	80
	For reason wyll ever it shuld so be	
	Wyse men to have folys in captyvyte.	

Marchaunt	Mary, as for wyt and subtell invencyon,	
	Myne auncestours wyth thine may make comparison.	
	For though my fader were a smyth, what than?	85
	Yet was he a mervelous quyk wyttyd man,	
	And coud work as well for hys part	
	As any in this land usyng that art,	
	And devyse new fassyons in thynges that he made,	
	That every man to bye hys ware was glad;	90
	And carve and grave in yron and stele	
	Both image and letters mervelously wele,	
	And ther on ley gold, and gylt it also	
	Fyne and pure as any gold smyth coud do.	
	My grauntfader also was a mason	95
	Of grete wyt as any in thys regyon	
	And coud byld a castell and tour ryght well,	
	In whych some of thy kynnysmen now do dwell,	
	Wherein aperyth ryght good masonry	
	Wyth immagys and armys wrought curyously.	100
	My grete graundfadyr, lo, was a wever	
	Of wollyn yarn and of other gere,	
	And made mervelous pleasaunt workis to behold:	
	Lynyn, dyaper, sylk, and cloth of gold;	
	All such subtell thyngis as I have rehersyd, lo,	105
	Myne auncestours by theyr wyttis coud work and do.	
	And as for thyne auncestours, I know no thyng	
	Thei coud do bi their wittis worth of praisyng	
	But use, occupi, and wast evermore	
	Such thyngis as myn auncestours made before.	110
	And thou and thine auncestours, having thoccupacion	
	Of such thingis wrought bi the operacion	
	Of other men, oughtist not be praysed therfore;	A2
	But the prayse ought to be gyven ever more	
	To the artyfycer, whych by hys wyt	115
	It devysyd and so connyngly wrought it.	
	Wherefore, yf thou sey that wyt and polesy	
	Be the thynges perteynyng to gentry,	
	Thyn auncestours may never compare wyth mine,	
	For theyr actys prove them wyser than thyne.	120
	For thyn dyd never no thyng in theyr days	
	Concernyng quyk wyt that was worthy prays.	

Knyght	Yes, iwis, lewd Javell, I wold thou knewist it!	
	Myn auncestours have had more wysedome and wyt	
	Than thyne have had and coud do also	125
	Many thynges that thyne coud never do.	
	For in the contrey at sessyons and syse	
	They have be electe to be justyce,	
	And, for theyer wyt and grete dyscressyon,	
	They have juggyd and donne correccyon	130
	Uppon thyne auncestours – artyfycers	
	That have made false warys and ben dysseyvers –	
	And holpe for to maynteyn every thynge	
	That ys to the comyn welth perteynyng.	
	They have ben also in tyme of warr	135
	Both in thys land and other contreys farr	
	Dukys and leders of the hole army	
	And, by theire wyttis and warly polycy,	
	Study, forecast, and dilygent travayle,	
	Have won many a grete fyld and batayle.	140
	And thyne auncestours that were there	
	Were never able to bere shyld nor spere,	
	And were never but soldyars and pyoners,	
	Nor never had wysdome to be rulers.	
	But because myn auncestours have ever be	145
	Dyscrete and wyse, they have had auctoryte.	

Marchaunt	Nay, nay, thyne auncestours cam never all	
	To auctoryte for wysdome princypall,	
	For though some were wise, yet some of them agayn	
	Had small discression, lyttyll wyt or brayn.	150
	But because of the long contynuaunce	
	Of theyr grete possessions by enherytaunce,	
	By the folysh maner of the worlde, we see	
	For that cause ever they have had auctorite.	

Knyght	And I say that good reason agreth to it,	155
	For though the fader have no grete wyt,	
	The sone that is wyse shuld never the more	A3
	Lose hys land or auctoryte therfore.	
	For he that by study, dylygens, and payn,	
	Grete landys or possessyons doth attayn,	160
	Hys owne lyfe is to shorte and to lyte	
	For to take the frute of his meryte.	
	Reason wolde therfore that after hys lyfe	
	Hys heyrs before straungers have prerogatyfe.	

And the contynuaunce of such possessyons 165
Makyth noble men and gentyll condycyons;
And they whos blode hath long contynued,
As gentylmen so they shuld be honoured.
And so myn auncestours long tyme have be
Grete possyssyoners and in auctoryte. . 170
Therefore consyderyng my grete lynage
My blode, my noble byrth and parentage,
Thou art not able to compare with me
Nother in gentylnes nor in nobylyte.

Here the Plouman commith in with a short whyp in
hys hand and spekyth as folowith:

Plowman   Now here is bybbyll babbyll, clytter clatter! 175
I hard never of so folysh a matter.
But by Goddys body, to speke the troth,
I am better than other of you bothe.

Knyght   Avaunt, kankerde chorle! fro whens commyst thou?

Plowman   Mary, folysh pevysh daw, even fro my plow. 180
How sayst, woldyst any thyng therewithall?

Marchaunt   Ye, mary, thou lewyd vyllayn and rud raskall!
It is for the full yll besemyng
To perturb any gentylmens talkyng.

Plowman   Gentylmen! ye gentyl men? Jak Heryng! 185
Put your shone in your bosome for weryng!
I accompt my self by Goddys body
Better than you bothe and more worthy.

Knyght   Avaunt, knave, get the out of the gate,
Or I shall lay my sworde on thy pate! 190

Plowman   That shall I prove, I make God avow,
Never in better tyme – have at the now!

Et verberat eos.

Marchaunt   Now holde thy hand, felow, I the pray,
And harkyn what I shall to the say.

Plowman   Sey, knave, say what canst sey? 195

Marchaunt   Holde thy hand, I pray the, and com no narr —
I am a marchaunt and no man of warr.

Knyght   Thou art not honest, I tell the playnly, A3ᵛ
To make any quarrel here so sodaynly
To perturb our communycacyon. 200

Plowman   Here ye may se, syrs, by Goddys passyon,
Two proude folys make a crakkyng,
And when it commyth to poynt, dare do no thyng.

Marchaunt	Our commyng hyder and our entent	
	Ys not to fyght but by way of argument	205
	Every man to shew hys oppinyon,	
	To see who coude shew the best reason	
	To prove hym self noble and most gentylman.	

Plowman	By God, all the reasons syth ye began,	
	That ye have made therof, be not worth a fly.	210

Knyght	No, syr? I pray the than, tell me why?	

Plowman	Furst, as touchyng noblenes, I say	
	Ther is nother of you both dyd prove or lay	
	Ony of your actys, wherby that ye	
	Shulde in reason prove you noble to be,	215
	Or therby deserve any maner praysyng.	
	But all the effect of your arguyng	
	To prove your noblenes was but only	
	Of the deddys and actys of your auncestry.	
	And of the actys that your auncestours did before.	220
	Ye ar the nobler never the more.	

Knyght	As touchyng my self, I dare make comparison	
	Of as noble dedys as he hath any done,	
	For I am and have ben one of the chevalry	
	At the commaundement of my prynce ever redy,	225
	And every tyme of warr have be captayn	
	And leder of a thousand men or twayne,	
	And with hors and harnes, spere and sheld,	
	Have jopardyd my body in every felde.	
	And rentis of my landys have spende lyberally,	230
	And kepte a grete house contynually,	
	And holp to ponyssh thevys and brybers alwey,	
	To the grete tranquylyte of my contray.	
	And you, maister Marchaunt, wyl never take labour,	
	Except it be for your proffet and lucoure.	235

Plowman	Go to, go to, now master marchaunt,	
	There is a reason that gyvyth you a taunt,	
	I trow, more than you can answere well.	

Marchaunt	Nay, iwys, pyvysh and rude Jak Javell,	
	I can make an answere so substancyally	240
	Wherto nother of you is able to reply.	

Knyght	If thou canst answere my reason, do.	A4

Merchaunt	That can I well doo.	

Plowman	Then go to, fole, go to!	

Marchaunt	I say the comyn well of every land	
	In fete of marchauntdyse doth pryncypally stand,	245
	For if our commoditees be utteryd for nought	
	In to strange landis, and no ryches brought	

Hydyr therfore, we shuld come to beggary,
And all men dryffyn to lyf in mysery.
Then we noble marchauntis that in this reame be,   250
What a grete welth to thys land do we:
We utter our warys and by theyrs good chepe,
And bryng them hyder, that grete proffet
And pleasure dayly commyth to this regyon
Too all maner people that here do won.   255
Forthermore, ye see well with youre eyes,
That of straynge landis the commodytees –
We have such nede of them that be there –
That in no wyse we may them forbere:
As oyle, sylkis, frutis, and spyces also,   260
Golde, sylver, yryn and other metallis moo,
All drammys and druggys longyng to physyke,
Whych men must nedes have when they be seke,
Whych in thys reame can not well grow –
Our contrey is to colde and not hote inow –   265
Without whych thyngis we shulde lyfe in mysery,
And oft tymes for lak of them we shulde dye.
And I spende my studi and labour contynually
And cause such thyngis to come hyder dayly
For the comfort of thys land and commen welth,   270
And to all the people grete proffet and helth.
And for such noble dedys, reason wyll than
That I ought to be callyd a noble man,
And nother of you both that here now be
In noblenes may accompare with me.   275

Plowman   Now well hit! by Goddes body, well hit
Of one that hath but lyttyll wyt!
Answere me one worde furst, I pray the:
What is the noblest thynge that can be?

Knyght   What saist thou therto thi self, let see?   280

Plowman   Is not that the noblyst thyng in dede
That of all other thyngis hath lest nede,
As God which reynith etern in blysse?
Is not he the noblest thyng that is?

Knyght   Yes, mary, no man in reason can that deny.   285

Plowman   Well than, there is no reason therof why   A4ᵛ
But because he is the thyng omnipotent,
And is in him self so suffycyent,
And nedyth the helpe of no nothyr thyng
To the helpe of hys gloryous beyng;   290
But every other thyng hath nede of his ayde.

Marchaunt	Mary, that is very trough and well sayde.
Plowman	And lykwyse that thynge that hath most nede
	Is the thyng that is most wreched.
	So, suffycyency is ever noblenes, 295
	And necessyte is ever wrechydnes;
	And he, that hath more nede of that thyng
	For the preservacyon of hys lyvyng
	Then his felow hath, his felow must nedys be
	By thys same reason more noble than he. 300
Knyght	What than?
Plowman	By the same reason, it provith, lo,
	Ye be but caytyffys and wrechis, both two.
	And by the same reason prove I shall
	That I am the noblyst man of us all.
	For I have nede of no maner thyng 305
	That ye can do to help of my lyffyng;
	For every thyng whereby ye do lyf,
	I noryssh it and to you both do gyf;
	I plow, I tyll, and I ster the ground,
	Wherby I make the corn to habounde, 310
	Whereof ther is made both drynk and bred,
	Wyth the which dayly ye must nedis be fed.
	I noryssh the catell and fowlys also,
	Fyssh and herbis, and other thyngis mo.
	Fell, herr, and woll, whych the bestis do bere, 315
	I noryssh and preserve, which ye do were;
	Which yf ye had not, no dowt ye shuld
	Starve for lak of clothis, because of colde.
	So both you shulde die or lyve in necessite,
	If ye had not comfort and help of me. 320
	And as for your fyne cloth and costly aray,
	I cannot see whi ye ought or mai
	Call your self noble because ye were it,
	Which was made bi other menis labour and wit.
	And also your dilicate drinkis and viand 325
	Bi other menis labours be made so pleasand.
	Therefore, mayster marchaunt, now to you I sei,
	I can not see but I am able, and mai
	Lyf wythout you or your purveaunce,
	For of fode and cloth I have suffisaunce 330 A5
	Of my self for lyffing necessary.
	And now, sir Knyght, to you I sey playnly,
	I see not that ye can any thyng do
	For the commyn well, or ought longyng ther to.
	But ech man, beyng in auctoryte, 335
	Havyng wit, may do it as well as ye.
	Therfore, to spek now of necessyte,
	Ther is nother of you both but ye be

In more nede than I; therfore I sey playn,
I am more noble than other of you twayn. 340

[Marchaunt] Now that is a folysh reason, so God me save,
For by the same reason, thou woldyst have
Everi best, fyssh, and other foule than
To be more noble of birth than a man.
For man hath more nede of bodely coveryng 345
Than they have, for they nede no thinge.
The bestis have herr and also a thik skin,
The fissh, skalis or shells to kepe theyr bodyes in;
The foulis, fethirs, and so everi thing
Bi nature hath his proper covering, 350
Save man him self, which is born all nakyd,
And therfore he shuld be than most wrechyd.

Plowman Mary, no man can make a better reason,
For that is a sure and a trew conclusyon.
For if a child, when he is furst born, 355
Were not holp and coveryd, he were sone lorn.
He hath no strenght to help hym never a dell,
Yet bestis have power to help them self well.
So, consideryng manns body, in dede
A best is more noble, and man more wrechyd, 360
Because he hath nede of many mo thyngis
Than bestis have to help of theyr lyffyngis.
Also, man must dayly labour and swete,
To get hym sustynaunce, as drynk and mete;
The grownd he must dyg, and the bestis kyll, 365
For brede and mete his bodi to fyll,
Grapis, frutis, and herbis norssh dyligently
To make good drynkis to refressh his body.
But all brut bestis have coveryng natural,
Sufficyent to cover their bodyes with all, 370
And fynd theyr fode ever on the grownd redy
Without any payn, labour or study.
So everi man, by reason of hys body, A5ᵛ
Is more wrechyd and in more mysery
Than bestis be. Yet this not wythstandyng, 375
Man is most noble of creaturys lyvyng,
Not by hys body, for that is impotent,
But by hys soule, beyng so excellent.
For, by reason of hys soule intyllectyve,
He subdewyth all other bestis alyve, 380
And compellyth all other bestis that be,
By hys wit, to releve his necessyte.
But bestis have no wyt them self to defende,
Nor can get no more than God hath them send.
For take any best that weryth heer, 385
And do clyp it of bare agayns wynter;

That best hath no maner of polecy
To get other coveryng for hys body
Of cloth nor skyns, nor hath no wyt
To put it uppon hym thaugh one have made it,   390
Nor can byld no house nor kyndyl no fyre
To warme hys body yf nede shuld requyre.
But yet a man hath wyt and understandyng,
For to help hym self in every such thyng.
So man for his soule intellectuall   395
Is most noble creature of bestis all.

Marchaunt   That is a verey good and pregnant reason;
Yet me thynkith thou makist a degression
From the argument that we furst began,
Which was to prove who was most gentylman,   400
Whych we disputyd. I wold thou haddist hard it.

Plowman   Tussh, I hard what ye seyd everi whit.

Knyght   Then shew thy reason therin or thou go.

Plowman   Nay, be God, I have some what ells to do.
I must go by me a halporth of gresse,   405
The spokes of my cart therwith to dresse.
Trowe ye that I wyll leve my bysynes
For your babelyng pomp and folysshnes?
Nay, by Sent Mary, I wyll not do so,
For I can now to the merket goo   410
And for an halpeny as much gresse by
As shall cost me in our town a peny.
And I tell the playnly without any bost
A halpeny is as well savid as lost.

Marchaunt   Straw for an halpeny! therin is no wast.   415
Tary with us a while, perhapps thou mast
By our acquayntaunce now here get more   A6
Than thou gatist with thi cart this monyth before.

Plowman   Straw for thi councell, torde, a fart!
Trowist I will gyf up my plow or cart   420
And folow thy folish appityte and mynde?
Nay, I am not yet so mad nor so blynd.
For when I am at my cart or plow
I am more meryer than other of you.
I wold not chaunge my lyf nor my lyffyng   425
For to be made a grete lorde or a kyng.
There is no joy nor pleasure in this world here
But hyll bely, fill bely, and make good chere!
Be it prynce, lorde, gentilman, or knave,
Hit is all the joy that here he can have.   430
But these covetous and ambicious wretches,
They set there myndys in honoure and ryches

So much, that they be never content;
So they lyf ever in payn and torment.
But a man that can this meanys fynd,   435
To have fode and cloth and a mery mynde,
And to desyre no more than is nedefull —
That is in this worlde the lyf most joyfull;
Which lyfe in this worlde no man shall acquire
Tyll he subdew his insaciat desyre.   440

Marchaunt   I see well thou hast a curst apysh wit.
Then yf thow wylt depart, I pray the, yet
Come agayn when thy bisines is doo.

Plowman   For what intent now shuld I do so?

Marchaunt   For we will in oure olde argument prosede: 445
Who shulde be callyd a gentylman in dede,
And we wolde be glade to here thy reason.

Plowman   I wyll come agayn uppon a condicion
That ye wyll wayt uppon me both twayn,
And be not out of the way when I come agayn.   450

Knyght   We wyll not be farr hens.

Plowman   Then I wil not fayle.

Marchaunt   Then I pray the let not thi promyse quaile.

Plowman   Lo, here is my fynger, now trust me well.
I will come agayn yf I have my hele,
For, by God, I promyse you one thyng: 455
I am as trew of my worde as the kyng.
But if I fynde you not here, then, by my trough,
I shall call you oppenly false knavys both.

Marchaunt   Thou shalt fynde us trew in every thyng.

Plowman   I thynk so, except lyeng and stelyng.   460

Knyght   Then farwell for a season, a dew!   A6ᵛ

Plowman   Then fare ye well both — I dare say, as trew
As some that be tyede at a post in Newgate.   *[Exit]*

Marchaunt   Well, now he is gone, God sped well his gate!
But what shall we do now the meane season?   465

Knyght   Let us take now some recreacyon,
And come agayne here and kepe our poyntment.

Marchaunt   Now therto I am ryght well content;
And in the meayn wyle, good Lord, of thy grace
Preserve all the people here in this place.   Amen. 470

Finis prime partis   *[Exeunt]*

[Enter] The Plouman

Plowman	Here I may walk and wander to and fro,
	But I se not them whych I wold speke to.

[Enter the Merchant and the Knight]

Marchaunt Yes, by the rode, here we be both twayn,
To whom thou dydyst promys to mete here agayn
To dyspute the questyon that we began: 475
Whych of us coud prove hym most gentylman.

Knyght Thou seydyst thou hardyst our argumentes all.

Plowman So dyd I nother good nor substancyall,
For thy folyssh and pyvyssh oppynyon
Was, because of the grete domynyon   480
Of the landis and rentis wher to thou wast bore,
Whych thyn auncestours had long tyme before,
Thou thynkyst thy self a gentylman to be;
And that is a folyssh reason, semyth me.
For when Adam dolf and Eve span,   485
Who was then a gentylman?
But then cam the churll and gederyd good,
And ther began furst the gentyll blod.
And I thynk verely ye do beleve
That we cam all of Adam and Eve.   490
Then, to speke by reason, grete possessions
Make no gentylmen but gentyl condycyons.
That is the cause and best reason why
One shuld be callyd a gentylman truly.
And forthermor mark well this reason then: 495
If a mannis auncestours have be gentylmen
And verteous and good to commyn well,
That ought to be reputyd never a dell
To the prayse of the chyld whych doth refuse
Such good condycyons and the contrary use.   500   B1
But he ought to be dyspraysyd the more
Because hys auncestours hath shewid hym before
A precedent of gentylnes and vertew,
Whych good example he dothe not insew.
For the gentylnes of hys blode cler[l]y   505
In hym doth decay and utterly dye.
So he that usyth condycyons verteous,
Though that hys auncestours were vycyous,
Ought not to be dyspraysyd therfore,
But ought to be honoryd and praysyd the more.   510

Knyght Yet me thynkyth more honor shulde be gyffyn
To hym whych ys of noble blood and kyn.

Plowman	Then yf thou wylt loke honoured to be	
	Because of thy blod, then mark well and see	
	The vylyst beggar that goth by the dore —	515
	Had ye not both one God and creature?	
	Ye cam of one furst stock and progenye,	
	Both of Adam and Eve, ye wyll not denye.	
	The beggar and thou wer both, dowtles,	
	Conseyvyd and born in fylth and unclennes.	520
	Thy blood and the beggars of one colour be;	
	Thou art as apt to take seknes as he.	
	Yf thou be in the body woundyd,	
	Thy flessh is as yll as his to be helyd.	
	Alas, I have knowen many or thys,	525
	So proud of theyr byrth that all theyr lyffys	
	Wold gyf them to no labour nor lernyng,	
	Whych brought them to myserable endyng,	
	That in poverte wrechydly dyd dye	
	Or fallyn to theft and hangyd therfore full hye.	530
	So I sey vertew and good condycyons than	
	Is that whych makyth the very gentylman.	
	And though the fadyr may bequeth to hys son	
	Hys ryches, hys land and hys possessyon,	
	Yet may he nother gyf nor bequeth	535
	Unto hym in no wyse after hys deth	
	Hys vertew nor hys gentyl condycyons:	
	They can not descend as other possessyons.	
	And yf thou wylt be a gentylman, nedys	
	Thou must than use vertew and gentyll dedys.	540
Knyght	Why desyre men, then, prayse evermore	
	Of the actis of theyr auncestours done before?	
Plowman	One cause therof ys for lak of lernyng;	
	They perceyve not the reason of the thyng.	B1ᵛ
	Another is because ther be many	545
	That call them self gentylmen unworthy,	
	Whych lyfe voluptuously and bestyall	
	And do no good in the world at all,	
	But lyfe in pryde, slouth, and unthryftynes.	
	And because they have no maner goodnes	550
	Nor properte nor vertew in them wherby	
	Any man shulde thynk them any prayse worthy,	
	Therfore they seke for commendacyon	
	Of the actys that theyr auncestours have done.	
Marchaunt	Then I mervell men desyre to be callyd	555
	Of the blode of them that excellyd	
	In worldly honour, as kyngis and emperours,	
	Where some were tyranttis, some were conquerours;	
	And few desyre to be callyd of their blod,	
	Whych have ben callyd just men, verteous and good,	560

	And usyd indyfferent justyce and equyte,	
	Mekenes, abstynens or wylfull poverte.	
Plowman	Yf I shuld tell the the verey cause trew,	
	It is because they love no such vertew;	
	Whych vertew and gentyll condycyons shuld be	565
	Longyng to gentylmen of properte.	
Knyght	If gentyl condycyons be the cause, lo,	
	Then wyll I compare with both you two.	
	For I have usyd ever gentyll maner,	
	And so have myn auncestours that before were.	570
	For furst of all when thys worlde began,	
	Long after ther were but few people, than	
	Men had suffycyent of every thyng	
	Wythoute gret labour for fode and clothyng.	
	All thyng was in commyn among them, doutles,	575
	But after warde, when people dyd increse,	
	Ich man to increse hys pleasure and volupte	
	Of goodis and landes desyryd properte,	
	Wereof grete stryf and debate dyd aryse.	
	Then such as mine auncestours were that were wyse	580
	Did studi to make laws how the people myght be	
	Lyffyng togedyr in pease and unyte,	
	And agayns enmiys alwey defendyd	
	The people that tyllyd the ground and laboryd.	
	The people perseyvyng than theyr goodnes,	585
	Theyr gret wyt, dyscressyon and gentylnes,	
	Were content to gyfe them part of the proffet	
	Comyng of theyr landis whych they dyd get,	
	As corn, catell, and such thyngis as they wan.	
	But after, when that coyn of money began,	590
	They chaungid those revenuse and were content	
	To gyfe them in money an annyell rent.	
	So for theyr good and verteous condycyons	
	They cam furst to landis and possessyons.	
	So possessyons began and were furst found	595
	Uppon a good and resonable ground.	
Plowman	By Gogges swete body, thou lyest falsely;	
	All possessions began furst of tyranny.	
	For when people began furst to encrese,	
	Some gafe them self all to idylnes	600
	And wold not labour, but take by vyolence	
	That other men gat by labour and dylygence,	
	Than they that labouryd were fayne to gyfe	
	Them part of theyr gettingis in peas to lyfe,	
	Or elles, for theyr landis, money a porcyon.	605
	So possessyons began by extorcyon.	

B2

111

And when such extorsyoners had oppressyd
The labouryng people, than they ordeynyd
And made laws mervelous strayte and hard,
That theyr heyrys myght injoy it afterward. 610
So the law of inherytaunce was furst begon,
Whych is a thyng agayns all good reason
That any inherytaunce in the world shuld be.

Knyght   That is a shamefull opynyon, semyth me,
For when I have labouryd and by grete study 615
Gat and purcheysyd landys truly,
It is good reason that I have lyberte
To gyfe those landis to whom it lyketh me,
Or elles to let them descend lynyally
To my chyld or cosyn of my blod most nye. 620
For inherytaunce must nedys be a good thyng
Because so much good therof is procedyng,
Every man to hys blod such love doth bere.
Because the land shall descend to hys heyre,
He wyll byld theron and the land improw 625
And make corn and grasse to encrese and grow,
Graft frute, set trees, and norysh tymber
And to incresse fyssh make pondys wyth water,
Stok busshis and wedes whych dystroy herbage,
And all baren ground bryng to tyllage, 630
And amend the hye wayes that be ther about,
And do many other good dedis, no dowt,   B2ᵛ
For the profet of hys heyrys that shalbe,
And for the commyn welth of his countre.
Which thyngis surely he wold never intend, 635
Yf the land shuld not to hys heyre descend.

Plowman By thy reason no nothyr thyng is ment
But a good dede uppon an yvell intent.
When men for love or pryd do such good dedis,
The dyvell therfore shall quyt them theyr medys. 640

Knyght   Whyder God or the devyll quyt them therfore,
Is now to our purpose never the more,
For theyr myndys and intentis no man can tell.
But touchyng inherytaunce, thys I wot well,
Much good commyth therof and dayli doth grow. 645

Plowman Nay, mych ill commyth therof, I shall prove how:
For these men that be of gret possessyons
Unto theyr blod have such affeccyons,
Yf any land lyke them that lyeth nye them
Of theyr pore neghbors, they wyll distroy them 650
Or by extort meanys they wyll them compell
The land for half the worth to them to sell.

	And when they lake money they wyl alwey	
	Ever borow and never wyllyng to pay.	
	And when they shall dye ye see thexperience:	655
	Few of them have remors of consyens	
	To make any maner restytucyon	
	Of any land so wrongfully gotton.	

Knyght   Thou hast spoke sore agayns gentylmen,
But what seyst thou of marchaundis then?   660

Plowman   Many be good and worshipful also,
And many charitable dedis they do —
Byld churchys and amend the hye ways,
Make almyshowsys and help many decays.
But some be covetous, and full falsely   665
Get theyr goodis by dysseyt and usury,
And when they have a thousand pound in theyr cofers,
They wyll rathyr suffer theyr neyghbers
To sterve for hunger and cold and to dye,
Or they wyll gyfe to help them a peny.   670
And yet, more over, when any of them be
Promotyd to rule or auctoryte,
They dysdayn all lernyng law and reason,
And jugge all by wyll and affeccyon.

Marchaunt   Thou art but a rayler, to speke so sore   675
Agayne gentylmen and marchauntis evermore.
Be not plowmen and other that dryfe the cart
And such rusticall felows as thou art
Fals shrews, and lyfe as vycyously also
As gentylmen of landis and marchauntis do?   680

Knyght   Yes, this vylleyn carters almost echon
Have nother conscyens nor devocyon,
For brybe and stele every thyng they wyll,
If they may secretly come theruntyll.
And as for prayer and dyvyne servyce,   685
They love them in no maner wyse,
Nor nevyr wolde labour nor work do
If nede of lyffyng drofe them not therto.

Plowman   Yet gentylmen and the rych marchauntis that be
Use mych more vyce and iniquyte.   690

Marchaunt   Why, thynkyst all marchauntis and gentylmen nought?

Plowman   Nay, I sey not so; that is not my thought.
I am not yet so folysh nor so mad,
For I know many good though some be bad.
Yet some wyll suffer hys detis unpayd to be   695
And dye and jeopard hys soule, rather than he

113

Wyll any of hys landys mynysh and empayre,
That shuld after hys deth come to hys heyre.
And some of them so proud be of theyre blod
And use small vertew and doo lytyll good,   700
But gyfe all theyre myndys and theyre study
To opprese the pore people by tyrrany.
And some of them thynk thys for a surete,
It is the most honour to them that can be
To be able for to doo extorcyon   705
And to mayntayn it wythout punycyon.

Knyght   Bi Goggis swet bodi thou art a stark knave,
            Noble men and gentylmen so to deprave.

Plowman   What, thou proud horeson fole, whom dost thou knave?
            I trow thou woldist a good blowe or two have   710
            Wyth a good whypstoke to tech the curtesy.

Knyght   Avaunt beggerly knave, I the defye!

Plowman   What, wylt thou wage battell by and by now?
            That shall I prove strayght, I make God avowe.

                                    Et hic verberat eos.

Marchaunt   Kepe the peace, masters, hold your handys, for shame!   715
            To make thys besynes ye be gretely to blame.
            Ye wyll dysturb all thys hole company.

Plowman   Nay, mary, it is a cause to make them mery,
            To walke such a proude foole is but sport and game.   B3ᵛ

Knyght   By cokkys body, were not for worldly shame,   720
            I shuld cut thy flesh or elles see thy herte blode.

Marchaunt   Sir, hold your tong, your wordis be nothyng good.
            We lose here with thys lewyd altercacyon
            Mych good pastyme and recreacyon.

Plowman   Why, what better pastyme her canst thou have,   725
            Then to here one to call an other knave
            And see such a proud foole walkyd with a whyp?

Marchaunt   But I love it not; therfore, of felyshyp,
            Leve thys brablyng and with good argument
            Trye the matter that is most convenyent.   730

Plowman   Nay, I wyll trye it how so ever he wyll,
            Be it with wordys or dedys I wyll answere hym styll.
            For, be God, yf he wyll not be content
            To be concludyd by good argument,
            I wyll conclud hym one way, or that I goo,   735
            Or I shall prove it on hys pate, that shall I doo.

Knyght	Thow spekyst lyk a clerk that hath lyttyll wyt.
	When a case is put, yf he can not soyle it
	By no maner reason that he can ley,
	Then wyll he answere hym thys wyse and sey, 740
	'Beware what ye sey, syr, now I advyse you,
	For it is treason or herysy that ye spek now,'
	To thentent to rebuke hym opynly
	Before the unlernyd people that stand therby.
	And yf he can no colour of such thyng fynd, 745
	Then wyll he vex and chafe in hys mynd
	And cast owt some lewd wordis of quarelyng,
	To torn the hole matter to chydyng and fyghtyng,
	And so dost thou now lyke one that were mad.
Plowman	Nay, I wold thou knewist, thou folysh lad, 750
	I am nother mad nor dronken yet.
	For myn oppynyon I have well provyd it
	By substancyall reason and argument,
	That enherytaunce is not convenyent,
	And shewyd better reasons than thou canst doo. 755
Knyght	Nay, thy reasons may soone be answered unto.
	For God defende that estates of enherytaunce
	Shuld be dystroyed, for by that good ordynaunce
	Gentylmen of landes undoutydly
	Brynge up theyr chyldren full honourably: 760
	Some put to the scole to lerne connynge
	To instruct the people in vertuous lyvynge,
	Some made to be actyfe in marcyall dedys, B4
	Able to defend the land when nede is;
	And the rustycall people that have no land 765
	Such thyngis be not able to take in hand.
	Wherfore yf we shuld dystroy enherytaunce,
	We shulde dystroy all good rule and ordynaunce.
Plowman	But such men as have gret rentis and landys
	And no estate but terme of theyr lyvys, 770
	And every thyng theron wyll norysh and save,
	For the grete zele and love that they only have
	To the commyn welth of theyr contrey
	And for God sake – lo, these people be they
	That be worthy to have possessyons. 775
	And such people of vertuouse condycyons
	And no nother shuld be chosyn governours,
	And thei shuld have landys to maintain their honours
	Terme of theyr lyvys as long as they take payn
	For the commyn welth; thys is good reason playn. 780
	So that no man owght to have any land
	But such as be apt and have charge in hand

115

For the commyn welth, as pryncys, and rulers,
Bysshoppys, curates, prechers, and techers,
Jugges, mynysters, and other offycers,   785
That of the commyn welth be executers,
And valyant men of the chyvalry,
That be bounde to defende the people dayly.
Such men as be apt to all such thyngis
Shuld have landys to mayntayne theyr lyffyngis.   790
So enherytaunce is not besemynge
To let them have landys that can do no such thing.
Nor I thynk it not resonable nother,
One man to lyf by labour of an nother,
For ych man is borne to labour truly,   795
As a byrde is to fle naturally.
Nor a man ought not to have such lyberte
To lefe landys to hys chyld, wherby that he
Shall lust for to lyfe in slouth and gloteny,
Compellyd to do nought but lyfe voluptuously.   800

Marchaunt   There is alway good remedy for that:
That is to compell them to do somwhat,
So that ych man havyng enherytaunce
Have some auctoryte and governaunce,
Wherein he shulde take payne and besynes   805
To constrayn hym to eschew idelnes.

Plowman   Then thys grete myschef shuld folow of hit: B4ᵛ
Oft tymes they shuld rule that have lyttyll wyt
Or disposyd to be proud and covetous
Or to lyfe after theyr lustis voluptuous.   810
Which, yf such men had auctoryte,
Many thyngis no dowte mys orderyd shuld be:
Where justyce shuld be, there wold be tyranny,
Where peas shuld be, warr, debat and envy.
So there is no good reason that I can se   815
To prove that any enherytaunce shuld be.

Knyght   Yes, that shall I prove by good auctoryte,
For rede in the byble and thou shalt therin see,
God sayd to Abraham, 'tibi dabo
Terram hanc et semine tuo.'   820
Whych is as much to say, to expounde yt trew,
'I shall gyfe thys land to the and thyn yssew.'
Here is a good prove that it was Goddes wyll
That Abraham and his blode shulde continew styl
As possessyoners and have the governaunce   825
Of that lande as theyr propre enherytaunce.

116

Plowman	Thou answerest me now even lyke a fole,
	As some of these fonde clarkes that go to scole.
	When one putteth to them a subtyll questyon
	Of phylozophy to be provyde by reason,
	Whan they have all theyr wyttes and reason spende
	And can not tell how theyr parte to defende,
	Than they wyll aledge some auctoryte
	Of the lawes or elles of devynite,
	Whiche in no wyse men may denye.
	And yet ye knowe well that of phylozophy
	The pryncyples oft contraryant be
	Unto the very groundys of devynite.
	For the phylozophers agre here unto:
	Quod mundus fuit semper ab eterno,
	And devynys: *quod in principio omnium*
	Creavit deus terram et celum.
	But thou dydest promyse openly, even now,
	Onely by naturall reason to prove how
	That enherytaunce ought for to be had.
Marchaunt	By Gogges body, syrs, I holde you bothe mad.
	Ye be lyke some woman that I knowe well,
	When they wolde any matter unto a man tell,
	They wyll tell twenty talys by the way
	Nothynge to purpose to the matter that they
	Dyd furst intend to tell and declare.
	And in lyke maner now both ye do fare,
	For ye dyspute now whytheyr enherytaunce
	Be a resonable thyng or a good ordynaunce,
	Whych is a matter no thyng perteynyng
	To the questyon movyd at the begynnyng.
	For the questyon was whych of us all thre
	Coud prove hym selfe most gentylman to be.
Knyght	As touchyng that, we have all spoke and sayd
	Ich man for his part as much as can be layd.
Plowman	Nay, I have yet reasons laft wherby I can
	Prove my selfe of us all most gentylman,
	That nother of you both can voyde by reason.
Marchaunt	If thou have ought elles to say, now speke on.
Plowman	Then to you both, answer me thys short clause:
	Is not gentyll condycyons the most princypall cause
	To make one to be a gentylman?
Knyght	Paradventure it may be so, what than?
[Plowman]	'Paradventure,' quod'a!
	Nay, I shall prove that by examples many on:
	For musyke makyth one a musycyon,

830

835

840

845

850   C1

855

860

865

870

Grammer to be good gramareon,
And also geomytry a good geometrycyon,
And chorlysh condycyons a chorle for to be,
And so of every other estate and degre.   875
And where gentyll condycyons be, doutles,
In any person there is gentyllnes.
Than as vertew makyth a good man,
So gentyl condycyons, a gentylman.

Marchaunt   All those poyntys I thynk must nedys grauntyd be.   880
             What arguyst more therof, forth let us see.

Plowman   How seyst than to pryde, wrath, and envy?

Knyght   They be nought and evyll, I thynk verely.

Plowman   What is mekenes, pacyens, and charyte?

Knyght   Everychone a gentyll and good properte.   885

Plowman   What is covetous and lyberalyte?

Knyght   The furst good, the other nought, for surete.

Plowman   What is gloteny, sloth, and lechery?

Knyght   They be nought all, who can that deny?

Plowman   What abstynens, good besynes, and chastyte?   890

Knyght   Verteous and gentyll propertees they be.

Plowman   Syth ye have grauntyd thys, I shall prove playn
             I am a gentylman, so is none of you twayn.
             Furst, for pryde, your rayment shewyth what ye be,
             For ye wyll never be content except that ye   895   C1ᵛ
             Have the fynest cloth and sylke for to were
             Of oryent colours, and all your gere
             So costly; your housys gylt gloryously,
             As though ye wold therin your self deyfy.
             Ye covet evermore goodis, landis, and rent;   900
             What so ever ye get, yet never content.
             Wrathfull, ye be movyd to anger anon,
             And envyous, dysdaynyng every man.
             And as for me, I am content alwey
             Wyth a pore cotage and symple aray.   905
             I dysdayn no man and yet pacyently
             Can suffer to be callyd knave and not angry;
             Somtyme I call hym knave agayn in hast,
             And when I have sayd, my anger is past.
             Ye have your beddys so pleasaunt and soft,   910
             Wherein ye ease your self to long and to oft,
             Whych makyth your bodyes so tender to be
             What ye can not endure labour lyke me.
                              118

Wyth no maner course fode ye wyll be fede,
But wyth pleasand wynys and most whytest brede,   915
Wyth flesh and fysh most dylycate and fat,
All frutis and spyces that can be gat.
And when ye have had such pleasaunt refeccyons,
To aswage your carnall insurreccyons,
What so ever she be – wyfe, wedow or mayde ——   920
If she come in the way, she shalbe assayd.

Marchaunt   Thou liest, sklanderours chorle, for I think of troth
Thou usyst sych vyse more then we both.

Plowman   Nay, by cokkys body, I use no sych lyfe,
For I am content wyth blak Maud my wyfe.   925
Trow ye that I care for these nise proude primmys,
These paintyd popagays that hold up their chynnys
And loke so smoterly, as who say they wold
Have every man woo them that doth them behold?
Tote, man, for all sych venereall werk   930
As good is the foule as the fayre in the derk.

Knyght   Thou sayst trew – drafe is good inough for swyne.

Plowman   Yet thou answerest to no reson of myne.

Knyght   Thy reasons all, ryght well answere I can;
For I sey it becommeth a noble man   935
To have rych apparell and clothyng
And goodly housys of costly byldyng,
And that ych man accordyng to hys degre
Be knowyn from other and what they be.   C2
For yf such costly thyngis were not made,   940
Work for pore peple coud never be hade
And many folkys than shuld fall to idylnes,
Whych is the moder of vyce and wrechydnes.

Plowman   Ye, but I delyte noo sych vanytese worldly.
I delyte nother in sloth nor gloteny.   945
I dyg and delfe and labour for my lyvyng,
Never ydyll but somwhat ever doyng.
Dayly I ren and go bere, swete and swynk,
I ete broun brede and drynk small drynk,
Content with cours mete, what so ever it be,   950
So it quench the hunger, it suffysyth me.
These poyntes I use wych I have rehersyd now ——
Be not these gentyl condycyons I pray you?

Marchaunt   If thou use them, nede compellyth the therto,
For if thou coudist, hardli thou woldist other wise do.   955

Plowman   What I wold doo then ye can not tell.
It is not to purpose, but thys I wot well:

	Syth that I use my lyfe in such good maner	
	Whyth such gentyll condycyons expressyd here,	
	More then ye both do, styll contynuyng,	960
	And syth that gentyll condycyons is the thyng	
	To make a gentylman, the cause pryncypall,	
	Wherin I use my lyfe most of us all,	
	Who can by any reason denye than	
	But that I am of us all most gentylman?	965

Knyght In feyth, yf thou be a gentylman therfore,
Thou art a gentylman agaynst thy wyll full sore.

Marchaunt Syth I see he standyth in his own consait so well,
That opynyon we shall never expell
From hym by no argument nor reason.   970
Therfore now for a lytyll season
Let us depart from hym, I hold it best;
Then we shall have wyth hym some rest.

Knyght I agre therto, for Caton sayth this:
Contra verbosos noli contendere verbis.   975
Contend nor argu never in no matter
With hym that is full of wordys and clatter.

Marchaunt Wherfore for a season let us both depart.

Knyght I am agreid therto with all myn hart.

Plowman Why, syrs, than wyll ye depart and be gon? 980

Marchaunt Ye, that we wyll; farewel for a season.
For to tary here lenger we see no grete cause.

Et exeant.

[Plowman] Then fare ye well – as wyse as two dawys!   C2ᵛ
And I pray God sende you such grace both twayn
To be stark cokecoldys or ye come agayn.   985
Now masters, they be both gone away.
Therfore one worde, now harke what I sey.
We see well now by playne experience
When a man is set in a wylfull credens
All to fortefye hys owne oppynyon,   990
If God hym selfe wold than wyth hym reason,
In effect it shall nomore avayle
Than wyth a whyp to dryfe forth a snayle.
Therfore no remedy is that I can see,
For yvell men that be in auctoryte.   995
But let them alone tyll God wyll send
A tyme tyll our governours may intend
Of all enormytees the reformacyon,
And bryng in theyr handis the rod of coreccyon,

120

And the reformyng of injuryes them self see,   1000
And wyll sey precysely, 'thus it shall be'.
For exortacyons, techyng, and prechyng,
Gestyng, and raylyng, they mend no thyng.
For the amendement of the world is not in me.
Nor all the grete argumentes that we thre   1005
Have made syth we resonyd here togedyr
Do not prevayle the weyght of a fether
For the helpyng of any thyng that is amys.
We can not help it, then syth it so is,
I wyll let the world wagg and home wyll I goo   1010
And dryf the plowgh as I was wont to do,
And praye God send us peas. I wyll no farr mell,
Therfore, masters all, now fare ye well.   *[Exit]*

Hic miles et mercator iterum intrant.

Knyght   Now, by my troth, I am glad that he is gon.

Marchaunt And so am I, by swete Seynt John.   1015
I hard not a chorll thys sevyn yere
Shew so curst reasons as he hath don here
For the mayntenaunce of hys oppynyon.
Yet he hys dyssevyd for all hys reason,
For it is necessary that rulers be   1020
To have possessyons to mayntayn theyr degre;
And those few to dryfe the multytude all
Of the other people to labour to fall.
For yf the rulers drof them not therto
The peple wold be ydyll and nothyng doo.   1025

[Knyght] And most reason is that governaunce   C3
Shuld come to such rulers by inherytaunce,
Rather than to have them chose by eleccyon,
Oft tymys by drede, mede and affeccyon,
Men of evyll conscyens that grete tyrauntys be.   1030
Rede old cronyclys, the prove ye shall see.
And though they hafe grete wyt and lernyng,
Yet so proud they be therof, they fere nothyng,
Nother God nor man, but evermore styll
Without councell or advyse folow theyr own wyll.   1035
But th[e]y that by enherytaunce rulers be,
Though they have no grete lernyng, yet we see
Yt makyth them more ferefull and better content
To folow wyse mens councell and advysement.
And syth that yt hath ben so long contynuyd   1040
Enherytours to have rule, and so long usyd,
And that they have rulyd by as good dyscressyon
As the other that have be chose by eleccyon,
If that order of rule by successyon of blode
Shuld be dystroyd, it shuld doo hurte and no good.   1045

Marchaunt	That reason is so grete no man can debarr.
	Neverthelas that churllysh knave, that cartar,
	After hys fond oppynyon thynkyth thus
	Hym selfe more gentylman than any of us.
Knyght	And therin he lyeth, for by experiens we see 1050
	That gentyll condycyons most commenly be
	In them that be of noble blode borne.
	For take twenty carters wych never were beforne
	Aquayntyd, let them be togyder;
	Take twenty straynge gentylmen in lyke maner; 1055
	These churllysh carters, I dare well say,
	Wyll not agre togeder skant one day
	Without chydyng, quarellyng or fyghtyng.
	Ychone wyll stele from other and be pykyng
	And stryfe whych of them at the skot shall pay lest 1060
	And indever them who can play the knave best.
	But these gentylmen, I warant you, wyll study
	Who can shew to other most curtesey
	And of theyr gentylnes wyll profer to pay
	For the other and shew what pleasurs they may. 1065
	So, touchyng gentylnes, I say surely
	Men of grete byrth use it most commynly.
Marchaunt	There can be no truer sayng nor sentence
	And the cause therof we see by experience;
	For these pore wreches that have nothyng 1070
	Must be nygardys, churlysh and spayryng.
	But gentylmen be taught to be lyberall,
	And so they may be, for they have wherewithall.
Knyght	And as touchyng noblenes, that argument
	Whych the plowman made late provyth evydent 1075
	That gentylmen borne to land must nedys be
	For suffycyency of most nobylyte.
	For besyde Goddys gyftys of grace and of nature,
	As wyt and bodely stryngth, yet they be sure
	Of other ryches, as of land and rent, 1080
	To avoyd nede; so they be more suffycyent
	Of them self than other pore people doutles.
	Then yf nede of straunge helpe cause wrechydnes,
	And suffysauns be cause of nobylyte,
	Men born to gret landys must nedys most noble be, 1085
	For it is impossyble that noblenes
	Be in them whych lyve in nede and wrechydnes.
Marchaunt	A better reasone no man can devyse.
	And yet, forthermore, I thynk lykewyse
	He that hath grete haboundaunce of ryches 1090
	May use lyberalyte and gentylnes.

1070 C3ᵛ

122

And also it is ever necessary
That some lyfe in welth and some in mysery.
And let churllys bable and say what they wyll,
Hit hath ben so ever and wyll be so styll,   1095
For it is almyghty Goddys purveaunce
Wyse men of folys to have the governaunce.
And they that rule well, I besech Jhesu
Send them good lyfe and long to contynew.   Amen

[Enter] the Phylosopher

Phylosopher Ye soferayns all, dyscrete and excellent,   1100
             Before whom thys dyalog shewyd hath be,
             Touchyng thre poyntys by wey of argument —
             Furst what is gentylnes and what nobylyte,
             And who shuld be chose to hye auctoryte —
             Thys questyouns they be so hye and sottell   1105
             Few dare presume to dyffyne them well.

             Yet I thynk now, under your coreccyons,   C4
             The thyng that makyth a gentylman to be
             Ys but vertew and gentyll condycyons,
             Whych as well in pore men oft tymes we se   1110
             As in men of grete byrth or hye degre.
             And also vycious and churlyssh condycyons
             May be in men born to grete possessyons.

             And forther, as touchyng nobylyte,
             Yet standyth much part I thynk doutles   1115
             In suffycyencye, reason doth agre;
             But that suffysaunce makyng noblenes
             Must nedys be annexid unto goodnes,
             For suffysauns is not the cause pryncypall
             That God is noble, but hys goodnes wythall.   1120

             So vertue is ever the thyng pryncypall
             That gentylnes and noblenes doth insue.
             Then these hedys, rulers, and governours all
             Shuld come therto be cause of theyr vertue,
             And in auctoryte they ought not contynue   1125
             Except they be good men, dyscrete and wyse,
             And have a love and zele unto justyce.

             Wherfore, sovereyns, all that here present be,
             Now marke well these reasons here brought in
             Both agayns men of hye and of low degre   1130
             For thys intent only – to rebuke syn.
             For the best wey that is for one to begyn
             To convert the people by exortacyon
             Ys to perswade them by naturall reason.

For when that a man by hys owne reason   1135
Juggyth hym selfe for to offend,
That grudgyth his conscyens and gyffyth compuncyon
In to hys herte to cause hym amend.
But such blynd bestis that wyl not intend
To here no good councell nor reason   1140
Ought by the law to have sharp coreccyon.

But then yf the laws be not suffycyent
Whych have be made and ordeynyd before
To gyfe therfore condygne ponyshment,
The pryncys and governours be bound evermore   1145
To cause new laws to be made therfore,
And to put such men in auctoryte
That good men, just and indyfferent, be.

But because that men of nature evermore
Be frayle and folowyng sensualyte,   1150
Yt is impossyble in a maner therfore   C4ᵛ
For any governours that be in auctoryte
At all tymys just and indyfferent to be,
Except they be brydelyd and therto compellyd
By some strayt laws for them devysyd,   1155

As thus, that no man such rome ocupye
But certayn yerys and than to be removyd;
Yet that whyle bound to attend dylygently,
And yf he offend and surely provyd,
Wythout any favour that he be ponysshyd.   1160
For the ponysshment of a juge or offycer
Doth more good than of thousand other.

And untyll that such orders be devysyd
Substauncyally, and put in execucyon,
Loke never to see the world amended   1165
Nor of the gret myschefes the reformacion.
But they that be bounde to see the thynges done,
I pray God of his grace put in theyr myndys
To reforme shortly such thynges amys.

And though that I my selfe now percase   1170
Thus myn oppynyon have publysshed,
Or any of my felowes here in this place,
In any poynt here have us abused,
We beseche you to holde us excused.
And so the auctour hereof requyreth you all,   1175
And thus I commyt you to God eternall.   Amen.

JOHANES RASTELL ME FIERI FECIT
CUM PRIVILEGIO REGALI

124

Notes to the Plays

NOTES TO FOUR ELEMENTS

The Text

Original   *A new interlude and a mery of the nature of the .iiij. elementis.* [Anon.] 8° [J. Rastell, 1520]. One copy, imperfect. (*STC* 20722; Greg, Bibliography, No. 6.)

Facsimile   TFT, 1908.

Editions   J. O. Halliwell, ed., *The Interlude of the Four Elements*, Percy Society, London, 1848.

Julius Fischer, ed., *Das Interlude of the Four Elements*, Marburg, 1902.

J. S. Farmer, ed., *Six Anonymous Plays*, London, 1905. [Modernised text.]

R. Coleman, ed., *The Four Elements, as performed at the University Printing House*, Cambridge, 1971. [A cut and modernised acting text.]

The present text is that of the British Library copy (L). See the general note on Editorial Procedure (p. 28). Only substantial disagreements with Fischer's readings are noted. Where expansion or interpretation of original contractions is doubtful the original reading is recorded in the notes (marked L).

*   *   *

The preliminary pages of the surviving copy are missing. The copy was part of Edward Malone's collection of plays. Handwritten on the fly-leaf verso is 'This Interlude was bound with Rastell's Abrigem^t of the Statutes. 1st Impression dated 25th Oct. 11 Hen. 8th' [i.e. 1519]. This copy of the Abridgement was recovered by the British Museum in 1961 (see A. Hyatt King, 'Rastell Reunited', *Essays in Honour of Victor Scholderer*, Mainz, 1970, pp. 213–17).

Heading. The topics are listed like the chapters of a popular encyclopædia, in the manner of Caxton's *Mirrour of the World*, 1480. See Introduction, p. 11.

F.iii *phylosophy naturall*: the study of natural phenomena, as distinct from moral and metaphysical matters.

F.vi The cuts of *sad* (serious) matter proposed may be: *the messengers parte*: 1–147; *some of Naturys parte*: 148–203 or 217, 225–88; *some of Experyens parte*: e.g. 715–877, 1058 ff.

A lot more cutting is required to bring the time to 'not paste thre quarters of an hour of length'. The suggestion is·taken up by Roger Coleman in his edition of *FE* (as performed at the University Printing House, Cambridge, 1971).

F.x *Nature naturate*: the English form of *Natura naturata*, i.e. Nature in its created and creating power (see 153–4). Nature, as God's deputy, is here portrayed as a man.

F.xii *dysgysynge*: Mask, mumming, and disguising are not clearly distinguished in contemporary usage. An entry of masked dancers into the hall may be meant (F.1318) or possibly the bringing in of a mechanical spectacle to the accompaniment of music. (See G. Wickham, *Early English Stages*, I, i, 191; J. Stevens, *Music and Poetry in the Early Tudor Court*, p. 251.)

F.xviii *fyrmament*: probably in the Ptolemaic sense of the sphere carrying the fixed stars.

F.xix *circumference above 21,000 myle* (L *.xxi. M. myle*). Reckonings varied from Ptolemy's 22,500 to Mandeville's 31,000 miles. Caxton reports that ancient philosophers calculated the earth's circumference as 20,427 miles 'of whyche every myle conteyneth a thousand paas, and every paas fyve foot, and every fote xiiii ynches' (*Mirrour*, Pt. III, ch. xvii).

F.xxi *cosmography*: possibly the first English use to mean the science which describes and maps the general features of the universe (both the heavens and the earth), without encroaching on the special provinces of astronomy or geography. The older usage (1432) is for a *book* of description or representation of these matters. Cf. F.687.

F.xxv *hote fumes . . . bathys*. Rastell discusses the subject in relation to the city of Bath in his *Pastyme of People* (?1530). Cf. Caxton, *Mirrour*, Pt. II, ch. xxi.

F.xxxi *blasyng sterrys and flamys fleynge in the ayre*. Caxton (*Mirrour*, Pt. II, ch. xxx) treats 'Of the fyre and the sterres whiche seme to falle'.

F.6 *late made*: recently composed. On dating the play see Introduction, pp. 6–9.

F.14 'Consider only his intention and his well meaning.'

F.16–17 *What nombre of bokys . . . Of toyes and tryfellys*. Between 1476 and 1510 the total number of books printed in England was about 500. *STC in Chronological Sequence* (ed. W. A. Jackson and P. G. Morrison, Charlottesville, 1950) lists 54 titles for the year 1500. The annual total had risen to 214 in 1550. In 1520, John Dorne, the Oxford bookseller, had in stock broadsheets of ballads at ½d or 1d, single leaves of carols, prognostications at 1d, as well as poems of Robin Hood and romances. In contrast, Rastell's own stock at the time of his death was remarkable in its variety of serious intellectual interest, with nothing more trifling than *Jests of Wydow Edyth* (117 copies) and a 'sampler boke' – possibly for lace-making. (R. J. Roberts in *Library* 1979, pp. 36–9.)

F.34 *subtell sciens*: 'erudite knowledge acquired in the schools.'

F.39 *balates*: songs. See F.1375.

F.43 *after his fantesye*: 'As the fancy takes him, every man sets down his opinion, however ignorant.'

F.50–1 These lines read like proverb and gloss.

F.54 *a commyn welth*: here used in its modern sense of a community rather than the general good (common weal).

F.56 *count hym but a daw*: reckon him a fool (jackdaw). Cf. 62–3, 1136–7, and *Gentleness* 982–3.

F.93 'Unless he habituate himself by practising this procedure.' The theory of knowledge sketched here derives ultimately, of course, from Plato.

F.114 *Dysputynge of hye creaturis celestyall*. The Messenger's scorn is for the perennial and notorious scholastic debate about air and angels.

F.147 s.d. *portans figuram*: carrying a model. Lines 162–8, 225 ff., 283 and 320 refer to a model of the heavens, the earth, and the four elements, as depicted in Rastell's printer's device. The later demonstrations of the earth's roundness (348 ff.) seem to require a globe (cf. the picture of the lecturer in Caxton's *Mirrour*, fol. 23), but Experience's geography lesson requires a very detailed map or globe. See Introduction, p. 6, and note to 689.

F.152 (L *nauture naturynge*): creating nature. Hawes (*Pastime of Pleasure*, 1509, xliv, 216) plays on the grammar of creation as natural propagation: 'Nature . . . whyche naturynge hath tought Naturately right naturate to make.'

F.164 *etheriall regions*. Caxton (*Mirrour*, Pt. I, ch. xv) explains: 'And so the heven goth round aboute an ayer whiche is above thayer, the whiche in Latyn is called hester, this as moche to saye as pure ayer and clere, ffor it was made of pure and of clere purete.'

F.173 *They cause here*, i.e. here, on earth.

F.185 'All matter retains its own elemental substance.'

F.209–10 See note to *Gentleness*, 379.

F.224 (L *I shall Instructe*) The two examples of capital 'I' are in different types: the usual textura 93 and lettre bâtard. The mixing of type during distribution has been used to suggest that printing of *FE* was c.1526–7 (Greg, *Bibliography*, No. 6) but without comprehensive evidence.

F.229–31 'The earth is located at the world's centre point, adjacent to the concentric sphere of water, in turn surrounded by the spheres of air and fire.'

F.241 *rounde* is probably adverbial here. Thus, 'lying all around the earth in various places'.

F.242–3 'Yet the hills and mountains which stick out from the earth in no way alter its overall roundness.' *The yerth excesse* may possibly mean 'the earth's extremities', but *excesse* is better taken as adjectival (?*OED*).

F.244–5 Caxton had used the comparison of the oak apple: 'Ffor neyther montayne ne valeys, how somever hye ne depe it be, takyth not away fro therthe his roundenesse, no more than the galle leveth to be rounde ffor his prickis.' (*Mirrour*, Pt. I, ch. xviii.)

F.248 *joyntly*: together, but also, touching one another.

Notes to *Four Elements*

F.248–50 Cf. Caxton's use of the image: 'And thys ayer encloseth the water after, the whiche holdeth hym al aboute the erthe: All in liche wise as is seen of an egge, and as the whyte encloseth the yolke . . .' (*Mirrour*, Pt. I, ch. xvi.)

F.257–8 'Each star has its own sphere, and each sphere its own axis, and so moves in an individual manner.'

F.278–9 'The earth is set pre-eminent at the centre of the concentric spheres, set far apart from (? *abiect*) any kind of motion.'

F.279 (L *Formast abiect*). *Formast* is a common spelling; *abiect* seems to be a *pp.* derived from Lat. *abiectus*: thrown down. Fischer emends to *Formost object*.

F.287–8 'shall live with you constantly and shall continuously exhort you to learn more science.'

F.324 (L *shew ye more*).

F.338 *In the myddes of the fyrmament hengyng so small.* Copernicus's *De Revolutionibus* was not published until 1543, but there were Greeks (Philolaus and the Pythagoreans) who did not believe in an immobile and earth-centred universe.

F.351–4 (L a small tear in the page makes some words partly illegible).

F.353 (L *.xxiiij. houres*).

F.354 (L *To* [illegible] *est*) i.e. to the east.

F.363 (L *provytht*).

F.374 (L *whane it doth fu*) The corner is worn. Fischer reads fa[ll] but the *u* is distinct, though the rhyme is odd; *full*: 'become full' (*OED* full v² 1b).

F.373–7 'The eclipse of sun or moon is clear proof (that the earth is not plane) because it is never at its fullest at the same time in all places on earth. Yet the eclipse broadly seen in perspective (*generally*), happens at one instant in the universe (*hole world*).' The distinction is between what is visible from earth's surface and what occurs in the heavens.

F.393 (L *Cowbe prove*).

F.394 The earth's circumference is 24,899 miles. But see the note on the Heading.

F.395 (L *And* partly worn away).

F.396 *Thys instrumentys* (the *T* partly erased in (L)) for 'these instruments'. Fischer reads *Hys*.

F.405 On Sensual Appetite's folk-play antics see R. Axton, 'Folk Play in Tudor Interludes', in *English Drama: Forms and Development*, ed. M. Axton and R. Williams (Cambridge, 1977), pp. 8–11. The fool blessing and cursing his sons appears in later mummers' plays. The sons are 'jackdaws' in Lyndsay's *Satire of Three Estates*.

F.405 *Hykman.* Hikke was a traditional medieval name for English hostlers (cf. *Piers Plowman*, B, V.339).

F.411–411a (L printed as one long line).

F.412–15 Internal rhyme gives this passage the character of Skeltonics:
> 'Benedicite
> I grant to the
> this pardon
> And gyve the[e] absolucion.
> For thy soth saws
> stande up Jack daw.'

The parody is of both ecclesiastical and secular ceremonies, shrift and knighting.

F.416 ff. *Make rome, syrs*: the traditional exordium of popular players. Cf. 556. Sensual Appetite's speech is a sing-song patchwork of half-quotation, using the refrains of popular songs.

F.417 *huffa, galand*: traditional overture of the stage swaggerer. A fifteenth-century song satirises gallants with the refrain:
> 'Huff, a galauntt vylabele!
> Thus syngyth galauntys in theyre revele
> With huff, a Galauntt.'

(R. H. Robbins, *Historical Poems of the XIVth and XVth Centuries*, No. 52) Cf. the Digby Play *Mary Magdalene*, 491, and Skelton's *Magnyfycence*, 754.

F.417 *tyrll on the bery*: nonsense refrain, possibly 'pass round the wine, troll the bowl'. But 'tirl upon a pin' (*OED* tirl 3) is 'to make a rattling noise to gain admittance', which may be more apt.

F.419 *Synge fryska joly*. *Fryscas* and *gambawdes* (1249) are lively dances, and Sensual Appetite boasts that he 'can fryske it freshly' (1344). Cf. Bale, *A Comedy Concerning Three Laws* (c.1538), line 1794:
> 'Now shall I be able to lyue here peaceablye,
> And make frowlyke chere, with heyhow fryska Jolye.'

F.419 *with hey troly loly* is not the refrain of any particular song (See J. Stevens, *Music and Poetry*, pp. 413, 424).

F.423 *or be pope holy*: 'to become a pious hypocrite'. In Chaucer's *Romaunt of the Rose* 'an ipocrite . . . was clepid Poope-Holy' (*RR*, 414–15). The French *papelardie* probably meant glutton, from 'paper' (eat) and 'lard' (bacon). The English form is due to popular etymology.

F.455 (L *craturs*).

F.474–6 'Whatever pleasure the limbs take in feeling the qualities of softness and hardness, heat or cold, is worth nothing unless it is mediated through me.'

F.485 *Of hym*: i.e. from Sensual Appetite.

F.502 'The devil send you on your way!'

F.542 *Mary, at the dore, evyn here by*. This suggests indoor staging, perhaps with the stage or playing place set between the two doors of a typical Tudor hall screen.

Notes to *Four Elements*

F.551 (L *Than I be shrew ye page of thyne age*) 'Curse you, fellow, for being so old (and so slow).'

F.553 'Why do you make it so difficult?'

F.561–6 Most of the wines mentioned are 'hot', i.e. spiced, strong, and sweet, and not good to drink with meat: *ipocrase*: cordial of wine and spices, filtered through a 'Hippocrates bag'; *clary*: clarified honey with wine and spices; *sak*: white wines imported from Spain and the Canaries.

F.578 *The kyngys taker*: the king's officer who exacts supplies for the sovereign (*OED* cit. *FE*), with a play on the bawdy original sense (*OED* cites an Act of Henry VII (1486): 'Where wymmen . . . been oft tymes taken by mysdoers . . . takers and procurators').

F.582 *dyght*: 'prepared' with the Chaucerian sense of 'handled sexually'.

F.586 *stewes*: the word-play is closer than in later English, because *stewe* was still used for public hot bath houses as well as for brothels.

F.590 *wagtayles*: OED cites Lyly's *Midas* (1592) as the earliest example of 'wagtail' for a courtesan.

F.598 'the long and the short of it.'

F.599–600 This exact form of the proverb is not found earlier than *FE* (see Tilley, *Prov.*, W.676–7). The jest appears in *A Hundred Merry Tales* (printed by J. Rastell in 1526): 'A certayn artificer in london there was which was sore syk that coud not well dygest hys mete / to whom a physycon cam to gyve hym councell & seyd that he must trie to ete metis that be light of dygestyon as small byrdys / as sparous or swallous & especyall the byrd that ys callyd a wagtayle whose fleshe ys meruelouse lyght of dygestyon because that byrd ys ever mouyng & styryng. The sik man heryng the phesicion seyd so answeryd hym and seyd / Syr yf that be the cause that those birdys be lyght of dygestyon Than I know a mete mych lyghter of dygestion than other sparow swallow or wagtayle / & that ys my wyuys tong for it is never in rest but euer mouyng & styrryng' (*A .C. mery tales*, B1^v).

F.630 *evyn with the gretest*: in the manner of the greatest men.

F.648 *Agayne ye come therto*: in preparation for your return.

F.673 *the sowth sterre.* Amerigo Vespucci, in his Letter from Seville, 1500, tells of losing sight of the pole star as he passed the equator, and recalls Dante's celebration of the beauty of the stars about the South pole in *Purgatorio* I (J. H. Parry, *The European Reconaissance*, N.Y., 1968, p. 178).

F.677 (L speech heading *STU* misplaced by this line).

F.681 'to reckon the nearest way' (cf. 716).

F.683 (L speech heading *EX.* misplaced by this line).

F.689 (L *fugure*) See above, 147.

F.708–876 Rastell's geographical knowledge is discussed by J. Parr in *Philological Quarterly*, 27 (1948), 229–40, and by M. E. Borish in *Studies in*

Philology, 35 (1938), 149–63. Parr is undoubtedly right that Rastell was well informed and accurate according to contemporary geographers. Rastell's sources are of three kinds and no single 'source' accounts for all his details.

(1) *Writings*. Among cosmographical writings he had probably read (*pace* Borish) Gregor Reisch's *Margarita Philosophica Nova* (1506, 1512, 1517), parts of which were popularised in Stephen Hawes's *Pastyme of Pleasure*, 1509. Many of Rastell's details of the new world are found in the accounts of the voyages of Vespucci to Central and South America and of the Cabots to Newfoundland and Labrador, as recorded in Peter Martyr's *Decades of Ocean* (pr. 1511, 1516). Rastell's failure to mention Columbus is not decisive proof that he did not read Martyr. (*The Decades of the newe worlde or West India* were translated into English by Richarde Eden, and printed by W. Powell in 1555.)

(2) *First-hand reports and word of mouth*. The abortive voyage in which Rastell was a 'venturer' was organised under Sebastian Cabot and Sir Thomas Spert (see Introduction, p. 5). Following the Cabots' discovery of Newfoundland in 1497 a number of voyages to Labrador put out from Bristol between 1500 and 1505, organised by an Anglo–Azorean syndicate.

(3) *Maps, globes, and globe gores*. Rastell's 'fygure' was undoubtedly based on the most up-to-date models available. Borish claims he knew and used the map in the 1515 (Strasburg) edition of Reisch's *Margarita Philosophica*, which was based on Martin Waldseemüller's world map in his *Cosmographiæ Introductio* of 1507. I do not find Borish's arguments conclusive. In 1516, the year before Rastell's expedition, Waldseemüller printed a *Carta Marina*. Printed by woodcut in twelve sheets, it made up a world map almost 8 feet by 5, amplifying geographical features with lengthy descriptions of people, customs, and commodities, and showing pictures of the various tribes and crowned rulers enthroned in Europe, Africa, and Asia. (A facsimile is printed in J. Fischer and Fr.R.v.Wieser, ed., *The Oldest Map with the Name America*, Innsbruck, 1903.) A striking number of details tally with those given in *FE*: e.g. the conception of the New World as a continuous coast over 5,000 miles long; the picture of the northern natives wearing animal skins; their lack of iron; the approving mention of pine-trees and abundant fish in the north; the placing of Prester John's kingdom in India Maior; the prominence given to the throned rulers, Turco, Soldanus Egipti, Sophi Rex, and – the largest of all the woodcut portraits – Chaam Rex, the Great Khan of Cathay.

F.711 *occian see rownde*, i.e. the Atlantic, the *mare oceanum* of cartographers (e.g. Juan de la Cosa, 1505). This is the 'great Occyan' (733) surrounding the earth's land-mass, as distinct from the Mediterranean and inland seas. The name 'Atlanticum mare occidentale' is found in Reisch's world map (*Margarita Philosophica*, 1512 ed.) but was not in general use.

F.714 *Irelande, that holsome grounde*: hallowed by a long Christian tradition, and also healthy, St Patrick having driven out the poisonous snakes. Rastell may have written at least part of the play in Ireland during his enforced stay at Waterford in 1517–18.

F.715   i.e. the straits of Dover, the nearest (*next*) way to Calais and Boulogne.

F.720   *quart*: region, quarter. This may be semi-technical, since some geographers divided the earth into four quarters: Europa, Africa, Asia, and the New World.

F.726   (L *Gulfe of Uenys*).

F.727   'it' is understood.

F.730   *Iselonde, where men do fyshe*. English vessels, particularly from the east coast, continued to fish off Iceland in defiance of prohibitions issued from time to time by Denmark and the Hanseatic League. In 1528, 149 ships sailed for Iceland (*Letters and Papers, Foreign and Domestic, of Henry VIII*, IV, ii (1872), No. 5101). See below, 805–11.

F.733   *great Occyan*. See above, 711.

F.735   *tell it*: reckon its size.

F.736–7   (L *within this .xx. yere*) How exact is Rastell here? He seems to have known nothing of Columbus's voyages. If the date of writing is 1517 (see Introduction, p. 5) then the discovery of the new lands is placed at 1497 or later. This is the date given by Vespucci to his first voyage. Amerigo Vespucci, a great publicist, claimed to have discovered the 'fourth part' of the earth, and the name America was broadcast by Waldseemüller in his *Cosmographiæ Introductio* of 1507 and on its world map. But Rastell seems to be thinking specifically of the more northerly 'new found lands' discovered by the Cabots on behalf of Henry VII. See 772–4.

F.747–8   Rastell apparently refers to the northern part of the continent. There are no records that the hinterland had been penetrated by Europeans as early as this.

F.749–61   Experience's outline fits what is known of Rastell's misadventure of 1517 (see Introduction, pp. 5–6). A group of English venturers obtained King Henry VIII's consent to sail to the new found lands to discover what commodities there were. These speculators, who chartered ships and crew, were cheated by the professional mariners. The voyage to which Experience refers was clearly abandoned.

F.754   (L *they venteres*) 'the venturers'. Venturer has both senses given by *OED*, 1: adventurer, especially by sea; and 2: one sharing in a trading venture, especially sending ships overseas (this sense not otherwise recorded before 1557).

F.771–4   *so farre a grounde*: Experience describes the lands as a single continent (cf. 811–16).

F.773   (L *the .vij. Herry*).

F.775–80   Letters patent from Henry VII (19 March 1501) to English merchants who sailed with João Fernandes (Lavrador) authorise the partners to take possession for the crown of England of any place 'unknown to all

Christians'. The opportunities for conversion are reiterated by Richard Eden in his prefaces to *Decades of Ocean*.

F.785 (L *The honour the sone for his great lyggt*) This was a commonplace related of both southern and northern inhabitants (R. Eden, *Decades*, Book I, 1555 ed., f.5^v, 318^v).

F.789 *wodes*: possibly dwellings of boughs, rather than merely woods to shelter in. *Cotes*: shelters, usually for animals.

F.790, 796 This lack of iron (observed among the W. Indians by Columbus) is noted on Waldseemüller's *Carta Marina*, 1516, in the region of Newfoundland.

F.793 *Copper they have*. This was true both of North and South. On his third voyage (1498) Columbus found that the Venezuelans possessed copper. In 1524 Verrazzano noted that the Wampanoags of Massachusetts valued plates of copper which they and the Hurons obtained from tribes in the Lake Superior region. It is true that native copper in a fairly pure form has been found there in lumps up to several hundred pounds.

F.799 (L *Great haboundauace*).

F.800 *pyne aple tre*: almost certainly the unexotic pine-tree, which, together with fir (*vyr*), by its profusion and size astonished explorers on the Newfoundland shore. Trevisa notes, in his translation of Bartholomaeus's *De Proprietatibus Rerum*, Lib. XVII, cap. cxxii: 'And for þe pynappil tree is strong, ofte þerof beþ mastes ymade for schippes' (Oxford ed., 1975, p. 1017). Although the modern pineapple was itself a source of wonder to Columbus and his brother in Cuba and Guadeloupe, the huge pines were also noted for their nautical value (S. E. Morison, *The European Discovery of America*, vol. I (1971), 207).

F.802 *Both pyche and tarre and sope asshys* All three products would come from a single process, the controlled burning of the wood. Bartholomaeus Anglicus (*De Prop. Rer.*, Lib. XVII, cap. cxxiii) describes the extraction of pitch for caulking ships and says that a more liquid pitch is made in Greece (possibly Rastell's 'eest landes' of 803). Alkaline soap ashes, cooked with fat, formed the base of soap. The Portuguese king granted to João Alvares Fagundes, who explored the south coast of Newfoundland, rights to set up soap factories in the region on 22 May 1521 (Morison, I, 229).

F.805–7 John Cabot took codfish off Newfoundland simply by letting down and drawing up weighted baskets. According to Richard Eden, Sebastian Cabot reported that tunny were 'taken and kylde with troute speares' (Morison, I, 203).

F.808–10 The Grand Bank fisheries were very early exploited by English, Portuguese, and French (specially Norman) fishermen, and the vast amounts of new world fish soon upset the domestic markets. Fleets of ships from Rouen, Fécamp, Dieppe, and St-Malo established a factory for curing stockfish in Newfoundland in 1519. By 1542 sixty vessels might sail for the

Grand Bank in one day. Rastell's grumble suggests that English fishermen felt the pinch by 1517 and resented competition.

F.809–10 'Yearly they load up more than a hundred sailing ships with fish.'

F.811–13 The nakedness of the central American peoples was widely commented on by Rastell's contemporaries.

F.814–16 The fifty-seven Beothuk Indians of Newfoundland captured by the Portuguese in 1500–1 are described appreciatively by Cantino as wearing deerskin garments (Morison, I, 215; cf. Eden, *Decades*, 1555 ed., f. 318ᵛ).

F.830–1 The length of the Mediterranean is underestimated by about 400 miles – an error common among map-makers who worked with Ptolemy's projection.

F.832 *The Soudans contrey*: 'the Sultan's country (Egypt)'. He is depicted on Waldseemüller's *Carta Marina* crowned and bearing a sceptre, just to the east of Cairo. Due north of him is shown 'Turco' (the *great Turke* of 833), champion of Islam.

F.837 *Ynde*: Asia.

F.838–40 Like his contemporaries, Rastell accepts Amerigo Vespucci at his own valuation (in the Soderini Letter) and recounts the tradition spread by Waldseemüller. An explanation deriving the name America from Americus appears in the text of Waldseemüller's *Cosmographiæ Introductio*. The name America also appears on the South part of the new continent on the Globe Verte of 1515 (Bibliothèque Nationale). Rastell appears to apply the name to the whole of the 'new lands'.

F.841 Jerusalem is pictured as a towered city on the *Carta Marina* of 1516, as it was on most medieval maps.

F.842–3 Presumably Moses's song in *Exodus* 15.

F.844–6 Traditional geography named Asia north of the Ganges India Maior and south, India Minor. According to most authorities, the legendary Christian king Prester (Presbyter) John had his seat in Ethiopia. But there is no clear single tradition. Mandeville (whose *Travels* were printed in five editions between 1496 and 1504) makes Prester John king of India Major. The 1515 edition of *Margarita Philosophica* identifies Ethiopia as India Maior; so does the *Carta Marina*. The confusion seems to have arisen from the attempt to reconcile different traditions concerning Prester John's kingdom.

F.852 *Cane of Catowe*: the Khan of Cathay, a legendary survival from two centuries earlier, whom Columbus nevertheless expected to meet.

F.853 *the great eest see*: the China Sea.

F.859–61 The calculation of latitude is roughly correct. The longitudinal reckoning corresponds closely to the layout of the *Carta Marina*.

F.862 (L *tayle playne* corrected by a (?) sixteenth-century hand to *sayle playne*) 'sail directly along the same latitude'.

F.868 Experience's ignorance of the southern hemisphere 'on the other syde' is best evidence for the 'figure' being a globe. The *Carta Marina* shows equatorial America and Africa but otherwise nothing in the southern hemisphere, which ends at 50° S.

F.877 (L *wooderfull*).

F.878 s.d. 'And suddenly Studious Desire shall say.'

F.883 *mere*: merry (rhyming with Humanyté).

F.890 *Saynt Gyle*. Saint Giles, hermit (d. 714), was patron of cripples and beggars.

F.898 *farre oversayne*: much mistaken.

F.917–23 The tail-rhyme structure is just recognisable. Apparently *nyght / lyght* retain the fricative and sound different from *delyte / apetyte*.

F.927 *se to me*: look after me. Possibly *se* should read *so* ('I trust you will likewise take trouble for me').

F.934 *a knavys skyn*: a fool's coat? See below, 1188–9.

F.938–9 'You shall have another (knave's skin) so that we don't have to fight over the one.'

F.940 (L *Iohn*) possibly a misprint for *Ioha*. But cf. 846.

F.960 *a rounde*: a circular dance, about which little is known (Stevens, *Music and Poetry*, p. 245).

F.973 *or I go*: before I leave.

F.975 Proverbial?

F.976–7 'You are still set in your ignorant ways, as you always have been.'

F.988 'Do you find fault with me?' (*OED* ail, *v*.26).

F.990–1 'You are the sort who neither knows, nor wishes to learn, anything.'

F.997 *Tom Couper* is mentioned as a traditionally foolish type in *A Hundred Merry Tales* (No. 53).

F.1000–1000a (L printed as one line). Cf. 1004.

F.1004–1004a (L printed as one line).

F.1002 *ABC*. ABCs 'for to lerne rede' were among the stock of John Dorne, Oxford bookseller, in 1520, together with ballads of Robin Hood (see below, 1396). (H. S. Bennett, *English Books and Readers*, 2nd edn., Cambridge, 1969, p. 22.) The 1538 inventory of Rastell's stock includes 90 copies 'of the abces with sillables' (R. J. Roberts, *Library*, 1979, p. 36).

F.1028 (L *wha*).

F.1039 *In fewe wordes and shorte clause*. The virtue of brevity is attested in educational writing and proverbs of the period (Whiting, *Prov.*, W.799). Cf. *Mankind*. 102: 'Few wordis; few and well sett.'

F.1061–2 'However carefully you keep it under observation, you will hardly be able to see it change its place.'

F.1065–7 'You will think that it rises and has come nearer (*nere*) to the point immediately above your head.'

F.1084 'This experiment proves it true.'

F.1098–118 The demonstration parallels that in Reisch's *Margarita Philosophica* (1512 and 1517 eds.) where a woodcut shows a man in the crow's nest ('oculus superior') and another on the poop ('oculus inferior'), both looking across the sea to a tower on land. But Rastell would hardly need a picture in a learned treatise to suggest to him such a practical demonstration. The few lighthouses that existed at the beginning of the sixteenth century consisted of coal fires atop a tower.

F.1103 *in the see farre*: far out at sea.

F.1128 *Be this the seey.* Experience points to the globe, thus assuming what he is to prove.

F.1134 (L a whole gathering D1–8 is missing).

F.1135 (L *With argyng here theyr folyshe*) The corner of the page is badly worn. *Sawes* is suggested by Halliwell and Fischer. But in tail-rhyme stanzas the missing word would not normally rhyme with the short-line ending (*strawes*).

F.1150 (L *aboue .v.C.thowsand*) an indefinitely large number, about ten times the population of London in 1517, and about a fifth of the population of England. (I am grateful to Dr E. A. Wrigley for advice on this point.)

F.1152 'What has disturbed you to make you so out of breath?'

F.1159 (L At the bottom of E1[r] is written the name John Pulley, 1541.) The copy belonged to the Pulley family in Bridgnorth, Shropshire (See A. Hyatt King, *Library* (1971), p. 204).

F.1164 (L *Than thou hast made a cut hym purs*) apparently a printer's transposition rather than a neologism: cut-hym-purs is not found. (*OED* cites Palsgrave, 1530: 'His eares be cutte of, it is a signe he hath ben a cut purse.')

F.1166 *by the hard ars*: close to the buttocks. (Cf. *Nature*, I, 1276: 'by the hard kne'.)

F.1168–73 With this beheading foolery compare *Mankind*, 435 ff. (*The Macro Plays*, ed. M. Eccles, EETS, Oxford, 1969.)

F.1170 *troublid the more*: troubled thee more.

F.1174 'You have acquitted yourself like a bold knight.'

F.1184 (L The corner is badly worn; *its* has been inked in by hand.)

F.1185 'It would be charitable.'

F.1188–9 *For he is but an innocent, lo, | In maner of a fole.* Erasmus (*Praise of Folly*, ch. 35) speaks of 'innocent' fools, who are naturally foolish and blameless. Heywood makes the same point in *Wytty and Wyttles* (ed. de la Bère, p. 129): 'Wherever innosents innosensy dyspewt / For thowghts worddes or dedes god none yll ympewt'. The lady Science of Redford's *Wyt and Science* (c.1530) reproves Wyt, who is wearing a fool's coat and ass-eared cap, with a similar distinction:

> 'I take ye for no naturall foole,
> Browght up among the innocentes scoole,
> But for a nawgty vycious foole,
> Browght up wyth idellnes in her scoole.' (784–7)

(J. Q. Adams, ed. *Chief Pre-Shakespearean Dramas*, Cambridge, Mass., 1924.) It is possible that in the lost part of *FE* Ignorance dresses Humanity in a fool's costume.

F.1194 *Huddy Peke* is the name for a proverbial fool in Medwall's *Nature* (I, 724) and Bale's *Comedy Concernyng Thre Lawes* (ed. Schroeer, line 224). There may be some possible connection with a fool's cap (hood-with-a-peak).

F.1197 *I warrant you*: I am your protector, you may rise.

F.1213 (L *appyte*).

F.1213–15 'He must now and then join in and consent to the pleasures that they delight in.'

F.1244 *angellys clere*: the purity of angelic voices rather than angels' brightness may be implied.

F.1246 *bluddys*: rakes, sparks (earliest use in *OED* is 1562).

F.1249 *With fryscas and with gambawdes round*. See above, 419. Contemporary French *gambade and frisque* are also used synonymously. *OED* takes *gambawde* to be a form of gambol (2: caper, leap). *Round* may be adverbial ('all around') rather than describe a precise kind of *gambawde*.

F.1267 *a trull of trust*: a reliably lusty wench. Cf. *Fulgens*, I, 842–3: 'I tell you it is a trull of trust / All to quenche a mannes thrust.'

F.1287 *chefe mershall*. The marshall of a Tudor household was responsible for seating and domestic arrangements in the hall. Cf. *Fulgens*, I, 149.

F.1289 *Nowe set thy hert on a mery pyn*: be merry! The origin of the expression, which dates to Chaucer (*Mer. T.*, 272) is obscure. The *pyn* may hold an ornament or a wind-wheel toy. Later the pin is associated with the tuning pegs of a musical instrument (Skelton, *Bowge of Court*, line 386).

F.1292–4 'And so I shall . . . join in amongst them.'

F.1306 'They don't care for anything learned.'

F.1312 (L After the s.d. a blank stave is printed, presumably for a musical incipit, if needed.) The possibility of musically incompetent performers is envisaged (*or ellys they may say it for nede*).

F.1319–24 *Tyme to pas with goodly sport* is the only song with music to survive in an early Tudor interlude. The version given here is a new one made by John Stevens and differing slightly from his transcription in *Musica Britannica*, XVIII, *Music at the Court of Henry VIII*, No. 10. The original barring is marked above the stave (,). Professor Stevens discusses the song in *Music and Poetry*, p. 258: 'It is a three-part song, not merely after the style of the simpler chordal pieces of *Henry VIII's MS* but actually adapted from one [i.e. H9:

"Adew madame et ma mastres"]. It was clearly sung unaccompanied.' The 'original', then, is attributed to King Henry VIII. Professor Stevens suggests a date of composition c.1515 and argues that the MS was commissioned by Sir Henry Guildford, Controller of the King's household.

(L: Music for the three-part song is printed on E5^r (3 staves), E5^v (3 staves) and E6^r (4 staves). The words are printed under the top part and the incipit only under the tenor and bass. *Wyth goodly sport our sprytys to* has been filled in by a sixteenth-century hand in both lower parts. The hand may be that of the signature on E1, but the pen is thicker and the ink blacker.)

One other fragment of printed music from the period is ascribed to Rastell's press (*STC* 20700.3). For a discussion of this in relation to *FE* see A. Hyatt King, *Library* (1971), 195–214.

F.1328 'It doesn't matter not having a minstrel.'

F.1332 'Watch out! (I'm going) among you!' If the expression *by this lyght* is not merely conventional then Humanity carries a torch in an evening performance.

F.1334 *dauncyth with all*: he dances at the same time (withal).

F.1335 *Praunce we, praunce we* is printed as the first 'echo'. This gives the dance-song 11 paired lines or movements. It may be that the first answer should be *Daunce we, daunce we*, and that Sensual Appetite should then lead again with *Praunce we, praunce we*. This would give 12 steps.

(L: In the l.h. margin by the printed text of the song appears the following note in a sixteenth-century hand: 'Sensuall appetite must syng thys song, and hys cumpany must answere hym lykewyse.')

F.1337 *gyngerly*: daintily (*OED* 1st ex.).

F.1339 *pranke*: prance (cf. prink, to dress up, make a display).

F.1341 *kroke*: twist or bend (*OED* crook *v.* 2).

F.1345 *loke it lordly*: make my glance like a lord's.

F.1350 *a kyt or taberet*: a small fiddle or a tabor. In England a favourite combination for accompanying dancing was lute, rebec, pipe-and-tabor.

F.1363 *the mean season*: meanwhile.

F.1364 (L A blank stave for music is printed here.)

F.1365 repeats the cue line almost verbatim.

F.1368 s.d. 'They leave singing.'

F.1375 *Some lusty balet*. The basic metre of popular ballad ($a_4b_3c_4b_3$) is barely discernible in 1396–1419. The term *balet* covers a wide range of sophisticated and popular Tudor songs.

F.1378 *All suche pevysh prykyeryd song*. The argument here is over the propriety of prick-song (i.e. written part-music in measured notes) in divine service. The notorious feature in England was the use of elaborate melismas (parodied in line 1387). Wyclif had scorned 'smale brekynge', 'knackynge and tatterynge' of the divine office. Bale railed at 'fresh descant, pricksong, counterpoint, and fa-burden . . . the very synagogue of Satan' (cited by Stevens, *Music and Poetry*, pp. 78–9).

F.1394 (L *care not fo* The corner is badly worn.) Fischer reads *to* [*me*].

F.1389 *Robyn Hode.* In *A Hundred Mery Tales* (D1^r-v) there is the story of an idle young man who asks a friend: 'therffore I pray the teche me my Pater noster / and by my trouth I shall therfore teche the a song of Robyn hode that shall be worth .xx. of it.'

F.1396–19 *Robyn Hode in Barnysdale stode* is recognisably the proper opening of the *Geste of Robyn Hode* which had been printed in several versions by 1518. The third stanza of the Lettersnijder edition (probably printed by Jan van Doesborch in Antwerp, c.1510–15) begins:

> 'Robyn stode in Bernesdale,
> And lenyd hym to a tre;'

but the remainder of the song in *FE* bears little relation to the *Geste*. Stevens notes, 'fools sing a miscellany of popular nonsense, obviously quoting popular songs (probably with bits of tunes)' (*Music and Poetry*, p. 255).

Rastell uses the same technique for writing some nonsense verses against J. Frith in his *New Book of Purgatory*:

> 'In the beginning of this year
> John Frith is a noble clerk
> He killed a millstone with his spear
> Keep well your geese, the dogs do bark.'

(cited by Reed, *Early Tudor Drama*, p. 22).

F.1408 (L *I broke*).

F.1409 *wryguldy wrage.* The sense seems to be 'Has anyone quarrelled with you (done the wryguldy wrag *to thee*)?' In Lancashire dialect 'wrigglety wry' means awry; *wrag* (scold, accuse) and *wraggle* (dispute) support the conjecture.

F.1416 (L *.lx. bowes and ten*).

F.1419 *So merely pypys the mery botell.* *Botell* seems to be a substitution for the expected 'throstle' (thrush). To the rioters the gurgling of the bottle is music. But *botell* may be a form of *boterel* (toad).

F.1443 Probably only a few lines have been lost from the conclusion. All that the plot requires is Ignorance's banishment, Humanity's repentance, and reinstatement with his former tutor Studious Desire.

The Text

Original	*A new commodye in englysh in maner of an enterlude* [Anon] 2° (J. rastell me imprimi fecit,) [c.1525]. One copy and fragments. (*STC* 20721; Greg, *Bibliography*, No. 10.)
Facsimile	*Calisto and Melebea*, TFT, 1909.
Reprint	*The Interlude of Calisto and Melebea*, ed. W. W. Greg, Malone Society Reprints, Oxford, 1908.
Editions	H. Warner Allen, ed., *Celestina, Translated by James Mabbe, 1631, with An Interlude of Calisto and Melebea*, London, 1908.
	J. S. Farmer, ed., *Anonymous Plays*, ed. J. S. Farmer, London, 1905. [Modernised spelling.]

The present text is that of the Bodleian Library copy (B). See the general note on Editorial Procedure (p. 28). A complete list of irregular and doubtful readings, including obvious printer's errors, such as inverted type and words oddly separated, is given by Greg in MSR. My examination of the fragments in the British Library's Bagford Collection revealèd no variants. Substantial differences from Warner Allen's accurate and conservative transcription are noted (WA). Where expansion or interpretation is doubtful, the original reading is given in the Notes (marked B).

The source book

The relation between the interlude and *La Celestina* has been studied by H. D. Purcell (*Bulletin of Hispanic Studies*, 44 (1967, 1–15), whose general conclusions I endorse. On the adaptation of the Spanish and its dramatic purpose, see the Introduction above, p. 17. Where the Spanish has apparently been misunderstood by the English playwright it is quoted from *La Celestina, tragicomedia de Calisto y Melibea*, ed. D. S. Severin (4th ed., Madrid, 1976). Where the Tudor English is merely cloudy, I have cited as gloss the parallel passage in James Mabbe's lively and scholarly translation of 1631 (*Celestine or the Tragick-Comedie of Calisto and Melibea*, edited in its earliest and most literal manuscript version by G. M. Lacalle, Tamesis Books Ltd, 1972).

★   ★   ★

C. Title. *A new commodye*. On this early use of *comedy* to describe an interlude see Introduction, p. 16.

C.1–12 The substance of Melebea's speech is taken from the Prologue of *La Celestina* and reverses the order of the authorities Heraclitus and Petrarch, the latter apparently better known to the English audience.

C.2–3 translate the Latin quoted in *La Celestina* from the Preface to Book II of Petrarch's *De Remediis utriusque Fortunae*: 'Sine lite atque offensione, nil genuit Natura parens.' De Rojas was steeped in Petrarch's writings and uses them to develop two commonplace themes: the contradictory nature of human love, and Fortune's opposition to human happiness. The nature of the debt is discussed by A. D. Deyermond, *The Petrarchan Sources of La Celestina* (Oxford, 1961).

C.4 *Eraclito*: Heraclitus, the Greek philosopher, to whom de Rojas attributes the saying 'Omnia secundum litem fiunt'.

C.5–7 'Strife is inherent in all created things, because no two objects on earth are identical in every respect' (because matter strives continuously to reach a state of unity and rest).

C.12 *Sory* and *sad* may be merely synonymous, but the sense of the line demands contrast, suggesting that *sad* here carries the older sense of gravity.

C.16 *sanguynyous*: blood-coloured, rosy (*OED* cit. *CM* as earliest ex.).

C.17 *do fewte*: do fealty, pay homage.

C.22 *sutes*: pleas of courtship.

C.24 *exclamacyons on Fortune*: the stock-in-trade of the Petrarchan lover (cf. 74 ff.).

C.25 *similitude*: adj. (?*OED*) simulated; apparently a neologism, translating Sp. *simulado*.

C.32 *Out of his daunger*: free from his power to do me harm. (Cf. Chaucer, *Canterbury Tales, Gen. Prol.*, 662: 'In dawngere had he att his owen gise / The yonge girles . . .')

C.33 (B *What a mys woman now crist? benedicite*) 'What, (I become) a wicked woman? may Christ's blessing forbid it!' *Mys* is *adj*. but WA interprets as 'amiss' and punctuates the line: 'What a mys, woman, now? Cristes benedicite!' assigning it to Calisto unnecessarily.

C.40 *I report me*: either, 'I appeal to you' (if she addresses the audience) or simply, 'I declare'. A reflexive use of *report* (*OED* 6).

C.45 *strene* (B final *e* blotted): progeny.

C.47 (B *woman hod*)

C.62–3 'if you flee from giving your final acquiescence to such a temptation.'

C.64–6 'I perceive that the drift of your speech is tantamount to an intention to subjugate my virtue and make me into such a (bad) woman.' The awkwardness comes from the author's twisting (or misunderstanding) the Spanish: 'Y el intento de tus palabras, Calisto, ha sido *como* de ingenio de tal hombre como tú, haber de salir para se perder en la virtud de tal mujer como yo.'

C.66 (B *be come*).

C.71–2 A couplet, signalling by its epigrammatic isolation a *leit-motif*.

C.77 *Dew gard*: 'Dieu vous garde! God keep you!' Sempronio greets the audience.

C.78–296 From the entrance of Sempronio the gist of the dialogue follows the first half of Act I of *La Celestina*.

C.83 'I had to attend to your house, your horse, and everything.'

C.91 *Phebus or Phebe*: sun and moon, Apollo and his sister Diana. The comparison and word-play are not in the Spanish.

C.93 *this wold make a wyld hors tame*. Sempronio plays on a proverb (Whiting, *Prov.*, B.148): 'A wyld beest a man may tame, / A womanes tunge will never be lame.' (Robbins-Cutler, *Index*, 106.5.)

C.97 (B *whych scyens I fynd the arte withont pyte*). The sense of the original can scarcely be justified by WA's punctuation: *Whych scyens, I fynd the, arte without pyte*. It is unlikely that *scyens* is a spelling of *syns* (since), but in that case a possible emendation would give: 'Whych, scyens I fynd *thou* arte without pyte, / Hy the, Sempronio', except that *whych* has no function here. However, if *whych* is a misprint for *wyth* (easily confused in a contracted manuscript form) then more radical emendation yields the good sense adopted in the text. Calisto's call for a scholastic stool completes the pose of learned lover.

C.105 *let pas awey the mare*. The *mare* was a kind of goblin (Lat. *incuba*: OE maere) supposed to produce nightmares by sitting on the sleeper's chest. A night-spell (c.1450) prays, 'Kepe the fro care, / And blesse the fro the mare' (Whiting, *Prov.*, C.38).

C.106 This may be spoken to the audience (Cf. *Mankind*, 555–6).

C.114–15 'All harmony is in every way discordant to me, as to a man whose will is not ruled by reason.' The crabbed inversion may arise from misunderstanding the Spanish ('Aquel en quien la voluntad a la razón no obedece') and might be rearranged: *whos wyll to reson is unruly*.

C.117 *Peas, warr, truth, haterad, and injury*. WA points out that *truth* may be a misprint for *truce*, and cites the Spanish, 'paz, guerra, tregua, amor, enemistad'.

C.119–21 Nero's love for Tapaya (Poppea?) is the classic example of the English playwright's linguistic incompetence. The Spanish song has:

> 'Mira Nerón de Tarpeia
> a Roma cómo se ardía:
> gritos dan niños y viejos
> y él de nada se dolía.'

which Mabbe renders correctly,

> 'Nero from Tarpei doth beholde
> How Roome doth burne all on a flame;
> He heeres the cryes of younge and old,
> Yet is not greiued at the same.'

C.123 *this foule*: this fowl. Calisto is also accused of being ignorant (145, 153), but fool is spelled *fole* (486, 508). The joke seems to be: 'What kind of a bird is this? – A love-bird.'

C.128 (B *lastytꝗ*) WA *lastytes*.

C.130 Mabbe comments here: 'Passions of the minde beyond all paynes of the bodie' (p. 122).

C.131 Spoken aside but overheard by Calisto.

C.133–5 'If the fire of purgatory burns as hot as my passion I had rather my soul transmigrate into brute beasts than go to purgatory in order to proceed to God.' i.e. Calisto prefers the Pythagorean idea of the soul to the Christian, and this is why Sempronio replies 'that has the flavour of heresy'. The existence and nature of purgatory had a special interest in England from the time of Henry's Defence of the Faith against Luther until the Edwardian reformation.

C.138–9 A deliberate parody of the creed, closely following the Spanish. Mabbe comments, 'O Atheist'.

C.140 *Wyth the*: in your eyes.

C.141 (B *I know on whych fote thou dost halt on*) 'I know what your weakness is.' The first *on* may be redundant. This proverbial expression appears also in the 1586 translation of *Lazarillo de Tormes* and so may originally be Spanish. (Cf. the English proverb, 'It is hard halting before a cripple.' Whiting, *Prov.*, H.50.) Sempronio may imply that love has wounded his master in the heel (symbolizing lustful love – cf. Spenser, *Shepheardes Calender*, March gloss) and so promises punningly in the next line to *hele* him.

C.148 (B *That kepyth in hym kepyth no order of counsell*) Cf. Dunbar's *Rewl of Anis Self*: 'He rewlis weill that weill him self can gyd.' (Whiting, *Prov.*, R.231.)

C.149 *Calisto his fire*: Calisto's fire. The poet shares the common and false assumption that the possessive derives from a contraction of *his*.

C.150 The English makes love feminine and gives her a net (cf. below, 203–4: 'yt is an old sayeng / That women be the dyvellys nettys and hed of syn').

C.151 'The steadfast pursuit of which (love) brings only inconstancy', or 'in whose (Love's) purpose is only inconstancy'.

C.152 *Elicea* is one of two whores dropped from the cast of *La Celestina*.

C.154 (B *obeysanus*).

C.154–5 'Because thou dost submitt the dignitie and worthines of a man to th' imperfection and weakeness of a frayle woman.' (Mabbe, p. 124.)

C.157–9 The lameness of this seems to come from mistranslation. Mabbe (p. 124) renders correctly: 'I beliue her to be a god, though I believe also that there is a supreme god that raignes in heaven, but she the only god that remaines amongst vs.'

C.160 'In comparison to God a woman is the lowest-born slave.'

C.164 *Nembroth*: Nimrod, the 'mighty one in the earth' and 'mighty hunter before the lord' of *Genesis* 10 : 8–9.

C.168–70 'Coward-like you despair of winning a mere woman', either, 'though numerous women have been had and lost' or, 'by whom many men have been begotten and undone'. (A figurative sense for *ungotten* is not recorded in *OED*.) The drift is unclear because the English poet has detoured around the topic of bestiality that is central in the Spanish. Mabbe (p. 125) translates: 'you . . . dispayre notwithstandinge in obteyninge a woeman, manie of whome, hauinge bene seated in high estate, haue basely submitted themselues to the embracementes of Muletters . . . and other some not ashamed to haue accompanied with brute Beastes'.

C.170 (B *hardꝫ*) i.e. heardest. WA's expansion *hardes* and suggestion *hardly* make little sense.

C.171 *It is resytyd in the fest of Seynt Jhonn*. The epistle recited on Midsummer Day (St John the Baptist) dwelt on the consequences of the fall of Adam and the 'ancient curse of women'. Cf. Mabbe, p. 126: 'Haue you not read the festiuall of Saint Iohn, where it is sayde: This is woman, that auncient maligner of man, who drave Adam out of Paradise: this is shee that did thrust the whole generation of mankinde into Hell: this is she that dispised Elias the prophet, etc.'

C.173 'Who but a woman was to blame?'

C.175 *She put man to payn whom Ely dyd dispyse*. The English poet seems to have misunderstood the Spanish (see note on 171), unless *whom* (for *who*) is the subject. *She* is apparently the widow of Sarepta speaking to Elijah ('O thou man of God, art thou come unto me to call my sin to remembrance, and to slay my son?' I *Kings* 17 : 18).

C.176–7 'Since Adam put himself in the hands of women, am I so superior to him that I can hope to do better?'

C.178–80 'It would be wise to seek remedy by following those men that subdued women and not those who were overcome by them.'

C.181 (B *begīnyngꝫ*) WA notes that *begilynges* makes better sense, and translates the Spanish *engaños*.

C.183 'They observe no moderation, but are uncompromising whether their purposes be fair, foul, or unreasonable.'

C.185 'However carefully you guard them, they will show themselves in public, finding subtle ways to give love-tokens.'

C.190–1 'O what trouble it is to please their tastes and satisfy all their capricious desires.'

C.196 *janglyng not mewde*: chattering not controlled by being cooped up, as hawks are.

C.197 (B *wylenes*: ? wiliness, possibly vileness (Spanish *suciedad*).

C.199 *enbawmyng*: cosmetics.

C.203–5 Cf. Whiting, *Prov.*, W.530.

C.206 *by me*: of me.

C.210–12 'and furthermore, Fortune has shared her powers with you in every particular (*yche whyt*) so that you can be a generous spender.'

C.216 (B *Noman*).

C.217 (B *And thought*).

C.222 *hye portly corage*: noble, dignified character.

C.226 *rehersyng of my style*. Calisto signals a rhetorical set-piece. The topos of *descriptio* by itemising a beautiful woman from top to toe is taught in the *Artes Poeticae* (See D. S. Brewer, 'The ideal of feminine beauty in medieval literature', *MLN*, 50 (1955), 257–69).

C.230–2 'I believe the sun's colour may concede pre-eminence to hers, so that whoever had grace to behold it would say that nothing can stand comparison.'

C.234 *raylys* is transitive, though the line could be read: *O, what foule comparison! this fellow raylys.*

C.235 *glasyng*: a nonce-usage as *adj.*, 'glass-like'. Cf. a 'glancing eye'.

C.236 'Her nose is well-proportioned and lacks nothing of shapeliness.'

C.239 *tetys . . . is*. It is common at this period for a plural subject to take a singular verb.

C.243 *in meane maner, this is no trow*: of middling size, this is no mere supposition.

C.246–7 'worthy because of her beauty to have the apple that Paris bestowed on the goddess Venus' (preferring her to Juno and Pallas, and thus precipitating the Trojan war).

C.253–4 In Christian neo-Platonic philosophy form or idea preceded matter as Adam preceded Eve in creation.

C.257–8 'It is also possible that you maye one daye hate her as much as you nowe love her' (Mabbe, p. 129).

C.258 (B *abbor*).

C.265 'I shall not grudge any labour or care.'

C.267 *adquire*: acquire (?*OED*). Sempronio plays on *things* (services Calisto requires of him) and *thing* (himself as instrument).

C.269–70 'May God bring that to pass, I am happy to hear you say so, though it is too much to expect you will be able to accomplish it.' Calisto hedges his bet to urge her on.

C.279 Cf. Whiting, *Prov.*, M.408: 'Such mayster, such servaunt', and M.410: 'Too early master, the sooner knave.'

C.282 (B *a M vyrgyns*) Sp. 'cinco mill'.

C.287 *All onely*: solely.

C.292 *let rewardis go*: be open handed.

C.302 *my hart* is the object.

C.304–5 The device for removing Calisto from the stage is not, of course, found in the Spanish. The reference to *myne orchard* has eagerly been taken as an indication that performance was at More's house in Chelsea, because it had a celebrated orchard.

C.306 (B *comyn*).

C.310 Spoken to the audience.

C.311–12 On the satirical purpose of Celestina's Mariolatry see my 'Folk Play in Tudor Interludes', in *English Drama: Forms and Development*, ed. M. Axton and R. Williams (Cambridge, 1977), 20–3.

C.313 *homely*: abruptly, without preamble.

C.314 *a woman universall*: a fac totum.

C.319–73 Celestina's *prety game* of Elicea and Crito economically puts into monologue form an episode which de Rojas wrote in his usual dramatic dialogue (*La Celestina*, Act I, Mabbe, pp. 130–2). See my 'Folk Play', pp. 17–18.

C.322 'Yesterday (or, the other day) we both came close to being openly disgraced.'

C.331 *among the brome*: among the sweeping brooms (hence the noise at 354). But is there an association with Celestina's witchcraft here? Cf. the ME riddle-poem:

> 'Say me, viit [creature] in the brom
> Teche me wou I sul don
> That min hosebonde
> Me louien wold?'
>
> (C. Brown and R. H. Robbins, *Index*, 3078)

C.334 *As who seyth*: as if.

C.345 'Impostumes, plagues, pox, and botches be thy ende.' (Mabbe, p. 131.)

C.368 A strip neatly cut from the page has removed parts of this line and of 410. 'Well, seeinge you will needes knowe, it is the fatt fryar's wenche.' (Mabbe, p. 132.)

C.378 (B *a perte*).

C.384–5 'I have the purpose of the enterprise in hand and you will prosper better if I do not let you flounder further.'

C.390 Cf. Whiting, *Prov.*, H.475: 'If hope wer not hert shulde breke.'

C.396 'Are you the people my master so sorely longs for?'

C.400 *ellys Goddes forbod*: God forbid it be otherwise.

C.401 'Her authority over my life is equal to God's.'

C.403 (B *ars*) *ears* is supported by Spanish (¿Y tú piensas que es vituperio en las orejas de ésta?). Sempronio asks, 'Do you think there is any modesty in Celestina concerning what she is told?'

C.404 'Never stand bail for the man who would tell you otherwise.'

C.410 Defective line, the reverse side of 368. *day* is just decipherable. ('It is a greate whiles a-goe, since my mother . . . dyed in her parish.' Mabbe, p. 134.)

C.414 (B *I dare well se*).

C.415 'Let's see who can allege the contrary.' (*OED* lay v. 26.)

C.419 'The things that she has to deceive people with.'

C.421–2 'And yet worse than that, a practice that can never be given up – not only a bawd but a witch by her craft.' i.e. Once a witch, always a witch.

C.425 *Hark hydyr*: listen here.

C.432–5 'You are able to renew my delicious hope of achieving my purpose, my regeneration here on earth.' The parody of the beatitude, 'Blessed art thou among women' is obvious.

C.442 'You are able to revive my dead spirits by advancing my cause.'

C.446 *Wordes are but wynd*. Cf. Whiting, *Prov.*, W.643.

C.448 'Money makes the success of the merchant who has to put on a display.' Cf. Whiting, *Prov.*, M.629, Skelton, *Magnyfycence*, line 1574.

C.452 'that I should be mistrusted by such a good woman as you are.'

C.458 *wedes among corn*: proverbial (Heywood, *Dialogue*, 132).

C.459 *suspecious*: suspicious people. But possibly the type is inverted and the word should be *suspicions*.

C.460 Or ? read *For*.

C.482 *among*: 'in company' (the primitive ME sense) or, simply, 'also'.

C.482 (B *What a old*).

C.485 s.d. 'And let them sing.' There is no indication of music in the text.

C.485 'But don't pitch it too high.'

C.486 Does Celestina call the audience's attention to Parmeno's antics? At 493 and 508 she fondly addresses him again as 'lyttyl fole'.

C.491 Cf. *Ludus Coventriae*, p. 123, 25: 'And looke ye rynge wele in your purs, / For ellys your cawse may spede the wurs.'

C.492 'He shall be taught to sing *sol-fa* that women's flesh is expensive.'

C.502 s.h. (B *M.* in error).

C.505–6 *And thy moder* (B speech heading lacking). Celestina surely speaks 505, unless *thy* is an error for *my*. I give 506 to Parmeno because it seems unlikely that Celestina swears by, or curses, herself. ('Now the fyer of the Pox consume thy bones, for thy mother was as old a whore as I.' Mabbe, p. 143.)

C.506 *wyld fyre*: pox, venereal disease. Cf. *Fulgens* I, 1006–7: '*A*: Set even such a patche on my breche! *B*: A wyld-feyre thereone!'

C.512 'It would be a charitable thing if you were dead.'

C.520 (B *Elders*) 'Follow the teaching of your elders and their counsel.'

C.524–5 'Don't put too much trust in employers; they cannot be relied on (to help) once your own money is spent.'

C.528–30 'Thy master, men say, and I think too, is – but never mind! It's not my business who he employs. There will be no lack of flattering words, but rewards for service will be small, believe me.' My punctuation is tentative, but avoids both emending the text and running the sense over the line ends. The broken syntax reflects Celestina's deliberate change of direction. She avoids criticism and makes her inuendo by means of a proverb (Cf. 'Ffare wordys may ther be / bot luf is ther none': *Towneley Plays*, XIII, 569). *Lak* is intransitive: 'be lacking'. *Karych* ('care I') could be an error for *karyth*, easily misread by the compositor. If so, one might interpret:

> Thy maister, men sey, and as I thynk he be
> But lyght, karyth not who come to his service.

'Your master, who men say is insubstantial – and I think so too – doesn't care who he employs.'

C.533 *kepe thys*: 'heed this'.

C.538–9 Cf. Whiting, *Prov.*, R.120: 'Rychesse yll goten cometh to yll ende'.

C.540 (B *yoyfull*).

C.542–8 'Truth and honesty are riches in name, but certain wealth lies in the possession of real riches; second most important is the acquisition of fame through friends' report; this is surely true. Then I cannot commend a friend more highly than Sempronio. I do this in order to prosper the wealth of both of you. That task is now in my hands if you agree.'

C.550 'And who loves Arusa?'

C.554–5 'A man should be acquainted with men who do evil in order to know their ways but should himself intend to do good' – closer to an epigram of humanist counsel than a true proverb.

C.556 *Sempronyo hys*: Sempronio's.

C.559–61 'Is not sin readily spied out in a person who is sunk in self-indulgence? How can he protect his reputation against the power of virtue?' Celestina's answer is 'keep on the move' (563 ff.).

C.563–84 This second of Celestina's set-pieces follows closely her praise of delight in the Spanish, Act I (Mabbe, pp. 147–8).

C.573 *now mume, now hem*: 'now silent, now speaking' . Cf. Heywood, *Dial.*: 'I will saie nought but mum'; Shakespeare, *AYLI*, I, 3, 20: 'if I could cry hem and have him'.

C.578 *Behold her better*. WA suggests a misprint for *letter* (Sp. 'mira su carta').

C.584 s.d. 'Here Calisto enters again'.

C.590 (B s.h. misplaced at 591).

C.602–4 Either 'my belief in this old woman' or 'the optimism of this old woman tells my heart that comfort will shortly come as I hope and desire, or else let death come and make an end of me!'

C.615–16 Whiting (*Prov.*, H.324) cites various examples of the proverb 'to know more than one's left heel'.

C.617–18 'In my keeping your well being is secure though you are extravagant.' Parmeno plays on *large* meaning 'prodigal' and 'at large'.

C.623 *I wyll chaunge my copy*: 'I will adopt another role.' (*OED* copy 11: matter for printing.)

C.628 'I will act just as he does, which ever way he goes.'

C.631 'get goods by stirring up lechery.'

C.633 Melebea addresses the audience: 'Tell me please, did that woman ever come in here before me?' But this reading suggests that Melebea has sought out Celestina. In B the line is badly printed. If *this woman* is a plural form then Melebea may more plausibly be saying: 'Have women ever come in here before?', suggesting that the playing place (hall?) is a predominantly masculine preserve (cf. 637–9).

C.636 'I am sure I shan't be defended against so many of you', where *had* is possibly a variant of *held* (preserved or defended). This sense seems contrary to her confidence at 635. Line 636 is carelessly set, and perhaps should read *lad*: 'I am sure I could not be led away or astray from such a company.'

C.640–919 The dialogue of Celestina and Melebea follows *La Celestina* (Act 4) more sustainedly than any other scene in the play.

C.646 (B *yough and pusell age*) i.e. youth and time of maidenhood. The first English usage (Fr. pucelage) suggests literal etymology.

C.647–79 This proverbial dispute of age and youth follows *La Celestina* (Mabbe, pp. 169–70).

C.649 'The final resting place for all unrelieved anxiety.'

C.652 'Suffering, disease – age welcomes all.'

C.653 *small charge*: light weight.

C.656 *as all of wyll*: wilfully.

C.658 'in order to live, because death is so loathsome.'

C.662 *His*: its, not necessarily a personification of Age.

C.665 *faynt of goyng*: feebleness in walking.

C.668 'Mother, you have suffered a great deal in growing old' or 'you have taken great trouble to tell about age. What have you to say of youth?'

C.675–6 Proverbial (Whiting, *Prov.*, S.209), but the English follows *La Celestina* very closely (Mabbe, p. 171).

Notes to *Calisto and Melebea*

C.680   (B *I wys*).

C.681   *or thys*: before now.

C.683   *aray the*: arrayed (disfigured) thee.

C.696–702   Cf. Mabbe, p. 172.

C.700–1   Mabbe comments, 'Text of Scripture profaned'.

C.703–6   'Show me boldly the extent of your need.' 'As for all I need, I left it safely at home: my food and drink.' Celestina manages to beg even as she boasts of her self-sufficiency.

C.710   'Before I was a widow I never bothered about money.'

C.713   'But there! I must murmur when I cannot speak outright.'

C.743   'God forbid it be otherwise.'

C.750   'Those that have power to heal sick folk and refuse to do so surely cannot excuse themselves of causing their deaths.'

C.760–79   All these proverbial examples of natural affection – unicorn, dog, cock, pelican – are found in *La Celestina*.

C.765   *lo, se the gentyll kynde*: look how gentle (magnanimous) creatures are naturally. (*kynde* (sb.): nature.)

C.777–8   The pelican was supposed to feed its young with its own flesh and blood, demonstrating that the impulse to self-sacrifice is natural. The familiarity of this as a figure of the Corpus Christi strengthens the note of sacrilege.

C.780   'Is this the drift of the last part of your speech?' or 'Is this the drift of your riddling?' (*OED* conclusion 7b.)

C.786   *lewdnes*. The modern sense seems appropriate here.

C.787–8   (B *I se well*) Emendation to *sey* (say) is suggested by the proverb, 'Say well and do well end in one letter; say well is good, but do well is better' (Tilley, *Prov.*, S.122). Melebea says, 'I have been praised only for fair speech, but that is the vilest part of man and woman' (i.e. 'Now see my deeds!').

C.788   Proverbial (Whiting, *Prov.*, T.387) but also in the Spanish.

C.789–90   Punctuation *certayn Cause* is unlikely in view of the poet's metrical practice, though it yields good sense.

C.790   (B *bnedicite*).

C.791   Melebea appeals to the audience.

C.792   (B *me disseyue me*).

C.796   *in the dyvyll way*: along the devil's path.

C.798   Melebea plays against the proverb, 'Fayre promys makyth folys fayne.'

C.801   'Will you take wages for bringing me to ruin?'

C.807   *to long days*: many days too long.

C.820 Either, 'Any more exhibition of his sorrows is wasted, since I cannot be merciful,' or 'More showing of affection on my part would be wasted.'

C.823 'Ther ys no storme ne tempest ay doth lest' (Whiting, *Prov.*, S.798).

C.834 *Seynt Appolyne*. In Spanish St Appollonia. She was an aged deaconess when martyred in Alexandria in A.D. 249 and had her teeth knocked out by rioters. She is represented in Christian art by pincers or a gold tooth and was held to have special efficacy in curing toothache.

C.837 *so many holy relykys*. Note the earlier praise of Melebea as goddess (156 ff).

C.850 *malyncoly*: melancholy, condition of excess black bile, causing sullenness and depression.

C.851 *in fredome as Alexandre*. It is Alexander's generosity or nobility that is invoked.

C.856 *naturys forge*. Nature in the *Roman de la Rose* tradition is imagined at work with hammer and anvil creating species. The collocation with the Narcissus story (858) is made in *RR*, to which de Rojas was greatly indebted for his conception of the great bawd.

C.872 *pacyent*. WA suggests correction to *pacyens*, noting the rhyme and the Spanish phrasing: 'O cuanto me pesa con la falta de mi paciencia.'

C.881 *thoughtys be lyght*. Proverbial (Whiting, *Prov.*, T.239).

C.890 *thy water*: urine. Cf. Whiting, *Prov.*, W.78.

C.894 *bedfolkis*: beadsfolk, pensioners bound to pray for the souls of their benefactors.

C.899 Cf. Tilley, *Prov.*, T.380.

C.901 'Make known to this sick knight how far I am prepared to go for him.'

C.904 *my word or dede*. Cf. the proverb 'say well and do well' used at 787.

C.905 s.d. 'Let Melebea exit.'

C.910 *Now know ye by the half tale what the hole doth meane*. Whiting (*Prov.*, H.40) cites Paston Letters of 1461: 'For a man may her by the halfe qwat the hole menyth'. The poet of *CM* draws attention to his own truncation of the source. Celestina has as good as won; that the girdle signifies a maidenhead is made explicit in Act 5 of *La Celestina*.

C.911–12 Cf. 'Wynteris wether and wommanys thowt / And lordis loue schaungit oft' (Whiting, *Prov.*, W.374) and 'After the tempest the fayre wether'.

C.919 *arche dame*: a nonce-usage, parodic of the ecclesiastical sense.

C.920 – the end. The scene of Melebea's repentance and her father's speech of good counsel have no correspondence in *La Celestina* and seem to have been invented by the English playwright following popular tradition. See Introduction, pp. 17–18.

C.941 (B *me though y^t*).

C.952 'dragging her body along on the grass, and with her tail pressed down, made herself so sleek' (*OED* strake, earliest use).

C.971 s.d. (B *lamentabli*) 'Here Melebea shall not speak for a space of time but shall stare with a sorrowful face.'

C.971 *studious*: in a study, or state of abstraction.

C.982 s.d. 'And she shall kneel.'

C.1000 *that wo myght she be*: 'may she be sorrowful.'

C.1010 *on thing*: one thing.

C.1025 *myne one*: mine own.

C.1029 *and in wyll clerely*: clearly determined.

C.1032–87 On the attribution of the epilogue to John Rastell see Introduction, p. 18.

C.1046–87 With these sentiments compare *Gentleness*, 1010 ff. Both passages are commonplace. Cf. Edmund Dudley's *Tree of Common Welth*, 1509–10: 'And therefore ye noble men, for the better contynuaunce of your bloode in honour, set your children in youth, and that betymes, to learninge, vertue and conninge, and at the leaste bringe them up in honour and vertue; for verelie, I feare me, the noble men and gentlemen of Englande be the worst brought up for the more parte of any Realme in Christendome.' (Cited by Cameron, p. 18.

Colophon. 'John Rastell had me printed / By (royal) priviledge.' See Introduction, p. 15.

NOTES TO GENTLENESS AND NOBILITY

The Text

Original   *Of gentylnes & nobylyte a dyaloge* [Anon] 2° (J.rastell me fieri fecit,)
[c.1525]. Two perfect copies, two imperfect, two sets of fragments.
(*STC* 20723; Greg, *Bibliography*, No. 8.)

Facsimile   TFT, 1908.

Reprint   *Gentleness and Nobility*, ed. F. P. Wilson and A. C. Partridge,
Malone Society Reprints, Oxford, 1950.

Editions   K. W. Cameron, *The Authorship and Sources of Gentleness and
Nobility*, Raleigh, N.C., 1941.

J. S. Farmer, ed., *J. Heywood: The Spider and the Fly. Together
with an attributed Interlude entitled Gentleness and Nobility*. Early
English Dramatists, London, 1908. [Modernised spelling.]

The present text is the best corrected original copy, that in the Pepys Library
of Magdalene College, Cambridge (P). See the general note on Editorial
Procedure (above, p. 28). A list of irregular and doubtful readings, and of
variants in the printing of the Pepys, Bodleian, and Cambridge University
Library copies is given by F. P. Wilson and A. C. Partridge in the Malone
Society Reprint. Cameron's edition is based on the imperfect British Library
copy, some pages of which are from a modern reprint. It has occasionally been
helpful in suggesting punctuation. Only where transcription or interpretation
is doubtful are original readings given in the Notes (marked P).

★   ★   ★

G. **Title.** *compilid in maner of an enterlude*. Cf. Introduction, p. 2.

G. **Title.** *divers toys and gestis*: various inconsequential and entertaining
matters.

G.5 *fet*: course, transaction (*OED* feat 5). 'I have practised that liberty to
trade and have found the very knack of business.'

G.13 *in presence here*. This formula usually refers to the audience, which the
Knight implies to be socially distinguished.

G.19 *And may dyspend yerely five hundred mark land*: 'I can receive an income
of 500 marks a year from land revenues.' In 1505 the value of the mark was
fixed by statute at two-thirds of a pound, 'ilk mark contenand viij unce of gold'
(*OED*).

G.22 *for all thy krakkys*: for all your boasting.

G.27 *chorle*: churl, a serf or bondman in Norman times, but later the sense is
weakened to 'country labourer'.

G.68 *That is evyn a pyg of our sow*. This may be the earliest occurrence of a
proverbial phrase also included by Heywood in his *Dialogue* (1546).

153

G.69 *lordys and estatis*. The collocation suggests the highest ranks of society (*?OED* estate 6). Cf. *Nature*, I, 733–4. *Pryde*: 'My fader a knyght, my moder callyd madame, / Myne aunceters great estatys.'

G.70 *thartyfycers*: the artificers, typically elided.

G.81–2 Proverbial, cf. 1093–4.

G.100 'elaborately decorated with imagery and heraldic devices.'

G.104 *dyaper*: linen or an inferior fabric, woven with a small simple pattern formed by different directions of the threads, used for napkins and table-cloths.

G.104 *cloth of gold*: tissue of threads, wires or strips of gold, usually woven with silk or wool.

G.123 *lewd Javell*: ignorant rascal. Cf. 239. The name *javell* is associated in ME with *chavel*: jaw; hence, perhaps, 'jawing' or gossiping. The devils in the *Towneley Plays* (*Judgement*, 337) gloat over sinners who sit 'all nyght with hawvell & Iawvell'.

G.127–8 'In the country [i.e. not in London] they have been elected as justices of the peace at courts of sessions and courts of assize.'

G.131 (P *auncestours artyfycers*) possibly a witty coinage (cf. master-masons).

G.134 *the comyn welth*: the common good (often spelled *weale, wele*). Cf. 244.

G.143 *pyoners*: foot-soldiers who clear and excavate in advance of the main army.

G.175 *babbyll babbyll, clytter clatter*. Cf. Skelton, *Colin Cloute*: 'He prates and he patters / He clytters and he clatters.'

G.185–6 *Gentylmen! ye gentyl men? Jak Heryng! / Put your shone in your bosome for weryng!* Jack Herring was a traditional figure (sometimes a puppet) dressed in leeks and herring skins, paraded and pelted in carnival processions. He is associated with Lenten misrule (a song of the mid-sixteenth century tells how 'Jacke-a-Lent comes justlynge in, / With the hedpece of a herynge') and he is a simpleton ('A gentleman nay, a iack hearing / As honest as he that carries his hose on his neck for feare of wearing'; *Apius and Virginia*, 1575, E.iv). Nashe, in *Lenten Stuff*, 1599, compares him to Jack Straw. In *Gentleness* the Plowman reverses the social expectation, saying: 'You two gentlemen! you are such idiots that you would carry your shoes in your shirt front so as not to wear them out, like Jack Herring.'

G.189–93 The boasts and comical combat of Plowman and Knight are repeated almost verbatim at 712–15.

G.192 s.d. *Et verberat eos*: he beats them. From the dialogue it seems that he beats only the Knight before the Merchant interrupts.

G.193–5 A triplet. Cf. 278–80.

G.239 *Jak Javell*: 'wrangler' (cf. 123), an alliterative formula on the pattern 'Jack Juggler'.

G.252 *and by theyrs good chepe*: buy theirs at a bargain. Note the rhyme of *chepe* and *proffet*.

G.278–80 A triplet. Cf. 193–5.

G.292 *that is very trough*: that is very troth, i.e. perfectly true.

G.306 *to help of my lyffyng*: to help me in my life. Cf. 331.

G.329 (P *Lyve wythout you or your purveyaunce* is repeated at the top of A5).

G.341 (P speech head lacking, 'M' written in by hand).

G.357 (P *strenght*).

G.357 *never a dell*: not a bit.

G.367 *Grapis, frutis*: two separate items, not the as yet unknown grapefruit.

G.367 *norssh*: nourish, cultivate.

G.379 *soul intyllectyve*. According to Aristotle, the part of the soul capable of understanding is peculiar to man. Hawes (*Pastime of Pleasure*, ch. XXII) distinguishes 'Beastes, with soules sensative, / And man also with soule intellectyve.'

G.414 *A halpeny is as well savid as lost*: earliest example of the proverb (Whiting, *Prov.*, H.42).

G.415 *Straw for a halpeny, therin is no wast*. 'There is no squandering in spending an extra halfpenny' – perhaps an allusion to the proverb 'haste makes waste'.

G.428 *hyll bely*: 'cover belly'. 427–8 evidently play on the 'olde Proverbe . . . That from a full bellie proceedeth sounder counsel' (Whiting, *Prov.*, B.294).

G.441 *a curst apysh wit*: a vicious, mischievous mind. The sense of *apysh* here seems to be 'clever, mischievous' rather than 'silly, fantastic' (*OED* 2).

G.453 *Lo, here is my finger*: a rustic pledge, more wary than offering the hand.

G.460 *except lyeng and stelyng*. The Plowman may be playing with the proverbial phrase 'true as steel'.

G.458 *trough*: pronounced *troth*, to rhyme with *both*.

G.463 *Newgate*: the prison where offenders might be tied to a whipping-post for public correction. Black jokes about Newgate are traditional in the early Tudor drama (Cf. *Youth*, 230 ff.).

G.470 'The end of the first part.' Actors leaving the 'place' bless the audience in medieval religious drama and in the tradition of itinerant mumming plays.

G.471 *Here I may walk and wander to and fro*. The same device is used in the *Towneley Second Shepherds' Play*, 46–7: 'It does me good, as I walk thus by myn oone / Of this warld for to talk in maner of mone', where it also introduces 'complaint' and satire.

G.485–6 *For when Adam dolf and Eve span / Who was then a gentylman?* This rhyme, attested in Brinton's *Sermons* (1374), was used as a slogan during the Peasants' Revolt of 1381 (see Brown & Robbins, *Index*, No. 3922) and preserved in popular carols (Greene, *Early English Carols*, No. 336). The occupations assumed after the Fall are traditional (cf. *Ludus Coventriae*, 29, 415 *Eva*: 'Ye must delve and I xal spynne'). The proverb is quoted by Heywood in *Spider and Flie*, ch. 44, st. 27. See also below, 517–18.

G.487–8 '(No one was gentleman until) a low fellow came along and amassed wealth, and so the first "gentle" blood began.' The lines were not apparently a proverb (but cf. Chaucer's *Pars. Tale*, 761–2: 'Thynk eek that of swich seed as cherles spryngen, of swich seed spryngen lordes', and Lydgate, *Minor Poems*, II, 564: 'A cherle of berthe hatith gentil blood').

G.498 (P *neuer adell*) 'not a whit'.

G.505 (P *clery*).

G.552 'think them worthy of any praise.'

G.561 *indyfferent justyce*: impartial justice.

G.638 'a good deed done with an evil intention.'

G.640–2 'The devil shall requite them with their rewards. Whether God or the devil reward them for it has no bearing on our present purpose.'

G.649–50 'If any land nearby belonging to their poor neighbours is pleasing to them, they will ruin them' (i.e. the poor neighbours, forcing them to sell; or possibly, 'they will ruin the lands' to the same end).

G.664 *almyshowsys*: charitably endowed houses for the poor.

G.664 *decays*: arrears, or possibly those who have fallen in arrears (?*OED*).

G.667 (P *haue a.M.l'i. in*).

G.674 'They give judgment selfishly and partially.'

G.709 'Who are you calling knave?'

G.714 See above, 189–93.

G.719 *walke*: to beat or press woollen cloth in the felting process, hence to beat or drub a person (*OED* 2). So Heywood, *Johan Johan*, line 40: 'Walke her cote, Johan Johan, and bete her hardely.'

G.730 (P *nost cōuenyent*).

G.807 *hit*: it.

G.819–20 *semine* in error for *semini*. 'Unto thy seed will I give this land' (*Genesis* 12 : 7).

G.841 (P *in principio oīm*).

G.840–2 'Philosophers agree "that the world has always eternally existed", whereas divines maintain "that first of all God created heaven and earth".' The first statement is typical of Aristotelian scholastic philosophy in the Middle Ages and I have found no specific source. The second is a recasting of the familiar opening of St John's gospel: 'Hoc erat in principio apud Deum. Omnia per ipsum facta est.'

G.844 *by naturall reason*: as opposed to the revealed truth of scripture.

G.847   *woman* i.e. women.

G.869   (P *paduenture qd a.* speech head lacking). ' "Perhaps", says he!', in a mocking tone. The line is uniquely unrhymed.

G.871–3   *musyke . . . grammer . . . geomytry*: three of the four subjects of the quadrivium. The Plowman uses the logical method of the schools.

G.882   *pryde, wrath, and envy*: the first three of the seven deadly sins in Chaucer's and Langland's classification. Each has its appropriate remedial virtue: *mekenes, pacyens, and charyte* (884). *Covetous* is paired with *lyberalyte* (886) and *gloteny, sloth, and lechery* (888) have counterparts in *abstynens, good busynes, and chastyte* (890). The pairs are pictured in a Cambridge Chaucer manuscript (CUL MS, Gg. 4, 27). In Medwall's *Nature* (II, 1066 ff.) Reason prescribes the same seven remedies and these personifications then appear on stage.

G.887   The Knight seems to damn himself in preferring covetousness to liberality (generosity). To be true to type he ought to be open-handed. Probably *furst* should read *last*.

G.892   (P *graüytyd*).

G.898   *housys gylt* probably refers to copper or brass gilt used in roofing and ornaments, appropriate to churches (hence *deyfy* of line 899).

G.918–19   *refeccyons . . . insurrecyons*: a traditional connection of gluttony and lechery. (Cf. *Nature*, II, 561–2: 'For hote drynkys and delycate refeccyon / Causeth flesshely insurreccyon.')

G.922   (P *skladerours*) i.e. slanderous.

G.925   *blak Maud*: a dirty skinned old hag.

G.928   *smoterly* (?*adv.*) prettily. (Cf. *FE*, 42: 'feyr and smotter of face'.) The sense of sexual provocativeness in G.929–30 sheds a new light on Chaucer's single usage, hitherto glossed as 'besmirched'. Symkyn's wife's pride springs from some attractiveness: 'And eek, for she was somdel smoterlich, / She was as digne as water in a dich.' (*Reeve's Tale, CT*, A. 3963–4).

G.926   *primmys*: pretty girls, paramours, with a suggestion of commonness. (Cf. *The Book of Mayd Emlyn*, c.1520: 'Thys lytell prety mouse / The yonge lusty prymme / She coude byte'.)

G.928   *as who say*: as if to say.

G.931   *As good is the foule as the fayre in the derk*: earliest (?) example of a proverb quoted by Heywood (*Dialogue*, 27, 38): 'The fayre and the foule, by darke are lyke store.'

G.932   *drafe is good inough for swyne*. An exemplum in *Gesta Romanorum* (XLIX) shows the association to be traditional: 'The wolf fownde a swyne etyng draffe and drestes . . . They lovedyn draffe of lechery . . . men and women . . . that lovyn more draffe and drestes, that is lustes and lykynges of the flesshe.'

G.936–40   Cameron (pp. 30–1) cites the *Act agaynst wearing of costly Apparrell* of 1509–10. 'Servants of husbandry', shepherds and labourers were forbidden to wear any cloth 'wherof the broode yerde passythe in pryce twoo shillynges' or any hose 'above the pryce of x *d*. the yerde uppon payne of imprisonment in the Stokkys by three days'. He notes that when the Act was renewed in 1514–15 husbandmen were permitted to pay twopence a yard more for their hose cloth.

In *Fulgens and Lucrece* (I, 720–64) the servants A and B discuss the absurdity of extravagant fashions.

G.948 Cameron punctuates: *Dayly I ren and go, bere, swete and swynk*, to make *bere* a verb. But the Plowman's boast of going bare answers the Knight's riding in 'rych apparell and clothyng' (936). The phrase is colloquial, as in the sixteenth-century song, 'Back and side, go bare!'

G.949 *Small drynk*: weak beer.

G.955 'If you had any choice, you certainly would do otherwise.'

G.959 (P *Whyth*).

G.960 *still contynuyng*: 'and, continuing my peroration, since . . .' The Plowman's affectation of scholastic argument mocks him.

G.968 'has such a good opinion of himself.'

G.973 'We shall have some respite from him.'

G.974 *Contra verbosos noli contendere verbis*. Cato, *Distycha*, I, 10. It continues, 'sermo datur cunctis animi sapientia paucis'. Caxton glosses this:

> Ayenst woordy folk ay ful of wynde
> Stryve not at al. Yt may not the proufyte.
> Such rasshe folkes ben in conceytes blynde
> The witles wordes auayleth not a myte
> In fele wordes is ofte wisedam ful lyte
> For vnto euery wight is geuen speche
> And, yet the wyse ful ofte ben for to seche.

(*Paruus Cato, Magnus Cato*, trans. Benet Burgh, London, 1477.)

G.983 *as wyse as two dawys*: jackdaws, a favourite comparison in the period (cf. *FE*, 56), perhaps because they were kept as pets and taught 'to speke'.

G.985 *cokecoldys*. The spelling suggests a bawdy pun.

G.986 *masters*. The Plowman is civil but not deferential.

G.992–3 *wyth a whyp to dryve forth a snayle*: a proverbial image of futility (Tilley, *Prov.*, S.582) illustrated in Barclay's *Ship of Fools*. Skelton begins his *Colyn Cloute*, 'What can it avayle / To dryve forth a snayle?'

G.996–1001 The note sounded here suggests a date of composition earlier than 1523, when a long-awaited parliament met to discuss social reforms. See Introduction, p. 21.

G.1010 *let the world wagg* (Whiting, *Prov.*, W.659). *Wagg*: 'stir, be active' but in the proverbial phrase has a reduced sense 'go where it will'.

G.1012 *peas*: peace, with a possible pun on the traditional symbolism which gives peas to the fool of folk play.

G.1013 s.d. 'Here the Knight and Merchant re-enter.'

G.1017 *curst reasons*: vicious, dangerous arguments.

G.1019 *he hys dyssevyd*: he is deceived.

G.1020–3 'It is necessary that there be rulers and that they have possessions in order to support their position in society; and that those few should compel the majority of other people to undertake work.'

G.1026–30 'It makes best sense that government should descend to such rulers by inheritance, rather than that [people] should choose by election, often through fear, bribery, or favouritism, wicked unprincipled men who become notorious tyrants.' *Chose* for *chosen* is possible, in which case *them* would refer to *such rulers* and be in apposition to *men of evyll conscyens*.

G.1030 (P *tryaunts*).

G.1036 (P *But thy that*).

G.1038 *Yt* i.e. inheritance (as in 1040). (P *Yet* for *Yt* is probably due to the compositor repeating *yet* from 1037.) The argument is that inherited power makes men less self-confident, more likely to take counsel than if they seek power on their own merit.

G.1041 (P *wsyd*).

G.1049 *any of us* – including the audience.

G.1055 *straynge*: unacquainted.

G.1073 (P *wherewᵗall*).

G.1083–4 'If dependence on outside help is the cause of wretchedness, and if self-sufficiency is the cause of nobleness . . .'

G.1097 Proverbial. Cf. 81–2.

G.1099 Possibly the Knight and Merchant withdraw at this point, though the Philosopher's reference to 'my felowes here in this place' (1172) may be taken to mean that they remain in 'the place' (i.e. the acting area), in view of the audience.

G.1100–end Note the shift to rhyme royal, appropriate to prologues and epilogues in drama of the period, and the formal, legal vocabulary. See Introduction, pp. 20, 25.

G.1115 (P *yet standyth mnch pt I thynk doutles*) a badly set line. Possibly *yet* should read *yt*, by analogy with 1038.

G.1117–20 'That self-sufficiency which creates nobility must be connected to moral goodness, because self-sufficiency is not the principal cause of God's nobleness, but rather his goodness is.'

G.1120 (P *god his*).

G.1144 *condygne ponyshment*: appropriate punishment: a formal legal phrase used in Acts of Parliament (e.g. 25 Henry VIII, c.4 [1533–4]: 'Former statutes . . . for lack of condigne punishment . . . be little feared').

G.1156 'For instance, that no man should occupy a public position except for a fixed number of years, and then should be removed; during his tenure he should be bound to attend (all its sessions) diligently.' Rastell himself was MP in the Reformation Parliament of 1529.

G.1160 (P *ponyhysshyd*).

G.1173 'have abused our priviledge in any particular.'

G.1176 (P *thys*).

Colophon. 'John Rastell caused me to be made / With royal priviledge.' Rastell himself seems remote from the printing process, though his type and press were used (see Introduction, p. 20).

Glossary

Readers unfamiliar with early Tudor spelling will find that a large number of words readily yield their modern-meaning when they are sounded (e.g. **a pase**: apace, **fedys**: feeds, **neclygens**: negligence, **ones**: once, **pepyll**: people, **thauncestors**: the ancestors, **the**: thee, **weryst**: wearest, **yvyll**: evil), and many of these are not listed. Line references are normally to the first occurrence in the volume and subsequent references are given only where the meaning is different or in cases of special interest. The part of speech is noted only where there might be some doubt. An asterisk * indicates a Note on this line. The indication (?*OED*) means 'this sense apparently not recorded in *OED*'.

a (*pron.*) he (*quod'a* F.529*)
a (*prep.*) in (*a felashyp* F.1391: for fellowship's sake)
a (*v.*) have (*God a mercy* G.67)
abbor abhor C.258
abject (*pp.*) ? set apart from F.279*
abused (*pp.*) misbehaved G.1173
accompare compare G.275
accomplysh fulfil C.27
accompt reckon F.681
accordyng (*adv.*) appropriately C.592
accoyntanaunce acquaintance C.690
adnychelate annihilated F.182
adquire acquire F.288, C.267
affeccyon favouritism G.674
agayne, agayns (*prep.*) against G.676; in anticipation of F.648, 1290
Almayne Germany F.727
almyshowsys alms houses G.664*
alowable laudable C.745
alowith allows C.652*
altercacion dispute, rivalry C.255
alycaunt wine of Alicante F.564
amonge (*prep.*) amongst F.1294*
amonge (*adv.*) now and then F.28; meanwhile C.482
amys amiss F.621
amyte amity C.481
annyell annual G.592
anon eventually C.569
aperte apart, aside C.378
appelyd accused C.456
approbate authoritative F.33
apysh fantastic, mischievous G.441*
aray (*pp.*) disfigured C.683
arche dame See C.919*

argyng arguing F.1135
armys heraldic devices G.35, 100
artografye orthography F.998
as such as F.216
as lyf willingly F.424
assoyle dispel C.584
assoylid dispelled C.457
aswage shorten C.867
attons at once C.446
atwyght atwite, reproach C.882
auctour author F.12
auctoryte authority G.38
audyens reception F.1318
auncyon ancient C.172
avaunce promote F.1440; put forward C.177
avouchid promised C.839
avow(e) (*sb.*) oath C.857; promise F.992
ay so nearly C.1001

balates ballads F.39*
banket banquet F.1253
basse embrace C.569
baudry office of a bawd C.420; bawdry C.471
bawdry unchastity C.200
be by F.428, G.733
be it let it be so F.657
bedfolkis beadsfolk, C.894*
Bedleme Bethlehem C.298
beginnynges dealings C.181
benevolent desiring to do well F.222
berdyd bearded C.395
beshrew curse F.415
best beast F.1443

161

besynes   commotion G.716
blasyng sterrys   meteors, comets
   F.xxxi
blow (v.)   puff for breath F.1152
bluddys (sb.)   rakes F.1246*
bordon   undersong, accompaniment
   F.1392
bore   born G.481
borrow (sb.)   pledge, surety C.404
bote   cure, salvation C.838
botell   ? bottle F.1419*
bounsynge   big, strapping F.640
boweth   bends C.653
boy   rascal C.501
brablyng   quarrelling G.729
brent   burnt C.120
brome   broom(s) C.331*
brothell   whore C.796
brut (adj.)   beastly C.789
brynnynge   burning F.804
but   unless F.1118; that C.19;
   without C.755
bydyst   are you waiting? C.797

can   know F.13; know how to F.1325
Cane of Catowe   Khan of Cathay
   F.852*
capasyte   mental ability F.223
capryck   caprik wine F.563
caryd   cared, troubled C.710
caryed   managed, completed C.907
case   chance, occasion C.370
Caton   Cato G.974*
Catowe   Cathay (China) F.852
certayne (adj.)   particular F.197
charge (sb.)   weight C.653
chauns   bad luck C.74
chepe (sb.)   bargain G.252*
chere   entertainment F.1225
chevalry   mounted men-at-arms
   G.224
chorle   churl, peasant G.27*
clary   cordial, punch F.565
clause   proposition, legal article
   G.865
clene (adv.)   neatly C.907
clere (adj.)   shining F.1244*;
   illustrious C.775
clere (adv.)   completely F.1079
clerk(ys)   scholars F.21; philosophers
   F.113; C.4
clery   ? clearly G.505*

close (adj.)   guarded C.185
cloth of gold   See G.104*
cokkys   God's G.720
collyk   stomach ache C.713
colour   pretext G.745
combryd   harassed C.14
comely (adv.)   pleasantly F.1340
comforthe   comforteth F.1276
communycacyon   conversation F.886
commyn (pp.)   descended from G.34
commyninge   companionship F.824
comyn well   common good,
   prosperity G.244
commyn welth   community, state
   F.54*
commyxion   blending F.xvi
commyxyd   blended of different
   elements F.187
compasse (vb.)   encircle F.249*
compilid   put together G. Title
comyn (vb.)   converse C.306
conclud   confute, overcome G.735
conclusions   experiments,
   demonstrations, F.xvii, 8
conclusyon   speech, riddling C.780*
condycyons   behaviour, character
   G.492; disposition F.976
condygne   appropriate G.1144*
conjecture   by ~ in conclusion C.214
connynge   learning F.21; intelligence
   F.324
consentyd   consented to C.35
conseyte   conception, idea F.44
conseytis   imaginative inventions
   F.137
constellacyons   configurations F.172
contembtacyon   satisfaction F.399
conteyne   occupy F.v
convenyent   appropriate F.360; to
   the purpose G.730
copy (sb.)   text C.623
corage, courage   disposition C.222;
   spirit F.314; desire F.678
corrupcyons   disintegrations F.173
corruptyd   destroyed by dissolution
   F.180
cosmography, cosmogryfy   F.xxi*,
   687
cotes   shelters F.788
couchyd   laid flat C.840
coud   could, knew how to G.106
countenaunce (sb.)   pretence C.336

162

countenaunse (v.) behave F.1340
countervaylys is equivalent to C.232
cours (sb.) turn, dance movement
F.1329
cours (adj.) coarse G.950
crakkyng (sb.) boasting G.202
craturs creatures F.455
create (pp.) created C.3
creature creator G.516
crispyd curled C.228
cure (sb.) care F.220
curst vicious G.1017
curyous skilful, elaborate F.42
curyously elaborately G.100
cut purs thief F.1164

damaske rosewater F.1260
daunger power to harm C.32
daw jackdaw, fool F.56, G.180
decays ? arrears G.664*
defende forbid G.757
dell part, bit F.884, G.357
delycatys delicacies F.897
delyte (v.) take pleasure in F.1214
denayed repudiated C.812
depend hang together F.vii
deprave disparage F.436, C.708
determynacyon settlement C.62
dew gard dieu vous garde, God keep
you C.78
deyfy deify G.899
dictys writings, words of wisdom C.8
discordith is discordant C.114
distroy ruin G.650*
dole sorrow, pain C.817
dolent (sb.) wretch C.782
dolf (pp.) delved, dug G.485
dotage foolish affection C.14
doutfull fearful, suspicious C.461
dowtles doubtless C.545
drafe, draffe (sb.) swill F.610, G.932
drammys drams weight G.262
drede (sb.) fear G.1029
dres (v.) ? address C.913
dress (v.) attend to C.83
dure endure, live F.1441
dyaper cloth G.104*
dyght prepared F.582*
dyme dim C.263
dysgysynge entertainment, show
F.xii*
dyspend have income from G.19

dysport recreation F.1246
dyvers various F.iii
dyvylish diabolical F.67

effectis operative influence F.105
effectuously ? urgently C.655
eftsonys again, from time to time
F.180
ellys otherwise C.400
elygant refined C. Title
empayre damage G.697
enbawmyng cosmetics C.199
endarkyth dims, casts in shadow
C.242
ennewyd restored, tinted C.241
ensew follow, conform C.621
entent drift, purpose C.780
entercours commerce, traffic G.3
equivalent identical C.7*
ere whyle a while ago F.891
eshyvyd achieved C.647
estate condition of life F.515; rank
C.20
estatis ? the higher classes G.69*
ethereall, etheriall filled with
heavenly æther F.64*
everychone every one G.885
evydent (adv.) clearly F.26
excesse (? adj.) protuberant F.242*
executers administrators G.786
experience proof C.655
experymente proof F.373
extort (adj.) extortionate G.651
extromers astronomers F.1138
eyen eyes C.260
eylyst do you find fault? F.988*

fable (v.) deceive C.419
fablyng deception C.680
facyon (sb.) shape F.183
falls (adj.) false C.805
fantesye whim F.43
fantesys delusive imaginings F.1291
farr further G.1012
favour appearance C.685
fayn well-disposed C.798*
faynt (sb.) feebleness C.665
feate (adj.) graceful C.237
feleshyp company, companionship
F.1391
fell (sb.) skin, hide G.73
fet (v.) fetch F.1242, C.94

163

fet(e) (*sb.*) knack G.5; mercantile business G.245; conduct, custom F.816
fewte fealty C.17
flykkeryng (*sb.*) coaxing, seducing C.202
fold (*v.*) swaddle C.866
fole fool C.486★
folys fools C.613
fonde foolish G.828
for so that C.264
forbere do without G.259
forbod (*sb.*) interdiction C.400★
force (*v.*) care F.909
forecast (*sb.*) foresight G.139
formast pre-eminent F.279; chief F.1286
forse *no forse*, no matter C.605
foule (*sb.*) fowl C.123★
fray (*sb.*) affray, fight F.1153
fredome generosity, nobility C.851
froward ill-humoured, perverse C.573
frowardnes ill-temper C.663
fryscas ? dances F.1249★
fryska See F.419★
fryske (*v.*) leap F.1344
full (*v.*) become full F.374★
full (*adv.*) fully F.869
full ere much earlier F.969
fygour shape F.470
fygure bodily shape C.240
fyrmament heaven F.xviii

galand gallant(s) F.417★
gall (*sb.*) oak-apple F.245
gall (*v.*) become sore C.371
gambawdes round round dances F.1249★
gate path G.189, 464
gatist gottest (got) G.418
gederyd gathered G.487
generacyon origin F.105
generacyons births, formations F.173
gere material G.102
ges (*v.*) reckon C.112
gest fellow, ? jester F.587; stranger C.903
gestis jokes G. Title
glasyng (*adj.*) ? sparkling C.235★
glose write or speak speciously F.41

god evyn good evening F.407
Gogges God's G.597
gotten won C.170★
gramercy thanks F.937
grave (*v.*) engrave G.91
gresse (*sb.*) grease G.405
gretest (*adj. sb.*) noblest (company) F.630
grevys griefs C.293
grose massive F.344
grosyst grossest F.95
gruch (*v.*) be resented C.265★
grudgyth grieves G.1137
gyddys (*sb.*) guides C.598
gylt (*adj.*) gilded G.898★
gyngerly daintily F.1337★
gyrdle belt C.836
gyse manner C.532

hache hatch F.1105
had (*pp.*) ? hald, protected C.636★
halporth halfpennyworth G.405
happith happens C.764
hard ars buttock F.1166★
hardely, hartly boldly C.703; plainly C.771
hardli hardily, certainly G.955
hardyst (*v.*) heardest C.170★, G.477
hast (*v.*) hasten C.595
haterad hatred C.117
have amonge watch out! F.1332
havyns havens F.806
hed chief part, fountainhead C.204
hele (*sb.*) health, well-being G.454
helyd healed G.524
hengyth hangs F.xviii
hens hence C.626, 793
her here G.725
herbage pasture G.629
herdly hardily, assuredly F.999
here (*v.*) hear C.308
herr (*sb.*) hair C.227
heyrys heirs G.610
hit (*pron.*) it F.553
holdyn (*pp.*) beholden F.304
hole (*adj.*) whole C.126
hole (*adv.*) wholly F.231
holones hollowness F.240
holp(e) (*pp.*) helped C.866, G.133
holsome healthy F.714
holyn holly F.1405
homely (*adv.*) rudely C.313

164

hope (*v.*)   trust C.270
hors   hoarse C.491
Huddy Peke   blockhead F.1194*
huffa   See F.417*
hy (*v.*)   hurry C.98
hye (*adj.*)   exalted F.115; abstruse
F.106, 324, 700; loud F.889
hyeng   hastening C.594
hyet (*pp.*)   hit F.405
hyght (*pp.*)   is called C.92

ibroke   broken F.1408
ich (*adj.*)   each G.577
imagyn (*v.*)   plot C.379
imbassades   deputations C.599
importune (*adj.*)   importunate C.22
improw   improve G.625
inbrace   embrace C.514
incontynent (*adv.*)   immediately
F.1360
indever (*v. refl.*)   strive G.1061
indyfferent   impartial G.561, 1148
indyte   compose F.39
inferyall   mundane F.116
influens   power C.1082; destinal
power C.211
inow   enough G.265, F.617
inpostume   abscess C.345
insaciat   insatiable G.440
insew   follow G.504
intellectyve   understanding F.210,
G.379*
inure   bring by practice F.93*
invyron (*adv.*)   round about F.2
ipocrase   Hippocras wine F.565
iwis, iwys   for sure F.1184, G.14

Jak-heryng   See G.185–6*
janglyng   noisy chatter C.196
Javell   See G.123*
jet (*v.*)   strut, display C.448*
jomble   ? tumble about C.356
joyntly   together, in contact F.248*
juggyd   passed judgment G.130
just (*adv.*)   just so, rightly F.1133

kankerde   envious, crabbed G.179
karych   ? care I C.529*
kaytyffes   villains F.761
kind (*sb.*)   nature C.765
knave (*v.*)   call 'knave' G.709

krakkys (*sb.*)   boasts G.32
kroke (*v.*)   crook, bend F.1341*
kynde (*sb.*)   nature C.765
kyt   small fiddle F.1350

lade (*v.*)   load cargo F.809*
lack (*v.*)   lack G.653; be lacking
(*intrans.*) C.530
langour   sickness C.730
las   less F.203
lase   lase, ribbon C.228
late (*adv.*)   lately F.6
laude (*sb.*)   praise F.302, C.18
ledy   leaden C.886
lefe   leave C.424
leme   gleam C.301
leppyng   leaping C.956
lere   learn F.991
lese   lose C.802
lest (*v.*)   please, desire C.724
leude   ignorant F.989
lever   rather C.955, C.134
lewdness   wickedness C.786*
lewyd   ignorant, churlish F.976,
G.723
ley   allege, maintain C.415
loke   look F.1345*
long (*adj.*)   lasting C.390*
long on   attributable to C.173
longyng   belonging G.262
lordeyn   lout C.610
lorn   lost G.356
losophers   philosophers F.1137
lucoure   lucre G.235
lyf, lyfe, lyff (*v.*)   live G.329, C.540
lyf (*adj.*)   lief, rather F.424
lyght (*adj.*)   frivolous C.881*; ? trivial
C.529*
lyghtnes   agility C.210
lykkyd her   sleeked herself C.953*
lymmys   limbs C.667
lynage   descent, ancestry C.775
lyst (*sb.*)   desire F.571
lyst (*v. impers.*)   it pleases C.132
lyte   little G.161

mache   match F.1276
made   mad F.614
malvesyne   Malmsey wine F.563
malyncoly   melancholy C.850*
maner   habit G.569
manyfest   reveal C.49

marcyall martial G.763
mare nightmare C.105*
mark gold coin G.19*
Mary by St Mary F.542
mast (v.) mayest, may G.416
matrone woman, ? midwife C.512
matter substance F.185*
Maud See G.925*
maystres masters C.1063
meane (sb.) course of action,
 intermediary F.93; moderation
 C.183, 236*
meane (adj.) common, poor F.30;
 average C.243
mede bribery G.1029
medys rewardys G.640
mell meddle G.1012
mendys amends C.807
mere merry F.882
mershall marshall F.1287*
messe mass F.428
mestres mistress C.642
mete (adj.) suitable to F.126
mevyd angry C.341
mewde caged, cooped up C.196
moderly motherly C.691
mone murmur C.723*
muskyllys mussels F.1410
musing pondering F.67
myddys midst, middle F.xviii
mynyon (sb.) favourite C.625
mynysh diminish G.697
mys (v.) fail, be lacking C.1034
mys (adj.) wicked C.33*
myschyfe misfortune F.535
myte smallest coin F.40

narr nearer G.196
nather (adj.) neither F.175
naturynge creating F.152*
necessite poverty, need C.703;
 constraining power C.742
Nembroth Nimrod C.164*
nere, nerre nearer F.1066, 1106
nexte nearest F.427, 681
nise fastidious G.926
no nother no other F.655, G.289
norssh nourish G.367
nothyr other G.289
noticion knowledge C.979
nought wicked G.692

noyauns annoyance C.76
ny close to C.322

obeysauns subjection C.154
occian see Atlantic ocean F.711*
occupi seize, hold by force G.109
occupy remain in F.976
of off F.1166
on (prep.) at F.1101
on hye aloud F.543
on (adj.) one F.163, 1223, C.1012;
 united C.534
one (adj. 2) own C.1025
ones, onys once C.289, F.174
ony any G.214
or e'er, before F.568, 973, C.681,
 G.403, 670
orason prayer C.1006
orbycularly spherically F.249
oryent resplendent G.897
oryson horizon F.1075
other either F.1293
ought anything G.48
oversayne (pp.) overseen, mistaken
 F.898*

paradventure perhaps G.869
pardyse paradise F.1262
partener partaker F.102
partis (sb.) parts F.241
pastaunce pleasure, entertainment
 F.524; pastime C.692
paste more than F.vii
pate head G.190, 736
peas peace G.1012*
per case sometimes C.370; by chance
 G.1170
perde par dieu, indeed G.16
pere appear F.1099
perfyte perfect C.223
perseyve take note C.582
pesis pieces C.585
pevysh quarrelsome G.180
playne (adj.) flat F.367
playne (adv.) plainly F.895; directly
 F.862
plays, pleys flirtings C.189, 571
plyght (v.) swear C.776
poles axes F.258
polesy policy G.117
polycy deliberate cunning F.445
ponderosyte weight F.274

popagays exotic birds G.927
portly dignified, stately C.220
possyssyoners owners, occupiers G.170
postys supports C.598
poynt devyse at every point, perfectly F.529, 1259
poynted (*pp.*) appointed F.895
pranke (*v.*) prance F.1339★
preferr promote, advance C.442
prengnaunt fertile, inventive F.29
prest ready C.726
prikeryd prick-eared C.951
primmys pretty girls G.926★
profettys advantages C.547
proper true, admirable F.iii; good looking F.641
properist most admirable F.1085
properte disposition F.989
prove make trial of G.191, 714
provyde (*pp.*) proved G.831
provydence guidance, arrangement F.261
prykyeryd prick-eared F.1378★
pryk song prick-song F.1379★
publysshed (*pp.*) made public G.1171
punycyon punishment G.706
purtrayture painting, drawing C.245
purveaunce providence G.1096; government G.329
purvey provide F.948; engage F.1356
pusans power F.1142
pusell age time of youth, maidenhood C.646
pykyng thieving G.1059
pyne aple pinecone F.800★
pyoners pioneers, sappers G.143★
pyte pity F.1326; mercy C.51

quadrant (*adj.*) square F.368
quak quake C.923
quaile fail, lapse G.452
quantyte dimensions F.119
quart quarter F.720
quene whore C.999
quiknes liveliness C.650
quod'a, quoth'a quoth he, says he, used mockingly F.529, C.108, G.869
quyk lively G.86

rage (*sb.*) seizure C.868
rampyon wine F.562★

raspyce sweet wine F.564
raylys utters abuse, jests C.234★
reame, reme realm C.300, G.2
reasons arguments C.691
rede (*v.*) advise C.477
regarde (*sb.*) estimation, worth F.476
regardyd esteemed F.21
rehersyd related C.8
remember remind C.595
remove move from place to place F.1062
ren (*v.*) run G.948★
repayre return C.860
report (*v. refl.*) appeal, declare C.40★
resolucyon reduction, separation F.188
reynyd (*pp.*) reigned C.853
rode (*sb.*) rood, cross G.473
rok spinning staff C.333
romble toss about C.354
rome (*sb.*) space F.555, 741; position, office G.1156
round (*sb.*) round-dance F.961
rounde (*adj.* ? *pp.*) surrounded F.339★
rounde (*adv.*) around F.241★
rud, rude ignorant F.44, G.182
rudely ignorantly, unskilfully F.129
rumney Romney red wine F.564
rybaud good-for-nothing, ? bawd C.786
ryght (*adv.*) directly F.1132
rygour obstinacy C.183★

sad serious F.vi, 421; steadfast C.12★
sadnes seriousness F.135
salvys medicines C.387
sanguynyous rosy C.16★
saunce pere without equal F.643
saws sayings, arguments F.414, C.574
sciens knowledge F.34★, 221, C.96
scyens ? science C.97★
seasyth ceaseth C.862
seke (*adj.*) sick C.846
sentence thought, argument F.26, 133; meaning C.737
serpently serpent-like C.187
sessyons sittings of law court G.127
set (*v.*) plant G.627
set (*v.*) put to music C.490

167

set by   care for F.1306
severall (*adj.*)   separate F.628
severell (*adv.*)   in particular C.323
shame   modesty, decency C.403
shewyng (*sb.*)   demonstrativeness
   C.820
shone (*sb.*)   shoes G.186
shrewd   vicious F.1153
shrewe (*v.*)   beshrew, curse F.888,
   C.79
shrews (*sb.*)   rascals G.679
shyppys   sheep's C.676
sightynges   sighings C.189
similytude (*adj.*)   dissembled C.25*
skapyth   escapes C.289
skole   teaching F.1192
skot   reckoning G.1060
small   light, weak (drink) G.949
smotter   pretty F.642*
sod, soden (*adj.*)   boiled F.605, 910
soferayns   gentry G.1100
solf (*v.*)   sing sol-fa C.492
son   the sun's C.230
sore (*adj.*)   difficult F.1005
sore (*adv.*)   harshly G.659
sote   sweet smelling F.1258
soth   true F.414, C.361
soudan   sultan F.832
soyle (*v.*)   assoil, resolve G.738
space   distance F.188
sped   success C.274, 384
spence   pantry F.957
spende (*v.*)   consume C.302
spende (*pp.*)   spent G.230
spere   sphere F.257
sperycall   spherical F.238
spye   keep under observation F.1061
squalmys   scales C.418
stark (*adj.*)   bold G.707
ster (*v.*)   stir, rake G.309
sterker   bolder C.413
sterve   die (of hunger) G.669
stewes   brothel F.586
stok (*sb.*)   stem, trunk C.651
stok (*v.*)   root up G.629
stole (*sb.*)   stool C.95
straunge (*adj.*)   disdainful C.822;
   distinctive F.257; rare, obscure
   F.395; a stranger's G.1083
straykyng   dragging along C.952
strayt   strict G.1155
straytly   strictly C.523

strene   progeny C.45
strenght   strength F.210
studious   preoccupied, perplexed
   C.971*
study (*sb.*)   care, thought G.615
style   manner of speaking C.226*
styll (*adv.*)   continuously F.288
subtell   abstruse F.34
suerte   surety, certainty F.1372,
   C.271
sufferayn (*sb.*)   sovereign C.158
suffereyn (*adj.*)   paramount C.223
suffysaunce   self-sufficiency G.1117
supportacyon   assistance, favour F.5
suspecious   ? suspicious people
   C.458*
suspect (*sb.*)   anxiety C.118
sutes   solicitations C.22
suttelte   subtlety, craft C.200
swynk (*v.*)   toil C.948
syn   since C.633
syse   assize G.127
syth   since C.176

taberet   small tabor F.1350
take   lead, begin C.485
tal   bold F.1174
tell   reckon F.735
tend   attend C.379
termys   rhetorical language F.42
than   then F.1154; thence C.135;
   when C.769
the (*pron.*)   thee F.224, 288, C.140;
   to thee F.1409*
the (*pron.*)   they F.785
thest   the east F.354
they venteres   the adventurers F.754
this   these F.838*, 1137, G.681
thought   anxiety C.649
thrall (*sb.*)   slave C.66
thryft   welfare, careful management
   C.618
thyng   means C.268*
to   too F.106, 259, G.911
too   to G.255
toolis   tools G.56
toppe (*sb.*)   topmast, lookout F.1104
torn (*v.*)   turn F.1343
tost (*sb.*)   toast sop in wine C.712
tote   tut, tut G.930
totyth (*v.*)   toots, protrudes F.1195
tow (*adj.*)   tough, awkward F.553

168

toyes facetious compositions F.17; amusing matters G. Title
trace (*sb.*) dancing measure F.1331
triangle (*adj.*) triangular F.368
trough (*sb.*) troth G.292*, 457
trow (*sb.*) fancy C.243*
trowe (*v.*) believe F.614, C.342, G.710
trull of trust wanton wench F.1267*
trye (*v.*) prove true F.1084; consider G.730
tryfellys fictions, jests F.17
tyde time F.201
Tyre wine of Tyre F.563
tyrll (*v.*) trill, spin F.417*
tythynges tidings C.925

undeservyd undeserving C.474
unethe, unneth with difficulty F.1061; scarcely, F.19
ungotten (*pp.*) not obtained, ? destroyed C.170*
universall experienced C.314
unshamefastnes immodesty C.199
usyd (*adj.*) customary F.109
utter (*v.*) offer for sale G.247

vengennis vengeance C.841
venteres venturers, adventurers F.754*
Venys Venice F.725
verey true C.1074; perfect G. Title

wagg (*v.*) stir, go its way G.1010*
walke (*v.*) beat G.719*, 727

wan (*pp.*) won, earned F.589
warely (*adj.*) cautious, prudent G.138
warrant (*v.*) protect F.1197
wawe (*sb.*) wave F.1099
wether whither C.39
whether whither C.695
which (*sb.*) witch C.817
whychcraftys witchcrafts C.198
whyder whether G.641
whyt (*sb.*) bit C.114
whytheyr whether G.853
with all also F.339; at the same time F.1334 s.d.
without (*adv.*) outside F.1312
wodes (*sb.*) ? copses, shacks F.787*
wold (*v.*) should C.1066
woll (*sb.*) wool G.73
won (*v.*) dwell G.255
wore (*sb.*) ore F.798
wot (*v.*) know F.537
wottyst do you know C.393
wrygyldy wrage See F.1409*
wyght person C.922
wyld fyre venereal disease C.506*
wylenes wiliness C.197*
wylfull willing G.562
wyt intelligence C.221

yche each, every C.114
yche whyt every bit, wholly C.114
yerth earth C.159
yerthly earthly C.46
yl (*adj.*) evil C.555
yll (*adj.*) troublesome (G.524)
yough youth C.646